The fifteen years between the conclusion of the GATT Tokyo Round in 1979 and the finalisation of the Uruguay Round in 1994 witnessed a period of spectacular growth in East Asia. Many of the countries in the region have in the interim developed vibrant economies characterised by significant liberalisation and deregulation which has led to strong trading performances. They have become major actors in the world economy as they benefited from a liberal open multilateral trading system.

This volume provides a comprehensive assessment of the likely effects of the Uruguay Round agreements and the establishment of the World Trade Organisation (WTO) on the dynamic economies of East Asia. The rapid development of these countries owes much to the strong export performance and unilateral deregulation of their economies in recent years. Their major stake in maintaining the integrity of the global trading system was demonstrated by their active participation in the negotiations. The impact of the Uruguay Round liberalisation on East Asian economic development and policies is evaluated, including using sophisticated CGE models to estimate the effects on trade and income. The strengthening of trade rules and dispute settlement procedures are examined by leading world trade experts. They establish that some gaps and weaknesses in the multilateral trading system remain to be tackled (anti-dumping, regional discrimination) and that some new problems are pending (competition policy, investment).

Readily accessible to a wide audience, this book will be of great interest to political economists, policy makers and international trade experts.

East Asian trade after the Uruguay Round

TRADE AND DEVELOPMENT

A series of books on international economic relations and economic issues in development

Edited from the National Centre for Development Studies, The Australian National University, by Professor Ron Duncan.

Academic editor
Ron Duncan, *National Centre for Development Studies, The Australian National University*

Advisory editors
Ross Garnaut, *The Australian National University*
Reuven Glick, *Federal Reserve Bank of San Francisco*
Enzo R. Grilli, *The World Bank*
Mario B. Lamberte, *Philippine Institute for Development Studies*

Executive editor
Maree Tait, *National Centre for Development Studies, The Australian National University*

Other titles in the series
Helen Hughes (ed.), *Achieving Industrialization in East Asia*
Yun-Wing Sung, *The China–Hong Kong Connection: The Key to China's Open Door Policy*
Kym Anderson (ed.), *New Silk Roads: East Asia and world textile markets*
Rod Tyers and Kym Anderson, *Disarray in world food markets: a quantitative assessment*
Enzo R. Grilli, *The European Community and developing countries*
Peter Warr (ed.), *The Thai Economy in Transition*
Ross Garnaut, Enzo Grilli and James Riedel (eds.), *Sustaining export-oriented developments: ideas from East Asia*
Donald O. Mitchell, Merlinda D. Ingco and Ronald C. Duncan (eds.), *The world food outlook*
David C. Cole and Betty F. Slade, *Building a modern financial system: the Indonesian experience*
Ross Garnaut, Guo Shutian and Ma Guonan (eds.), *The third revolution in the Chinese countryside*

East Asian trade after the Uruguay Round

Edited by
DAVID ROBERTSON

Director, Trade and Development Programme
National Centre for Development Studies
The Australian National University, Canberra, Australia

382.095
E13

PUBLISHED BY THE PRESS SYNDICATE OF THE UNIVERSITY OF CAMBRIDGE
The Pitt Building, Trumpington Street, Cambridge CB2 1RP, United Kingdom

CAMBRIDGE UNIVERSITY PRESS
The Edinburgh Building, Cambridge CB2 2RU, United Kingdom
40 West 20th Street, New York, NY 10011-4211, USA
10 Stamford Road, Oakleigh, Melbourne 3166, Australia

n+

© Cambridge University Press 1997

First published 1997

Printed in the United Kingdom at the University Press, Cambridge

*A catalogue record for this book is available from
the British Library*

Library of Congress cataloguing in publication data

East Asian trade after the Uruguay Round / edited by David Robertson.
         p.   cm.
     Includes bibliographical references.
     ISBN 0-521-58318-7
     1. East Asia – Commerce.   2. East Asia – Commercial policy.
  3. Uruguay Round (1987–1994)   I. Robertson, David, 1935–   .
  HF3820.5.Z5E373   1997
  382'.095–dc20   96–9562
                                                                              CIP

ISBN 0 521 58318 7 hardback

SE

Contents

Figures

Tables

Contributors

Kym Anderson   Professor of Economics, Director, Centre for International Economic Studies, University of Adelaide, Adelaide, Australia

Joseph F. Francois   Economic Research and Analysis Unit, WTO Secretariat and CEPR, Geneva, Switzerland

Masahiro Kawai   Professor of Economics, Institute of Social Science, University of Tokyo, Japan

Kala Krishna   Professor of Economics, Department of Economics, The Pennsylvania State University, USA

Suiwah Leung   Director, Economics of Development Program, National Centre for Development Studies, The Australian National University, Canberra, Australia

Will Martin   Senior Economist, International Trade Division, The World Bank, Washington, DC, USA

Bradley McDonald   Economic Research and Analysis Unit, WTO Secretariat and CEPR, Geneva, Switzerland

Håkan Nordström   Economic Research and Analysis Unit, WTO Secretariat, Geneva, Switzerland

Frances Perkins   Assistant Secretary, East Asian Research Unit, Department of Foreign Affairs and Trade, Canberra, Australia

Geoff Raby   First Assistant Secretary, Trade Negotiations and Organisations Division, Department of Foreign Affairs and Trade, Canberra, Australia; formerly Division of Trade Policy Issues, Trade Directorate, OECD, Paris, France

J. David Richardson   Professor of Economics, Maxwell School of Citizenship and Public Affairs, Syracuse University, USA

David Robertson   Director, Trade and Development Program, National Centre for Development Studies, The Australian National University, Canberra, Australia.

Gary P. Sampson   Director, Regional and Preferential Trade, and Trade and Finance Division, WTO Secretariat, Geneva, Switzerland

Ling Hui Tan   The Brookings Institution, Washington, DC, USA

Graeme Thomson Principal Adviser, Trade Negotiations and Organisations Division, Department of Foreign Affairs and Trade, Canberra, Australia

Yongzheng Yang Fellow, Trade and Development Program, National Centre for Development Studies, The Australian National University, Canberra, Australia

NIA

Preface and acknowledgements

As the Uruguay Round negotiations approached their scheduled completion at the end of 1990, it appeared likely that the rapidly industrialising economies of East Asia would face a new world trading system that would be less accommodating to the aggressive marketing that had underpinned their export-led growth strategies. Further dismantling of tariffs by OECD countries would be offset by easier access to contingency protection provided by GATT escape provisions, which would discriminate against competitive exporters. In these circumstances, the export and growth prospects of the East Asian economies would suffer and new strategies might become necessary.

The National Centre for Development Studies decided that outcomes from the Uruguay Round negotiations needed to be assessed from an East Asian–West Pacific perspective. In 1991, the Research School of Pacific Studies provided funding for a research fellow for this project for three years and the Australian International Development Assistance Bureau (AIDAB) – now AusAID – generously provided finance for research assistance .

In fact, of course, the Uruguay Round negotiations continued for another three years. The agreements embodied in the Final Act in December 1993 were more far-reaching and more comprehensive than envisaged in 1990. Liberalisation of industrial and agricultural trade and new agreements on trade in services, on international property rights and on strengthening GATT disciplines have established a new trading system to be overseen by the World Trade Organisation (WTO). The original objective of the research remains relevant, but the Uruguay Round Final Act impinges more directly than had been envisaged on many aspects of economic development in East Asian countries. The research programme, therefore, was amended to take account of changing circumstances in East Asia and in the international trading system.

This volume is a review of the way selected aspects of the Uruguay Round Final Act will impinge on economic developments and policies in

East Asian countries. The increasing significance of the East Asian region in the global economy and its dependence on an orderly world trading system under the WTO affected the circumstances of the review in 1994. Although many uncertainties remain about the implementation of the Uruguay Round agreements, and the operations of the WTO, this volume comprises a review of key aspects of the agreements for the Western Pacific economies.

The National Centre for Development Studies wishes to express its thanks to the Australian International Development Assistance Bureau for the generous financial support provided for the research behind this volume.

Among the many people who assisted with the organisation and the editing of the papers, a special vote of thanks must be given to John Watts and Ruel Abello for their devoted support, 'go-foring' and goodwill.

David Robertson

Glossary

AFTA	ASEAN free-trade area
AIDAB	Australian International Development Assistance Bureau (now AusAID)
AMS	Aggregate Measure of Support
ANZCERTA	Australia–New Zealand Closer Economic Relations Trade Agreement
APEC	Asia Pacific Economic Cooperation
ASEAN	Association of South East Asian Nations
ASEAN4	Malaysia, Thailand, Indonesia, Philippines
CUSTA	Canada–US Trade Agreement
CAP	Common Agricultural Policy (EU)
CGE	computable general equilibrium
c.i.f.	cost-insurance-freight
CITES	Convention of Trade in Endangered Species
EADCs	East Asian Developing Countries
EAEC	East Asian Economic Caucus
EANIE	East Asian Newly Industrialising Economies
EC	European Community
ECSC	European Coal and Steel Community
EEA	European Economic Area
EFTA	European Free-Trade Association
EMS	European Monetary System
EU	European Union
FDI	foreign direct investment
FEER	fundamental effective exchange rate
f.o.b.	free-on-board
GATS	General Agreement on Trade in Services
GATT	General Agreement on Tariffs and Trade
GDI	gross domestic investment
GNP	gross national product
GSP	Generalised System of Preferences

GTAP	Global Trade Analysis Project
IDB	Integrated Data Base (GATT)
IIT	intra-industry trade
ILO	International Labour Office
IMF	International Monetary Fund
ITO	International Trade Organisation
LAIA	Latin American Integration Association
LDC	less/least developed country
LTA	Long Term Agreement on Cotton Textiles
Mercosur	Common Market of the Southern Cone
MFA	Multifibre Arrangement
Mfn	most-favoured-nation
NAFTA	North American Free-Trade Agreement
NGO	non-governmental organisation
NIE	newly industrialising economy
NTB	non-tariff barrier
OECD	Organisation for Economic Cooperation and Development
OLS	ordinary least-squares
OMA	orderly marketing agreement
PSE	producer subsidy equivalent
QR	quantitative (import) restriction
SAM	social accounting matrix
SII	Structural Impediments Initiative
SPS	sanitary and phytosanitary
TPRM	Trade Policy Review Mechanism (GATT)
TRIMs	trade-related investment measures
TRIPs	trade-related aspects of intellectual property rights
UNCTAD	United Nations Commission for Trade and Development
VER	voluntary export restraint
VIE	voluntary import expansion
WTO	World Trade Organisation

East Asian trade and the new world trade order

DAVID ROBERTSON

One consequence of the prolongation of Uruguay Round negotiations three years beyond the original 1990 deadline was that uncertainties surrounding the world trading system multiplied. Combined with the renewal of regionalism as an alternative to the multilateral approach to trade liberalisation, these uncertainties created conflicting forces in trade policy among industrial countries and between industrial and developing countries. During the Uruguay Round negotiations, which began in 1986, many developing countries experienced changes in policies, switching from mainly import-substitution strategies to accept new economic opportunities from trade liberalisation and financial deregulation. These revisions to established economic policies evolved partly from the educational effects of participating in the GATT trade negotiations, because more contracting parties were active participants in the Uruguay Round than in any of the previous seven rounds. In addition, the economic performance of some East Asian economies in the previous twenty years provided an incentive for other countries to adopt their export-oriented strategies, a challenge taken up by ASEAN and in Latin America. During the Uruguay Round negotiations, Vietnam, China and transitional economies in Central Europe also began to open to market forces and trade.

The changes taking place during the seven years of the Uruguay Round negotiations interacted with the negotiations themselves. Regionalism achieved renewed support in both industrial and developing countries, partly as a bargaining device in the negotiating process and partly as a protectionist counter to progress in the Round. The political debate about the costs and benefits of regional economic integration was re-opened. The movement for closer economic and political union in Western Europe took another step with the proposal to complete the internal market by 1992, announced almost as soon as the Uruguay Round began. This stimulated the Canada–US Trade Agreement (CUSTA) (1989), which evolved into the North American Free-Trade Agreement (NAFTA) (1992). Both were consistent with the shift of US policy towards more emphasis on reciprocity and managed bilateralism in trade relations. With these two major economic blocs dominating the international trade debate, just when the Uruguay Round negotiations moved into crisis in 1990, it was not surprising that defensive regional trade agreements became an alternative for other countries. European countries not members of the European Union (EU), including transitional economies in Central Europe, sought special trade arrangements, which resulted in the European Economic Area (EEA) coming into effect at the beginning of 1995. Mediterranean economies and the Lomé countries also sought closer trade links with the EU to protect their preferential access. Latin American governments tried to find ways to associate with NAFTA; enticed by ill-defined initiatives from the United States, they took up new regional agreements among themselves as preliminary steps to creating a western hemisphere trade bloc, along the lines of President Bush's Enterprise for the Americas initiative (1992).

One perverse development in the new regionalism was the acceptance that a new Asian trade bloc based on the Japanese yen would arise as a counterweight to the EU and NAFTA. This concept was employed with some success by protectionists in Europe and NAFTA to pursue policies to discriminate against exports from the highly competitive East Asian economies, with little regard for the economic and political realities of East Asian development. When the proposal for Asia Pacific Economic Cooperation (APEC) was made in 1989, the East Asian countries responded enthusiastically, mainly because it would create links with the United States, which remained much the largest market for their exports. It was links across the Pacific and the informal, consultative nature of the APEC proposal that appealed to the East Asian countries. This contradicts the conventional European and North American view about East Asia as a new trade bloc.

This combination of regional initiatives and new protectionism based on 'grey-area' measures and lax implementation of GATT rules was the climate into which the Dunkel draft of the Uruguay Round Final Act was launched in 1991. In spite of last-minute compromises among the major players and some weakening of the Dunkel draft in the closing stages, the completion of the Uruguay Round in December 1993 came as something of a surprise. The Final Act represented the most comprehensive agreement ever reached on international trade. It established a new institution, the World Trade Organisation (WTO) built on the foundations of the GATT, comprising not only rules governing merchandise trade but also agreements on trade in services, intellectual property and new dispute settlement procedures. The whole Final Act requires a single undertaking, meaning that ratifying countries have to accept it in its entirety. (Only the four plurilateral trade agreements on trade in civil aircraft, dairy products, bovine meat and government procurement were subject to separate signature and applied conditionally to adherents.) At the final Ministerial Conference in Marrakesh in April 1994, representatives from 120 countries signed the Final Act, and more have sought membership since.

Yet the euphoria of completing the Uruguay Round cannot hide the confusion into which the WTO has been born. There are evident weaknesses in the Final Act, notwithstanding the triumphs of including agricultural trade, phasing-out the Multifibre Arrangement (MFA), the framework agreement on trade in services, accords on intellectual property and counterfeit, trade-related investment measures and government procurement, plus improvements to existing codes such as safeguards and subsidies. Sources of new uncertainties are largely untouched by the Uruguay Round Final Act. Regionalism and the most-favoured-nation (Mfn) treatment embodied in Article I of the General Agreement were not reviewed in the Uruguay Round; only perfunctory amendments were made to Article XXIV on free-trade areas and customs unions. Furthermore, access to anti-dumping protection was probably, on balance, made easier by amendments on circumvention in the Uruguay Round code. The effectiveness of the new safeguards code in removing voluntary export restraints (VERs) remains to be tested.

The circumstances in which the WTO is to be implemented have been complicated by the so-called 'new trade agenda'. This comprises a collection of new trade issues that were raised during the closing three years of the Uruguay Round, after the breakdown of negotiations in Brussels in December 1990. They include trade and the environment, labour standards, investment policies and competition policies. The first two are only marginally linked to trade policy and the GATT, but they have become socially sensitive issues in industrial countries and accepted as considerations in determining any economic policy (Robertson, 1994). The latter two have become increasingly exposed as influencing trade flows as conventional border measures affecting trade have been reduced by successive rounds of GATT negotiations and other liberalisations.

The successful conclusion of the Uruguay Round should restore faith in the multilateral trading system. Order restored by the WTO should reduce the attractions of regionalism and discriminatory trade measures, even if the Uruguay Round did not entirely satisfy the need to strengthen GATT rules affecting these exceptions to Mfn treatment. The liberalisations agreed will be implemented over ten years and will bring significant gains in global economic growth and welfare, as quantitative estimates have already demonstrated. Moreover, several of the agreements include commitments to further negotiation; for example, agriculture and services. The trade climate should become less confused as the WTO becomes accepted and the Uruguay Round agreements are implemented.

The WTO and East Asia

The Uruguay Round Final Act will have far-reaching effects on the rapidly changing, dynamic economies of East Asia (the ASEAN4 – Indonesia, Malaysia, Thailand, Philippines; the 4 NIEs – Hong Kong, Singapore, Korea, Taiwan; and China). During the more than seven years of negotiations these economies underwent major changes. GNP growth rates of 8–10 per cent per annum were achieved; manufactured exports from rapidly growing and modernising industrial sectors became centres for growth; and their integration into the global economy, through trade and foreign investment flows, was established. Much research has been undertaken into the reasons for the high performance of these economies (World Bank, 1993, 1994b; Lau, 1990). In all cases a major cause was the rapid adaptation of economic policies to changing circumstances and underlying macroeconomic stability. For the first time all these countries participated actively in the GATT negotiations (Taiwan and China as 'observers'), undoubtedly influencing their policies and exposing them to the benefits from liberal trade.

By the time the Uruguay Round was completed in December 1993, the dynamic East Asian economies had become firmly established as exporters of manufactures, and China had become a major exporter and the largest single recipient of foreign direct investment (FDI) in the region. In circumstances of growing trade uncertainties, with new trade issues occupying industrial countries' negotiators even before the implementation of the Uruguay Round Final Act had commenced, it is important to assess the overall effects that the Uruguay Round outcome might have on the trade and economic development of East Asia. With so much uncertainty surrounding the WTO, with continuing negotiations on aspects of trade in services and the new trade issues raised in the final stages of the negotiations, any assessment of the effects of the Uruguay Round outcome are prone to risk. In the following chapters, attempts are made to evaluate some of the agreements achieved in the negotiations, but the treatment is necessarily selective and neglects many important accords, such as intellectual property and trade-related investment measures.

World trade after the Uruguay Round

The Uruguay Round Final Act contains twenty-two Agreements, covering goods, services, investment measures, intellectual property rights, dispute settlement and the trade policy review mechanism. In addition it contains eight Understandings, twenty Decisions, three Declarations and a Protocol. It is the most comprehensive and far-reaching trade agreement ever concluded, and its repercussions are still being assessed around the globe. Part I of this volume comprises four chapters that attempt to assess the effects of the Uruguay Round Final Act on the world trade outlook.

The results of the Uruguay Round are put in the context of world trade developments in chapter 2, by Kym Anderson, of the University of Adelaide. He notes that the outlook for East Asian trade is crucial for the global trading system. The dynamic evolution of East Asian trade has doubled the region's share of world merchandise trade over thirty years, because East Asia's exports of manufactures increased at three times the rate of world trade. In spite of rapid growth in trade among the East Asian countries (stimulated by strong economic performance generally), these economies remain highly dependent on trade with all regions. Hence, they are dependent on the strength of the WTO multilateral system and its capacity to supervise the implementation of the Uruguay Round results and to manage negotiations on new trade issues: those already nominated and some unforeseen. New challenges will be made to the WTO by lobby groups seeking to use trade instruments to pursue environmentalism, labour standards and harmonisation of competition policies. The success of the GATT in lowering border barriers to trade has placed such issues on the international agenda, so that national governments can avoid unpalatable policies by pushing such matters on to global negotiations and reconciliation. Although these new issues and potential bilateral disputes will be initiated mostly by the EU and the United States, Anderson points out that the increasing weight of the Western Pacific economies (East Asia plus Australasia) in world trade will give them a strong say in the new WTO, as long as coordinated strategies can be established. The scope for special interest groups of industrial and developing countries to cooperate in the pursuit of global trade agreements was demonstrated by the Cairns Group of agricultural exporters in the Uruguay Round. The challenge for the Western Pacific economies, Anderson concludes

> will be to convince the wider world community that trade liberalisation can be consistent not only with economic growth but also with sustainable development, improved labour and environmental standards, and even improved political freedom and other human rights.

The industrial countries' perspective on the Uruguay Round is presented in chapter 3 by Geoff Raby, formerly with the Trade Directorate of the OECD Secretariat in Paris. The OECD Ministers declared in June 1994 that the Final Act will advance trade liberalisation, expand and strengthen GATT rules and promote economic growth. Yet already some OECD governments are showing apprehensions. The new trade agenda is receiving increasing attention even as the implementation of the Uruguay Round agreements begins. By explaining the benefits to be expected from meeting these commitments, Raby draws attention to the dangers inherent in overloading the WTO with disputes and new issues with ill-defined links to trade, such as labour and environmental standards. Exerting too much pressure on the WTO structure before the Uruguay Round agreements are implemented could diminish their value and, more importantly, could create harmful divisions among the enlarged membership along North–South lines. This would be unfortunate, given that one of the major successes of the seven years of Uruguay Round negotiations was to draw many developing countries into active participation in the negotiations and greater acceptance of the mutual benefits that are provided by multilateral trade rules and disciplines. The danger is that just when the GATT founders' dream of universal acceptance of multilateral and liberal trade is within reach, some OECD countries are giving emphasis to regional and bilateral trade policies. Proposals to extend multilateral trade rules to new areas must not be forced before consensus is reached on both the nature of the problem and the rules required. Raby concludes that the success and scope of the Uruguay Round Final Act should not be interpreted as reason to hasten too fast on new issues.

Many uncertainties remain about the trade effects of the Final Act. The scope of the agreements and undertakings have justifiably been accepted in laudatory terms. The conventional measures of liberalisation indicate deeper percentage tariff cuts and more extensive tariff bindings than in any earlier GATT negotiations, and agriculture is included in the liberalisation for the first time. Basic agreements to restrict access to non-tariff protection were reached, including safeguards, subsidies, quantitative regulations, standards and phasing-out the MFA. Nevertheless, there are serious doubts about evasions of commitments in the Agreement on Agriculture – so long the stumbling-block in the negotiations – on anti-dumping and on textiles and clothing.

The 'continuing negotiations' left over from the Uruguay Round Final Act raise some serious questions, after the Tokyo Round negotiations continued in the Safeguards Committee failed to reach any conclusions. The framework agreement on trade in services contains several key areas where agreement was not reached and negotiations are continuing: shipping, finance, professional qualifications and accounting practices. At the same time, differences exist over interpretations in other agreements – for example, those on intellectual property, subsidies, safeguards, processes and production methods in the 'standards code', transparency in quarantine regulations and technical standards. By extending the coverage of the WTO with many new agreements, the Uruguay Round has created a permanent negotiating process in many traditional areas of trade, as well as opening the opportunity to raise new trade issues. The WTO will require a settling-in period during which the formula for dealing with continuing negotiations will have to be resolved. During this time, developing countries, including the East Asian economies, will need to form coalitions and establish positions to protect their interests on a continuing basis. As full members of the WTO, due to the 'single undertaking' requirement of the Uruguay Round Final Act, some of these countries' interests will no longer be protected by the 1979 Enabling Clause which provides special and differential treatment to developing countries. More attention will have to be given to day-to-day processes in WTO committees.

No review of the Uruguay Round as it affects East Asia would be complete without consideration of the MFA, because its quantitative restrictions have influenced industrial development throughout the region. Speculating about what phasing-out the MFA might mean, assuming the schedule agreed in the Uruguay Round is achieved, is best done using a CGE model (see chapters 6 and 7). Kala Krishna and Ling Hui Tan of the Pennsylvania State University and the Brookings Institution, respectively, have chosen in chapter 4 to question the relevance of a simple static competitive model as used in most empirical and policy studies. Export restraints are administered by governments and different methods of implementation influence the allocation of 'quota rents'. Using available data, Krishna and Tan assess whether the rents accrue to exporting countries completely, as usually assumed, and they then model the alternative allocation systems according to observable data.

The analysis in chapter 4 suggests that quota implementation and market imperfections (both among potential exporters at export quota auctions and on final markets for clothing) do affect the rent transfers between countries and producers. Such non-conventional distributions of licences and rents will influence the way phasing-out the MFA will affect producers' and consumers' welfare and redistributions of production.

The Uruguay Round Final Act includes for the first time recognition that policies affecting trade, international monetary issues and development need to show coherence. A Ministerial Declaration calls for the WTO to pursue and develop cooperation with the IMF and the World Bank to achieve greater coherence in global economic policy making. This comprehensive approach acknowledges the progress during the past decade in parallel liberalisation of trade and financial regulations. In particular in East Asia, authorities have recognised that exchange rate stability is necessary to support expansion of trade and economic growth.

Suiwah Leung, from the National Centre for Development Studies, reviews in chapter 5 the evidence linking exchange rate volatility to trade. After examining empirical studies, she finds there is no consistent systematic relationship between short-term exchange rate fluctuations and bilateral or multilateral trade flows. Even in periods where a statistically significant relationship existed, the actual impact is much smaller than other factors that affect trade. Leung argues that currency hedging provides a satisfactory instrument to overcome short-term exchange rate fluctuations.

The deregulation of financial markets in East Asia in recent years has facilitated trade expansion and economic growth, by increasing exchange rate stability in face of fluctuations in external economic imbalances. Continuing financial deregulation in the Asia Pacific countries will make financial hedging more available. Exchange rate risks can then be managed in a cost-effective manner. As regards the effect of currency misalignments on the growth of protectionism, Leung argues that there are major gaps in current knowledge about the causes of misalignments, the efficiency of foreign exchange markets, the working of sterilised intervention, and what represents an appropriate 'equilibrium' real exchange rate. Against these uncertainties, there are real risks of disruption to the payments system if political commitments to a stable exchange rate are ever put to the test. To the extent that misalignments have fiscal causes, international economic policy coordination focusing on exchange rates would not solve the problem, and could undermine policy credibility. The WTO will contribute more economic coherence by introducing more discipline into the use of trade restraints as contingency protection and for balance of payments reasons. Institutional cooperation that incorporates WTO officials into IMF and World Bank committees should also enhance policy coherence.

Modelling changes in world trade

A perennial question that plagues trade negotiators in all countries is: what will be the economic benefits arising from mutual reduction in trade protection? Or, how will the benefits from reciprocal multilateral bargaining to reduce protection be distributed among participating countries? The underlying logic is usually related to tariff reductions or similar easily quantifiable measures. Probably the largest change from the Uruguay Round is the strengthening of the multilateral trade rules and disciplines embodied in the GATT. Yet the benefits from many of these changes cannot be measured.

Notwithstanding difficulties in estimating the effects of trade liberalisation on economic activity, efforts must be made to show sceptics in the protectionist lobbies that substantial real gains come from trade liberalisation. Estimating techniques improve all the time. Part II of this volume contains three chapters that model the welfare effects of aspects of the Uruguay Round Final Act and their distribution among different regions. The simplifications made to produce manageable models are the key determinants of the results of trade-policy changes. The computable general equilibrium (CGE) models used in chapters 6 and 7 allow for interrelationships between sectors and economies, with complicated feedback mechanisms. Each employs a new sophistication to refine the results.

The most sophisticated model and most comprehensive coverage is used in chapter 6 by Joe Francois, Bradley McDonald and Håkan Nordström, of the WTO. This model forecasts gains in global output and trade expected by the year 2005, based on 1990 data. This analysis relies on a fifteen-sector, nine-region CGE model of the world economy. This general equilibrium approach, based on an input–output framework, links together all parts of the world economy through a network of direct and indirect relationships. The changes introduced as a result of the Uruguay Round are fed into this general equilibrium framework in three stages:

- Initially, the effects of tariff reductions and import quota liberalisation are analysed with constant return to scale (CES) technologies, competitive domestic markets for capital and labour but no international movements of factor inputs.
- Next, industry-wide economies of scale are introduced within each industry, allowing production costs to decline as aggregate output increases.
- Finally, the model incorporates imperfect competition and scale economies for firms in each industry. This allows two-way trade in specialised goods, rather than simple comparative advantage.

The model in chapter 6 estimates the trade and income effects of the market access outcomes of the Uruguay Round resulting from tariff reductions, phase-out of industrial quotas and agricultural reforms. According to which version of the model is used, the merchandise trade volume in 2005 may be 10 per cent (constant returns) or 22 per cent (increasing returns and monopolistic competition) higher after full implementation of these Uruguay Round changes. A similar range of results is obtained for increases in annual global income in 2005 (1990 prices); US$200 billion increasing to US$510 billion according to the assumptions. Estimates based on perfect competition and constant returns to scale, used in all earlier estimates of global effects of the Uruguay Round, assume away important multiplier effects in the inter-sectoral relationships (Goldin *et al.*, 1993). Yet even the third version of the Francois–McDonald–Nordström model ignores major dynamic effects on expenditures and incomes through international capital flows and investment flows. Moreover, if the model allowed for more disaggregation of 'regions' and 'sectors', additional linkages would introduce new multipliers. The model does not attempt to estimate some of the most radical reforms resulting from Uruguay Round agreements, affecting non-tariff measures, trade-related investment measures, intellectual property, trade in services and general tightening of GATT rules, which are not readily quantifiable.

Hence, the large benefits claimed from the Uruguay Round by the Francois–McDonald–Nordström model are still under-estimates. Increases in trade volumes and incomes expected in 2005, compared with what would have happened without the Uruguay Round (based on 1990 data and OECD no-change projections), will be multiplied by allowing for dynamic and spread effects. This makes the overall effects even larger than was estimated when the negotiations were completed: merchandise trade volumes are larger by one-quarter than otherwise, and global income is 1.4 per cent higher. The distribution of these gains shows, not unexpectedly, that the major regions (EU and United States) are the largest gainers – largely because of the dominant effects of the agreement on agriculture on those regions' highly distorted domestic agricultural sectors. (Subsequent estimates of the liberalisation in agriculture suggest that these gains have been over-stated, Hathaway and Ingco, 1996.) Developing countries together share welfare benefits equal (approximately) to each of the major industrial regions. (Since developing countries are treated as one region in the Francois–McDonald–Nordström model, the trade and income gains are probably under-estimated because within-group trade is not allowed for in the results.)

The East Asian economies have demonstrated strong linkages between export expansion and income growth for over thirty years (World Bank, 1993). In chapter 7, Yongzheng Yang, from the National Centre for Development Studies, introduces the growth effects and conventional resource allocation effects of trade liberalisation into a comparative static CGE model using export externalities. In this case, the effects of Uruguay

Round liberalisation depend on the export (and import) composition of different countries' output. This additional characteristic is introduced into a ten-region, ten-sector CGE model to measure the effects of the Uruguay Round. (Yang used the Global Trade Analysis Project (GTAP) model, Hertel and Tsigas, forthcoming, used by Francois–McDonald–Nordström, adapted to give more emphasis to developing country regions.) Yang shows that by allowing for export-driven technological change, the overall trade and income effects of anticipated changes resulting from the Uruguay Round are doubled. The industrial countries absorb a smaller share of these externality gains than under static assumptions, while developing regions receive more. This is consistent with expectations because technology transfers would tend to be from industrial to developing countries, and would be accelerated by increasing trade.

The enhanced benefits for developing countries from the Uruguay Round found by Yang are consistent with the results of the Francois–McDonald–Nordström model. The latter showed that as the competitive/constant returns constraints were progressively relaxed and economies of scale introduced, the gains in income, welfare and trade from implementation of the Uruguay Round agreements all increased. Yang introduces an additional degree of freedom by allowing for technological change linked to trade and specialisation. Estimates of the economic benefits derived from trade liberalisation increase when more realistic features are incorporated into the CGE models.

General equilibrium modelling of international trade flows and links to economic growth, resource allocation and income distribution is a comparatively recent area of study, promoted by developments in computer capacities. Since 1985, attempts to measure the potential effects of the Uruguay Round agreements on the world economy, and the impacts of NAFTA and the Single European Market on member countries and the rest of the world, have brought rapid progress in CGE modelling techniques. The CGE models used by Francois–McDonald–Nordström and Yang are the most sophisticated attempts yet to estimate the effects of trade liberalisation. These studies cover only some quantifiable reductions in protection resulting from the Uruguay Round. The benefits expected from improvements in rules and disciplines, and surveillance by the WTO, cannot be measured. Nevertheless, the model results provided here are entirely consistent with other modelling exercises and show that the benefits in terms of trade increases and economic growth from the Uruguay Round are very substantial, *ceteris paribus*.

Major aspects of the Uruguay Round agreements are not allowed for in conventional CGE models. World trade in services is now estimated to be equivalent to around 25 per cent of the value of world merchandise trade (GATT, 1989). The framework agreement on trade in services (GATS) represents a major step towards bringing trade in services under the same disciplines that have ruled merchandise trade for almost fifty years. The potential value of the GATS in terms of facilitating trade in services has not yet been properly estimated, largely because statistics on trade in services are inadequate. Although most countries estimate net inflows and out-flows of services such as transportation, insurance, tourism, etc. for balance of payments reporting, few attempt to measure the directions of these flows between countries.

The final short chapter in part II (chapter 8), by Will Martin of the World Bank, contains an assessment of the CGE modelling techniques and ways that the studies might be extended. Because the Uruguay Round agreements are so complicated, modellers have to reduce them to simple quantifiable changes. One problem is measuring simple tariff reductions when applied tariffs are below 'bound' tariffs. This chapter examines this problem (see also chapter 9). Martin's comments suggest ways for extending the effectiveness of CGE modelling, where progress can be expected to continue.

Trade issues for East Asia

Part III of the volume contains seven chapters on selected trade issues facing regional economics now the Uruguay Round is over. Despite the major increase in East Asian countries' participation in the Uruguay Round as compared with earlier GATT rounds, Gary Sampson, of the WTO Secretariat, shows in chapter 9 that their concessions on market access are less significant than might have been expected from countries that depend heavily on the rules-based multilateral trading system. Their export-led growth strategies stand to benefit from the tightening of disciplines covering subsidies, safeguards and grey-area measures, where they have frequently experienced discrimination in industrial countries' markets, as well as from the general improvement in market access and tariff liberalisation resulting from the Round. As Sampson explains, the actual concessions by East Asian developing countries, measured by applied tariff rates, are likely to be more liberal than the actual 'bound' tariffs. Even so, the binding of domestic unilateral liberalisation commitments is a positive result, because it limits governments' scope to reverse recent liberalisation, as well as incorporating reductions in average tariffs in many sectors. Furthermore, any reduction in GSP preferences in industrial countries' markets, resulting from reductions in their Mfn tariffs, are likely to be offset by increased access to industrial countries' markets. The conclusion that the East Asian countries could have done more to liberalise their economies during the Uruguay Round supports a recent World Bank study which indicates that Latin American economies are benefiting from policies of rapid liberalisation undertaken since 1986 (Dean *et al.*, 1994). If high 'bound' tariffs were retained to provide trade preferences within the proposed ASEAN free-trade area (AFTA), the consequence could be welfare losses from trade diversion.

The Australian experience provides some important pointers for other countries in the post-Uruguay Round trading system. In chapter 10, Graeme Thomson, one of Australia's negotiators in the Uruguay Round, presents a trade expert's view of the results for Australia. Australia's experience with unilateral liberalisation has shown the direct benefits to be earned from structural adjustment and the new opportunities this creates for exports. At the same time, the success of the Cairns Group in the Uruguay Round negotiations demonstrated that medium-sized economies can influence outcomes, and by providing such leadership the dominance of the major players may be tempered. Given the growing influence and enlarged role of the East Asian economies in world trade, these countries should be able to affect the operations of the WTO, and continuing negotiations in areas such as trade in services and the new trade agenda of issues (the environment, labour standards and competition policies).

Australia was a major player in the Uruguay Round negotiations because agriculture was a crucial issue. In addition, Australia undertook a programme to liberalise its industrial protection unilaterally during the Round. By adjusting ahead of schedule, Australian industries should be in a competitive position as new trade opportunities emerge from other countries' liberalisation. This unilateral liberalisation is in keeping with many other Western Pacific economies which have taken similar steps over the past eight years. Some areas of hard-core protection (motor vehicles and clothing) remain to be tackled throughout the region.

The progressive reduction of border trade measures has drawn attention to domestic policies affecting market contestability. Restrictive business practices, state-sanctioned monopolies and cartel agreements are identified as domestic policies that impede competition, and may invalidate liberalisation of trade barriers. Many multinational enterprises now identify domestic competition policies as impediments to international competition. Bilateral trade disputes arising from complaints about the nature or implementation of domestic competition policies intensified in

14   *David Robertson*

the course of the Uruguay Round negotiations. US complaints against Japan in the Structural Impediments Initiative were followed by US and EU approaches to a number of East Asian governments.

J. David Richardson, of Syracuse University, examines the general issues raised by domestic competition policies in chapter 11. He argues that the subject has to be limited to disputes relevant to trade which relate to differences among national policies that cause economic inefficiency. After reviewing the causes of global issues in competition policies, Richardson asks: what specific difficulties arise from competition policies in the Western Pacific region? Because the economic history of East Asia is different from OECD countries, conceptions of firms, markets, industrial organisation and capital markets result in misunderstandings about competition and industrial structures. These offer gains from convergence of policies and mechanisms for conflict resolution, but introduce philosophical and cultural differences. Bilateral approaches to competition policy disputes have not proved successful, and sometimes aggravate disputes. A multilateral approach, using the WTO structure, probably offers the most viable approach to resolving disputes over competition policies, because this is the only generally accepted forum for the Asia Pacific economies. Richardson, by explaining the nature of the issues behind disputes over competition policies, indicates the complex issues that arise over multilateralism and sovereignty. Concerns about competition policies are closely linked with issues such as subsidy policies, trade safeguards and anti-dumping, which remain some of the most contentious issues even after the Uruguay Round.

The internationalisation of production and markets has established closer links between trade policies and investment flows. The traditional view of trade and investment as alternative ways to penetrate overseas markets has been revised, with evidence that trade tends to generate FDI in the same direction. Within East Asia, the contribution of Japan as supplier of machinery inputs and consumer goods has given way to investments in neighbouring economies as labour-intensive production processes shifted to lower-wage countries as Japanese costs and the yen appreciation reduced competitiveness. In chapter 12, Masahiro Kawai, from the University of Tokyo, examines the nature of trade and investment links between Japan and neighbouring economies over the past twenty-five years. He establishes some highly significant two-way relationships between Japan's bilateral trade and FDI flows. The interdependence between Japan and East Asia is increasing, with two-way flows of both trade and investment expanding strongly.

The Japanese data reviewed in chapter 12 establish the complementary relationship between trade and investment flows, as more and more international trade occurs within multinational enterprises or affiliated companies, involving parts and components (Julius, 1990). East Asian economies have benefited from substantial inflows of FDI from OECD economies, especially Japan and the United States. More recently, flows of investment between East Asian economies have become the largest source of new investment, enlarged by investment in China from Chinese migrant communities in neighbouring countries (see also chapter 13).

Kawai's review of Japanese trade and investment patterns provides support for including the trade effects of investment policies on the new trade agenda. The TRIMs agreement in the Uruguay Round made a beginning by establishing commitments to eliminate some trade aspects of investment policies. Some aspects of the GATS also affect international investments through associated issues such as rights of establishment and national treatment. The WTO is likely to become a focus for further negotiations where investment policies affect trade. At the same time, national sovereignty is often used to restrict foreign interference in sensitive areas, such as the media and civil aviation. The interface between trade and investment policies is not always obvious or uncomplicated.

China's trade has grown very rapidly in recent years. As an observer at the Uruguay Round negotiations and still seeking re-entry to the GATT, China remains a major problem for the multilateral trading system. The outstanding negotiating issues to restore China's membership are complex and volatile, but their eventual resolution seems inevitable. Acceptance of China into APEC and increasing economic exchanges with her Asian neighbours make China an essential consideration for East Asia in the post-Uruguay Round trading system.

In the past fifteen years, China has achieved real export growth rates that match the most successful of the newly industrialising economies (NIEs) of Asia. The pace of this growth is increasing and looks set to continue. Most of this export expansion has come from non-state-owned enterprises in the four coastal provinces (Guangdong, Jiangsu, Shandong and Liaoning). In chapter 13, Frances Perkins, from the National Centre for Development Studies, uses original research materials and published data to identify the major determinants of export success in the coastal provinces and points to some policy obstacles to export growth in other provinces and enterprises. She finds that enterprises with high productivity growth are the most successful exporters. This indicates that China will continue to benefit from productivity growth as enterprises' exposure to foreign competition increases and the economy grows. Autonomy of decision-making was much higher in firms with export success, which indicates that further export growth is likely as planning and state-control of enterprises are reduced. Both these movements towards more competitive markets will increase when China is restored to GATT membership, a pre-requisite for membership of the WTO.

Market-driven economic integration in East Asia has generated widespread interest, although it is still treated sceptically in Western Europe. In chapter 14 David Robertson reviews the likely effects of the Uruguay Round agreements on East Asian economies. The strong economic performance in East Asia has also generated initiatives from Asia Pacific governments seeking to formalise the integration process. In 1989, APEC was established to provide a forum for consultation among regional governments. Any decisions taken require consensus among all eighteen member governments, which is the Asian way. It was a surprise, therefore, when at their meeting in November 1994, APEC leaders adopted the Bogor Declaration to pursue free and open trade and investment no later than the year 2020. (David Robertson's chapter 15, see below, contains a brief review of APEC and how its objectives relate to the post-Uruguay Round multilateral trading system.)

Chapter 14 examines the place of globalisation in East Asian economic development. Globalisation of production and markets became an increasing concern of the trade negotiation committees as the Uruguay Round progressed. Specific issues, such as TRIMs, TRIPs and GATS dwelt on the relevance of globalisation. The declaration on economic policy coherence was a significant response to growing concerns about relationships between different aspects of national and international policies. Finally the main items on the so-called 'new trade agenda' are all closely linked to globalisation – competition policy, investment and innovation policy, labour standards, regionalism, and trade and environment issues.

International trade has played a leading role in the spread of economic development in East Asia. Export-led growth was adopted in successive waves as successful exporters moved up the technology ladder and released labour-intensive, standardised processes to their low-wage neighbours. The success of this approach depended on imported equipment and technologies, and on openness to foreign influences, especially foreign investment and corporate affiliations, to sustain competitiveness on world markets. The open, multilateral trading system has been essential for this commercial approach to development to succeed. The East Asian economies, therefore, had an active interest in the Uruguay Round negotiations from their beginning. As the Round proceeded, the East Asian economies became more integrated into global production and marketing, requiring them to adopt a more active role.

The benefits accruing to the East Asian economies from the Uruguay Round Final Act will come principally from the support it gives to the multilateral trading system. Tariff reductions and bindings offer some new market opportunities. The major benefits, however, will derive from an orderly, rules-based system watched over by the WTO and its dispute settlement procedures. Contingency protection still casts a long shadow and uncertainties about anti-dumping and new issues in competition policy remain a threat. As corporate affiliations across frontiers intensify with globalised production, opposition to discriminatory trade barriers in OECD countries should increase, bringing benefits to East Asian exporters.

The studies in this volume had been completed when APEC leaders adopted the Bogor Declaration. Chapter 15 was added to cover this surprising new commitment to liberal trade by the world's fastest-growing economies. After all, major new undertakings were made when the Uruguay Round Final Act was adopted at Marrakesh only seven months before.

Although regionalism is a major force in the trading system, which may have uncertain consequences for multilateral trade, APEC does not fall under Article XXIV of the GATT. APEC governments have avoided any agreements that discriminate against non-member economies, by pursuing trade liberalisation and deregulation through unilateral actions. The Bogor Declaration continues that approach, requiring officials to establish suitable liberalisation to be applied in ways consistent with GATT Article I, non-discrimination. Because the APEC countries are planning to proceed faster than commitments made in Uruguay Round agreements, without discriminating against outsiders, there is no inconsistency with the WTO. In fact, chapter 15 suggests, APEC may have an important role in underwriting the implementation programme of Uruguay Round liberalisation and promoting further progress in the continuing negotiations and reviews. Because of their growing significance in global trade and production, the APEC countries will play a major role in the development of the agenda for a new round of trade negotiations. Their success with 'open regionalism' will help to determine when such a round will commence.

I

World trade after the Uruguay Round

2

The outlook for the world trading system beyond the Uruguay Round

KYM ANDERSON

For F13 019

The outlook for the world trading system and the outlook for East Asian trade are almost synonymous. Dynamic, export-led economic growth in East Asia has doubled the region's share of world trade during the past three decades. True, the share of East Asia's trade that is intra-regional has been growing, as have the intra-regional trade shares of both Western Europe and North America. But the dependence of each of those regions' economies on markets outside their own region remains high. Developments in the world trading system and in global trade are crucially important to the region, as a healthy global trading system is essential for a continuation of East Asian economic growth. At the same time, the region's potential for influencing those developments is growing. Indeed, continued prosperity in East Asia depends not just on how well people there respond to changes in the world economy, but also on how well their firms and governments manage to influence the evolution of policies affecting world trade, be they multilateral, regional, or unilateral.

At the multilateral level, successful implementation of the Uruguay Round is obviously of crucial importance. The new World Trade Organisation (WTO) has a full work programme, not least in monitoring that implementation and arbitrating disputes arising from it. But even if the Round were to be implemented without major problems during the remainder of this decade, the GATT rules-based multilateral trading system under the WTO will continue to come under strain. The irony is that those challenges – regionalism, environmentalism, concern about labour standards, and competition policy – are in part a result of the GATT's very success in fostering global economic integration over the past forty-seven years.

Regional integration initiatives in Europe and North America, in addition to influencing the multilateral trading system, are having direct impacts on East Asian trade and investment. And unilateral trade policy initiatives, particularly by the United States, are being keenly felt in East Asia as well. After analysing each of these sources of change in turn, some

Table 2.1. *Europe, North America and the Western Pacific in the world
economy, percentages*

	GDP		Merchandise trade[a]	
	1963	1992	1963	1993
Europe (incl. CIS)	34	37	50	46
North America (incl. Mexico)	45	29	18	20
Western Pacific	11	23	11	24
Rest of world	10	11	21	10
World	100	100	100	100

Note:
[a]Merchandise exports plus imports.
Sources: World Bank (1994); GATT (1994f).

of the options available to East Asia that might minimise the risks and
maximise the opportunities arising from the challenges facing the global
trading system are examined.

Asia's expanding role in world trade

Early in the 1960s, the Western Pacific (East Asia plus Australasia)
accounted for less than one-eighth of world GDP and trade. Today both
shares are almost one-quarter. The growth in importance of the region has
been primarily at the expense of North America in terms of output and
income, but at the expense of other developing countries with respect to
trade. This follows from the fact that the share of GDP traded internationally has grown rapidly for North America (table 2.1).

The Western Pacific's interdependence with the rest of the world is even
greater than these shares suggest because much of Europe's large trade
volume is with other European countries as a result of the preferential
regional trading arrangements of the EU, EFTA and (until it was disbanded
in 1991) Comecon (figure 2.1). When intra-bloc trade is ignored, the
Western Pacific is an even larger participant in world trade outside those
blocs. Indeed if the EU is treated as a single trader, the six East Asian
economies appear in the list of the world's top nine exporters in 1993, with
three more not far behind (table 2.2).

How regionalised is Asia's trade becoming, compared with Europe's
and North America's? In part (i) of table 2.3 it is clear that Asia's intra-
regional trade share had grown relatively little until the 1980s and only by
a fifth during the 1980s. This is despite the greater regionalisation of

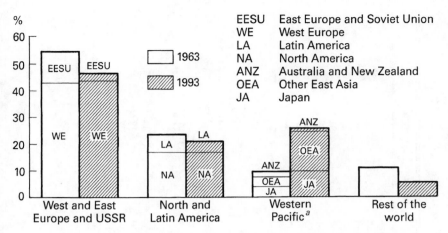

Figure 2.1 Regional shares of world merchandise trade, 1963 and 1993
Note:
*a*Japan; the market economies of Northeast and Southeast Asia plus China (collectively Other East Asia); and Australia and New Zealand
Source: GATT (1987; 1994f).

Table 2.2. *Leading traders internationally when the EU (formerly EC) is treated as a single trader and intra-EU trade is excluded, 1993, percentages*

	Share of world merchandise exports and imports (%)
1 EU-12	19.1
2 United States	18.0
3 Japan	10.2
4 Canada	4.8
5 Hong Kong	4.7
6 China	3.3
7 Korea	2.8
8 Taiwan	2.8
9 Singapore	2.7
10 Switzerland	2.1
11 Mexico	1.6
12 Malaysia	1.6
13 Sweden	1.5
14 Australia	1.5
15 Austria	1.5
16 Thailand	1.4
17 Saudi Arabia	1.2
18 Brazil	1.1
19 Indonesia	1.1
20 Russia	1.1

Source: GATT (1994f).

Table 2.3. *Trade shares and the intensity and propensity of regionalisation in world merchandise trade, 1948–90*

	1948	1958	1968	1979	1990
(i) *Intra-regional trade share (%)*[a]					
Western Europe	43	53	63	66	72
North America incl. Mexico	37	38	40	35	40
Asia	39	41	37	41	48
– Japan[f]	60	36	32	31	35
– Australasia[f]	14	25	31	49	51
– Developing Asia[f]	44	47	45	48	56
World, total	33	40	47	46	52
(ii) *Intensity of intra-regional trade index*[b]					
Western Europe	1.21	1.38	1.51	1.57	1.60
North America incl. Mexico	2.24	2.72	2.90	3.09	3.21
Asia	2.74	3.15	2.84	2.77	2.31
– Japan[f]	4.29	3.28	3.81	3.08	2.33
– Australasia[f]	1.08	2.00	2.47	3.32	2.47
– Developing Asia[f]	3.10	3.56	3.37	3.17	2.64
World, total[c]	2.43	2.65	2.81	2.64	2.62
(iii) *Share (%) of GDP traded*[a]					
Western Europe	35	33	34	48	46
North America incl. Mexico	11	9	10	19	20
Asia	25	26	21	27	29
– Japan[f]	8	19	17	20	18
– Australasia[f]	47	31	25	29	30
– Developing Asia[f]	25[e]	29	26	37	47
World, total[c]	22	22	22	35	34
(iv) *Index of propensity to trade intra-regionally*[d]					
Western Europe	0.30	0.46	0.50	0.75	0.73

North America incl. Mexico	0.25	0.26	0.28	0.60	0.63
Asia	0.67	0.83	0.60	0.76	0.67
– Japan[f]	0.28	0.53	0.31	0.55	0.42
– Australasia[f]	0.43	0.57 -	0.71	1.03	0.89
– Developing Asia[f]	0.84	1.07	1.09	1.23	1.21
World, total	0.54	0.57	0.61	0.91	0.88
(v) Index of propensity to trade extra-regionally[d]					
Western Europe	0.31	0.26	0.21	0.28	0.23
North America incl. Mexico	0.08	0.07	0.07	0.14	0.13
Asia	0.18	0.18	0.15	0.19	0.19
– Japan[f]	0.04	0.13	0.12	0.15	0.13
– Australasia[f]	0.46	0.27	0.19	0.17	0.19
– Developing Asia[f]	0.16	0.17	0.16	0.23	0.26
World, total	0.19	0.16	0.15	0.23	0.21

Notes:

[a]Throughout table 2.3, 'trade' refers to the average of merchandise export and import shares or intensity indexes, except that the share of GDP traded, and the propensity index refer to exports plus imports of merchandise. All values are measured in current US dollars. Turkey and the former Yugoslavia are included in Western Europe. North America refers to Canada, Mexico and the United States, and Australasia refers to Australia and New Zealand.

[b]The intensity of trade index for regions is defined (roughly) as the share of one region's trade with another region relative to that other region's share of world trade (see Anderson and Norheim, 1993, for a more precise definition of the indexes of intra- and extra-regional trade intensity).

[c]The world total intensity index is the weighted average across the seven regions (Africa, Eastern Europe, Latin America and the Middle East are not shown), using the regions' shares of world trade as weights.

[d]The propensity to trade index is defined as the intensity index multiplied by the ratio of exports plus imports to GDP (see Anderson and Norheim, 1993). The world total refers to the weighted average for the seven regions (Africa, Eastern Europe, Latin America and the Middle East are not shown), using the regions' shares of world GDP as weights.

[e]In the absence of reliable estimates of GDP prior to the 1950s for developing countries and until 1989 for Eastern Europe, 'guesstimates' have been made of the trade-to-GDP ratio for those regions. Given their small weights in world trade, the aggregates for the world will nonetheless be reasonably reliable. The ratio is estimated at current prices.

[f]The rows for Japan, Australasia and Developing Asia differ from the other rows in that they are treated not as regions themselves but as part of their sum which is the Asian region including South Asia.

Source: Anderson and Blackhurst (1993, appendix).

Europe's and (to a lesser extent) North America's trade and the large increase in Asia's share of world trade. The effect of changes in the regions' shares of world trade on intra-regional trade shares can be netted out by calculating the index of intra-regional trade intensity, roughly the intra-regional trade share divided by the region's share of world trade. Part (ii) of table 2.3 shows those indexes for Western Europe, North America, Asia, and the world as a whole (comprising also four other regions, not listed). These data confirm that Asia's regional trade pattern is different: while the intensity of intra-regional trade in Europe and North America has been steadily increasing over the postwar period, Asia's intra-regional trade intensity has been decreasing since the 1960s.

Do those differences in intra-regional trade intensity indexes mean that Asia has become more dependent on the rest of the world while Western Europe and North America have become more inward-focused? The answer is 'no', because what also needs to be taken into account is the overall extent to which each region's GDP is internationally traded. In this regard Asia has changed relatively little compared with Europe and America (part (iii) of table 2.3). Indeed, that share for Japan has grown hardly at all in recent decades (while doubling for North America and Developing Asia and rising by a third for Europe), and is partly why Japan has been singled out so much by the United States in its complaints about unfair restrictions on market access abroad.[1]

Anderson and Norheim (1993) have suggested a way to take those differences in trade orientation into account. It is to calculate the share of each region's GDP that is traded within its own region, and then to divide that by the region's share of world trade; and likewise to calculate the ratio of the share of each region's GDP that is traded outside that region relative to the share of the rest of the world in global trade. These ratios were called indexes of the propensity to trade intra- and extra-regionally, and they show the indexes to be equivalent to the product of the trade intensity index and the trade-to-GDP ratio. The calculated values for these propensity indexes are shown in parts (iv) and (v) of table 2.3. What they reveal is that on average Western European countries have a greater propensity to trade extra-regionally than do Asian countries, and that this difference has narrowed (but not greatly) during the past three or four decades. Those indexes also reveal that in the 1970s North America in this respect had been rapidly catching up with Asia – and has caught up with Japan – despite the much larger size and greater range of resource endowments and hence lesser need for the US economy to trade internationally.

In short, there are at least three things to note from these data and from table 2.4 (which simply shows the share of each region's GDP that is traded

Table 2.4. *Share of GDP traded extra-regionally, Western Europe, North America and Asia, 1958–90[a], percentages*

	1958	1963	1968	1973	1979	1983	1990
Western Europe	16	12	13	14	16	15	13
North America incl. Mexico	6	6	6	8	13	11	12
Asia	16	11	14	14	16	15	15
– Japan[f]	12	11	12	14	14	15	12
– Australasia[f]	29	27	23	27	27	22	28
– Developing Asia[f]	19	13	20	19	28	24	31
World, total[c]	13	12	12	14	19	17	16

Note:
See table 2.3, notes *a*, *c* and *f*.
Source: Anderson and Blackhurst, (1993, appendix table A7).

extra-regionally, averaging about one-seventh for Western Europe and Japan and one-eighth for North America). First, they reveal that the Western Pacific has become a more significant – indeed a major – participant in world trade, with its importance now exceeding Europe's and North America's when intra-bloc trade is excluded. But, secondly, this region's interdependence through trade with other regions is roughly matched by that of North America and Western Europe, notwithstanding the common claim that the latter are inward-looking trading blocs. That is, all three regions have a huge and still-growing interest in ensuring that prosperity flourishes outside their own geographic region and that extra-regional trade remains open, as a healthy multilateral trading system provides. And third, the latter is especially important for Asia because, unlike in Western Europe and now North America, this region does not have a free-trade agreement or customs union and so the WTO is important for maintaining and increasing openness not only of Asia's trade with other regions but also of intra-Asian trade. Yet, despite Asia being as important as Europe and North America in trade between regions, Asia has been much less assertive than the United States or EU in the GATT/WTO process.

Implementing the Uruguay Round agreements

For all its faults, the GATT rules-based multilateral trading system has served the world – and especially East Asia – very well. In particular, as a result of seven previous rounds of trade negotiations, import tariffs on manufactures have been wound down for most commodities to negligible levels in industrial countries. It is true that many non-tariff barriers (NTBs) are still in place and that some have risen as tariffs have been reduced. But the fact remains that the share of world GDP that is traded internationally has risen from just over one-fifth in the 1950s and 1960s to more than one-third since the late 1970s (part (iii) of table 2.3), only a part of which is likely to be due to the fall in international transport and communication costs and in the value-added share of output.[2]

The signing of the Uruguay Round agreements in Marrakesh in April 1994 brought to an end seven-and-a-half years of arduous trade negotiations. The struggle to reach agreement was not so much a sign of crisis in the multilateral trading system as a sign that, having reduced manufacturing tariffs so much in previous rounds, the time had come to turn to NTBs and to the trade policies of politically more sensitive sectors (agriculture, textiles and clothing, services) and to trade-related policies. These were the difficult items that had also often been ignored in unilateral and minilateral reforms. Certainly it is not very surprising that agreement on the extent and speed of farm and textile trade reform was difficult to reach. After all, assistance to agricultural, textile and clothing producers has been in place and growing for decades. So even a moratorium on further increases in protection levels in industrial countries for these traditional declining industries would be a significant change. And with trade in services also being brought under multilateral disciplines for the first time, not to mention progress in such trade-related areas as intellectual property and investment, the Round involved the relinquishing of a considerable degree of national sovereignty over policy. Conclusion of the Uruguay Round will not allow complacency with respect to the multilateral system. The new WTO has a full work programme of relatively routine matters, in addition to some major new challenges on the immediate horizon. Four routine activities are worth mentioning before turning to discuss some of the WTO's new challenges.

First, monitoring the implementation of the Uruguay Round agreements will be a major task in itself. There is plenty of scope in the agreements for different interpretations of what is required to comply;[3] a greater degree of policy transparency is required. Two aspects of the agreement on agriculture provide particularly striking examples. One is that since countries have to replace all non-tariff import barriers with bound tariffs, and they have done so by setting tariffs at rates well above the tariff equivalent of the previous NTBs (sometimes several times greater), it may well be that actual import barriers on some items will be higher at the end than at the beginning of the decade. The other is that while the Aggregate Measure of Support (AMS) via domestic farm policies is to be reduced under the

Agreement, increased price supports for industries that are 'supply-constrained' (for example, by land set-asides or dairy herd quotas) do not count in measuring changes in the AMS, even though we have clear evidence that higher prices induce higher yields per hectare or per cow. Thus, in addition to measuring the AMS continuing estimation of producer subsidy equivalents (PSEs) is needed and related indexes of actual protection, not least so that a proper evaluation of the leakiness of the Uruguay Round agreement can be used to negotiate a tighter outcome in the next round of farm policy talks, to begin in 1999 (Anderson, 1994a).

Second, because there is plenty of scope in the agreements for different interpretations of what is required to comply, as well as a large backlog of unresolved issues, the revamped dispute settlement mechanism for the WTO will be extremely busy as countries test the new rules and procedures.

Third, the WTO has to cope with the flood of new applications for membership. At present there are about 125 members, so potentially more than fifty countries could line up. The most important to cope with first is China, and that would then allow Taiwan to join immediately. Of Europe's former Comecon countries only the Czech and Slovak republics are full members, so a score of applications are or will soon be forthcoming from that region too.

And fourth, the task of tidying up unfinished business in the Uruguay Round (for example, in services) and beginning preparations for the next round of multilateral trade negotiations needs to get under way. Traditionally there is a honeymoon period before the task begins again, but that will not be the case this time. The US Congress has already raised some new trade concerns. The NAFTA was perceived to require side-agreements on environmental and labour standards before the US Congress would ratify it. So the United States is calling for a specific work programme on trade and environment and also on labour standards (see below).

Other challenges for the WTO

The GATT's successes since the late 1940s, together with rapid technological changes, mean that traditional barriers to international trade have become increasingly less important as determinants of international competitiveness. Those barrier reductions include not only governmental ones, such as import tariffs, but also natural ones such as transport and telecommunication costs. The latter are especially important in lowering the transactions costs of the banking/foreign exchange aspects of trade.

The resulting extra exposure of national economies to competition from abroad has caused attention to focus much more sharply on domestic policies that influence the international competitiveness of firms and industries. Two responses to that have been calls for (a) other microeconomic reforms which would increase competition domestically and lower firms' production costs, and (b) restraint on introducing further social policies that add to private costs of production. In the case of the first, if they are implemented multilaterally rather than unilaterally, those additional reforms are less painful for the groups that stand to lose (for example, trade unionists in the case of labour market deregulation, monopolies in the case of anti-trust policies, favoured domestic firms in the case of opening up government procurement). The reason is that the more other countries are reforming, the faster will be global market growth and hence the less need for contraction of any one sector absolutely (even if it were to decline relatively). The same is true in the case of governments needing to respond to calls for cost-raising social policies. For example, raising environmental or labour or other social standards is less threatening to producers of tradeables in one country if standards are similarly raised in countries with firms competing with those producers.

Not surprisingly, achieving agreement among countries to coordinate such reforms is easier the more similar are the tastes and preferences in the countries concerned. Hence their greater success among similar countries in a region than globally. Thus it was that Western European countries were able to use the EU for expanding their social charter via Maastricht. When the countries of a region are dissimilar, regional agreements tied to market access provide a vehicle. The United States, for example, was able to convince Mexico to sign side-agreements on environmental and labour standards in the course of getting the US Congress to approve the main NAFTA provisions.

When viewed in this light, the greater promise, as well as potential problems, associated with the deepening and widening of regional integration agreements, become more apparent (Lawrence, 1993). At one extreme there are those who seek to emphasise the problems, the biggest being the potential for the world to break up into three inward-looking trading blocs. And at the other extreme there are those who claim that these initiatives to encourage greater regional integration will, over time, be embraced at broader multilateral levels. The latter analysts would argue that regionalism is therefore a stepping stone rather than a stumbling block to an improved multilateral trading system and thereby to enhanced economic welfare. Certainly the pessimistic view that 'GATT is dead' is credible only in the sense that the GATT Secretariat has been replaced by the more substantive WTO. But the optimistic view about regionalism and the associated minilateral agreements on social issues, such as environmental and labour standards, needs to be tempered also. Consider first regionalism and then the two social issues.

Regionalism and the WTO[4]

There are several ways in which the proliferation of regional economic integration initiatives may be more of a stumbling block than a stepping stone towards freer world trade, even leaving aside for the moment the question of social issues. One is for the traditional reason that regional integration agreements can be more trade-diverting than trade-creating. The history of the West European arrangements (table 2.3) suggests this has not been a major problem in the past at least, in the sense that the propensity for Western Europe to trade with other regions has grown rapidly since the 1950s. Whether it will be a problem in the future is a moot point, however.

Supporters of NAFTA believe there is no cause for concern. They point, for example, to the effect that President Bush's offer to other Latin American countries (to consider forming a free-trade area with the United States) has had in encouraging those developing countries to push ahead unilaterally with their macroeconomic and microeconomic reforms (which would be necessary before the United States would consider their application). And Central and Eastern Europeans also know that before significant agreement to free up trade with Western Europeans can be reached, those formerly planned economies have to become much more market-oriented. However, people outside those regions believe there are causes for concern, not least because the text of recent regional trade agreements tend to be many hundreds of – rather than just a few dozen – pages. That is, they contain so many qualifications and exceptions that they fall a long way short of creating literally free-trade areas.

Snape *et al.* (1993) argue that a preferential trade agreement is more likely to complement and facilitate liberal multilateral trade the more it involves (a) full liberalisation of trade between participants in at least all products, if not also in productive factors; (b) no raising of external barriers to trade and investment on formation or subsequently, and a willingness and capacity to negotiate external barrier reduction thereafter; (c) homogeneous rules of origin and dispute settlement procedures; and (d) openness to new members on the same conditions as those faced by existing members.

 Clearly, not even EFTA or the EU, let alone NAFTA and the more recently negotiated and prospective regional integration agreements in

Europe and America, are close to fulfilling all these conditions. In fact the latest ones are more like 'hub-and-spoke' agreements, involving an ever-larger number of separate bilateral deals between the main or 'hub' economy (the United States, the EU-12, or Russia) and smaller 'spoke' economies. The likelihood is that the 'spokes' to be added in the future will be increasingly less natural trading partners than those added to date. And such agreements may then require those smaller spoke economies also to negotiate separate bilateral deals with other spokes. Rules of origin and dispute settlement procedures also become ever-more important elements in the administration of such trade agreements. The proliferation of hub-and-spoke agreements would not only increasingly distract participants' attention away from the multilateral trading system, but would also increase friction both among participants and between them and outsiders. It is difficult to imagine the world going very far down such a path without the global trading system coming under the sort of stress experienced in the 1930s.

Another way in which regional integration initiatives can be stumbling blocks to freer global trade is that their protagonists, by focusing on deeper and wider regional integration, divert the attention of government leaders and officials away from improving the broader multilateral system. Certainly the Uruguay Round suffered from Western Europe's preoccupation with furthering the EC Single Market and Maastricht processes during the 1980s and with deciding on how to proceed with the next enlargements and association accords. The Round suffered not just directly but also indirectly in the sense that American frustrations over getting the EC to the negotiating table led first to the Canada–US Trade Agreement (CUSTA) and then to NAFTA, both of which absorbed time of negotiators that might otherwise have been spent speeding up progress on the Uruguay Round.

And finally, as they widen and deepen, regional trading blocs tend to become more assertive towards other countries and blocs. Whether that helps or hinders progress toward freer world trade is an empirical question. In the early postwar years when the United States dominated the GATT, it was helpful that its inclination was predominantly (with some notable exceptions) in support of freer trade. Now that the United States has declined in relative importance and influence in the GATT and has become more protectionist in its rhetoric than in previous decades, and the EU has risen to become a counterweight economically but is unable because of its diverse membership to take up the leadership vacuum left by the United States, progress in liberalising trade multilaterally is more difficult. What this last point suggests is that there is scope for a third group of countries – most obviously one centred on the Western Pacific with or without North America – to take the initiative and contribute to the WTO process.

Environmentalism and the WTO[5]

The 'greening' of world politics accelerated substantially in the 1980s and is now much more pervasive in its effects on the world economy. It has changed the comparative advantages of different countries as the implementation of stricter environmental standards and higher taxes on polluters have greater effect in some countries than in others.[6] But because many of the more recent concerns of environmentalists go beyond national boundaries, and in some cases have to do with the global commons, they raise several questions about roles for trade policy.

One, which arose initially with the first wave of concern for the environment in the 1960s, has to do simply with the concern of firms in advanced industrial economies that their competitiveness is being eroded by the imposition of, say, stricter pollution abatement standards at home than abroad. Where the environmental damage caused by production is purely local, the calls by disadvantaged firms for trade restrictions or subsidies to offset the decline in their international competitiveness, because standards have been raised, has no economic logic: such assistance would tend to offset the desired effect of limiting by-product pollution. Nor is it reasonable to conclude that other countries are engaging in 'eco-dumping' if the imports they are able to supply are produced with laxer environmental standards, in so far as those lower standards are consistent with the preferences and natural resource endowments of those exporting countries (for example, because those countries are poorer and/or less densely populated and less urbanised). Even so, claims for protection against eco-dumping have political appeal and may result in higher import barriers or export subsidies than would otherwise be the case in advanced economies.

Trade-policy actions of this kind are more likely to occur, and to be more difficult to dismiss as inappropriate, when environmentalists in such countries view particular damage to the environment as unacceptable regardless of the nation in which the damage occurs. This case is even more problematic if the damage is not just psychological (as with animal rights) but also physical (for example, pollution blown across national borders by the prevailing winds), for then the relocation of production to a country with laxer environmental standards may worsen animal welfare, or pollution at home, in addition to reducing the profitability of the home firms: the infamous US–Mexico dispute over the use of dolphin-unfriendly nets by tuna fishermen comes to mind. In that case, the GATT ruled against the

US ban on imports of tuna from Mexico, partly because the ban did not discriminate according to which type of net was used – as it cannot, because an aspect of the production process rather than the final traded product itself is what is considered objectionable. The GATT panel ruled against the ban because to do otherwise would have created a huge loophole in the GATT for any country unilaterally to apply trade restrictions as a means of imposing its environmental standards on other countries. Such a loophole would work against the main objective of the multilateral trading system, which is to provide stable and predictable market access opportunities through agreed rules and disciplines and bound tariffs on imports.

Another concern is that, in addition to proposing the use of trade restrictions, some environmentalists also oppose trade liberalisation. They oppose the GATT's attempts to lower trade barriers on at least two grounds: that freer trade means more output and income, which they presume would mean more degradation of the natural environment; and that freer trade encourages the relocation of environmentally degrading industries to countries with lower environmental protection standards and/or more fragile natural environments.

Neither of these assertions is unambiguously supported by empirical evidence, however. The first, that income increases mean greater damage to the natural environment, may be true for some poorer countries (in which case, any additional environmental damage has to be weighed against the marginal economic benefits of higher incomes for poor people), but once middle-income status is reached people tend to alter their behaviour in ways that reduce pressures on the environment. One is that population growth tends to decline as incomes rise. Another is that education investment expands, and with it comes more skilful management of all resources including the environment. And, thirdly, modernising communities with rising incomes and improving education tend eventually to improve private property rights and put more stringent environmental policies in place (Radetski, 1992; Baldwin, 1995; Grossman, 1995). Clear-cut examples include Japan in the postwar period and Korea and Taiwan during the past decade.

The second assertion by environmentalists, that the relocation of production following trade liberalisation necessarily worsens the global environment, is even more questionable, for at least two reasons. First, we know from the law of comparative advantage that not all industries will be relocated from rich to poor countries when the former's trade barriers are lowered; some industries in the North will expand at the expense of those industries in the South. In any case, it cannot be assumed that relocating production in the South is necessarily worsening the environment.

A recent examination of the likely environmental effects of reducing government assistance to two of the North's most protected industries, coal and food, revealed that in both cases the global environment may well be improved by trade liberalisation (Anderson and Blackhurst, 1992). But evidently many more empirical studies will be required before the more extreme environmental groups alter their perception of, and publicity against, the WTO as an environmentally-unfriendly institution.

There is, however, one further way in which trade policy is being called upon to help achieve environmental objectives that has somewhat more validity. This is as a carrot or stick to entice countries to sign international environmental agreements. In the case of combating global environmental problems, such as ozone depletion or alleged climate change, the free-rider problem arises. One of the more obvious and possibly more cost-effective ways to reduce the free-rider problem is to write trade provisions into the agreement, as was done in the 1987 Montreal Protocol on reducing the use of CFCs and halons to slow ozone depletion (Anderson and Blackhurst, 1992). To date, no GATT contracting party has formally objected to that use of trade policy. Nor have they objected to the bans on trade in ivory and rhino horn that are part of the Convention of Trade in Endangered Species (CITES), or to the trade provisions in the Basle Convention on trade in hazardous substances and waste. Conflicts may arise in the future, however, if trade provisions are drafted into more contentious international environmental agreements (for example, to impose a global carbon tax).

Labour standards and the WTO

An even more recent and reluctant entrant on the WTO's potential agenda is the issue of labour standards. Like environmental standards, the linking of labour standards with trade originates with concerns in high-standard countries that lower costs of employing labour in other countries gives them a competitive advantage, from which producers in the high-standard countries (particularly unionised workers in low-skill industries) would like to be protected. The protection could come in the form of import barriers on the goods in question, or fines (as in NAFTA's side-agreement), or the denial of preferential market access (as the United States does with respect to its Generalised System of Preferences (GSP) to developing countries), or potentially even trade sanctions against countries not prepared to raise their labour standards. The concern ostensibly is not so much the average wage level difference as occupational health and safety standards, worker rights to form unions and seek a minimum wage level, the use of child or prison or forced labour, and the derogation from national labour laws in export-processing zones. Human rights activists and development non-government organisations (NGOs) often add support to these calls, believing that such action could reduce poverty and improve the quality of life in developing countries (even though in fact the raising of labour standards in the formal sector is more likely simply to drive employment into the informal sector where labour standards are even lower and/or to lengthen the queues of people seeking high-paid, high-standard formal-sector jobs). And as with environmental standards, traditional protection-ist forces are prompt to support any such calls for import restraint by high-standard against lower-standard countries.[7]

The International Labour Office (ILO) has been writing labour standards for seventy-five years. Why has this issue suddenly become entangled with the WTO and trade policy issues? In fact, it has been there for a long time,[8] in the background, and raises its head mainly when the trading system is in the news, such as when the International Trade Organisation (ITO) was being conceived in 1947, as well as at the end of the Tokyo Round and now. Partly it is coming under increasing discussion as a result of falling communication costs, which have meant that citizens of high-standard countries are increasingly able to get information on labour (and environ-mental) standards in other countries. That, together with the ever-greater sense of integration among the world's people (the 'global village' idea), allows and encourages the concern for human (as with animal) rights to spread beyond national boundaries, a tendency that might therefore be expected to continue indefinitely as global economic growth and integra-tion proceed.

But in addition the issue has become more prominent now because it became the subject of a side-agreement to the NAFTA.[9] The side-agreement was a price President Clinton paid to buy off opposition from labour groups to the NAFTA's passage through the US Congress. Having been encour-aged by their success in that regional trade liberalisation setting, and before that in some minor trade and investment agreements in the 1980s (Lawrence, 1994), the advocates for that side-agreement are now, like the environmental lobby groups, seeking to have an influence at the multi-lateral trade level. In both situations, the desire to reach agreement on trade liberalisation is to some extent simply being used opportunistically by these groups to further their own causes, despite the somewhat tenuous connection with trade. Their relative success to date is in large part because their causes have superficial popular appeal, while the downside in terms of the potential risk to the global trading system is far from obvious to the lay person.

In short, the 'greening' of world politics and the growing interest in worker and other human rights on more of a global scale are likely to put the WTO and trade policy under pressure to perform tasks for which they were not designed and are not well suited, and at a time when the WTO needs first to consolidate its role in the world and ensure the implementation of the Uruguay Round before tackling these new and much more controversial issues.

In addition to being affected indirectly by these new challenges to the multilateral trading system, Asian economic growth is also being affected more directly by several trade-policy developments. Two developments in particular deserve attention and are discussed below: the regional integration initiatives of Europe and North America, and the aggressive unilateral tactics of the United States.

Direct effects on Asia of European and American regional integration initiatives[10]

Apart from their systemic effects on the multilateral trading system, the deepening and widening of economic integration in Europe and North America have at least three important direct effects on excluded economies. The rest of the world's trade with those regions is affected by what the integration initiatives do to the integrating regions' rates of economic growth, to their comparative advantages, and – the focus of much attention in Asia – to their external trade and foreign investment barriers. Consider each of these in turn.

Effects on economic growth rates

It is impossible to be precise about the effects of closer economic integration on output and income growth in Western Europe and North America. But it is noteworthy that between the late 1950s and the late 1980s, Western Europe's share of global GDP rose from a quarter to a third. While this is less than the spectacular growth achievement of East Asia's market economies, it clearly outperforms much of the rest of the world; and at least some of that superior achievement may be attributable to the trade liberalisations associated with the formation of the EC and EFTA. Furthermore, a simulation exercise by Baldwin (1989) suggests, under various assumptions, that the EC1992 Single Market programme could raise the EC's GDP growth rate by at least a further 0.6 of a percentage point per year. Even more impressive gains are being suggested for Mexico as a result of NAFTA. Both Kehoe (1992) and McCleary (1992), for example, suggest that Mexico's GDP growth rate could be raised because of NAFTA by more than 1.5 percentage points per year. Mexico's economy is too small for its addition to the CUSTA to have a significant effect on United States and Canadian growth rates, but the effect nonetheless is likely to be positive.[11]

Effects on comparative advantages

These regions' faster economic growth, more efficient location and use of productive factors, and induced investment will be accompanied by changes in comparative advantages. Standard trade and development theory, such as provided by Leamer (1987a), offers a guide as to what to expect from the growth in the regions' effective availability of man-made capital relative to labour time and natural resources. Other things being equal, their integration initiatives are likely to strengthen their comparative advantages in capital-intensive (including skill-intensive) industrial and service activities at the expense of primary production and labour-intensive manufacturing.

Such changes would appear to be good news for resource-rich Australasia and for East Asia's developing countries which export either primary products or labour-intensive manufactures in exchange for capital-intensive goods and services: both their volume and terms of trade would improve. These changes would tend to have the opposite effect on many of Japan's firms, however, for Japan would face stronger competition from Western Europe and North America. A few empirical studies are available to provide estimates of the orders of magnitude that might be involved. One is by Stoeckel *et al.* (1990), using a straightforward non-dynamic CGE model of the world economy to estimate the welfare effects of the EC1992 Single Market programme. That study suggests that the gains to Australasia would amount to about 0.2 per cent of its GDP, that East Asia's developing countries would benefit by 0.1 per cent of their GDP, and that Japan would lose slightly, by 0.07 per cent of its GDP. A more recent and more detailed simulation study by Haaland and Norman (1992) provides almost the same result for Japan (a 0.08 per cent loss). But these studies ignore an important change in the past decade, namely, the emergence of Northeast Asia as a major net exporter of capital. Insofar as integration initiatives provide new foreign investment opportunities for excluded economies, this increased demand for its surplus savings would more or less offset the loss to Japan from greater competition in markets for capital-intensive goods and services.

Effects on external trade and investment barriers

There are legitimate concerns that these potential benefits for the Western Pacific, from faster economic growth and changes in comparative advantages in Western Europe and North America, may be offset by the raising of external barriers to trade and investment – a 'fortress Europe' or 'fortress North America' fear. Even the current external barriers create incentives for trade diversion as internal barriers are lowered. In the case of North America, for example, NAFTA will effectively provide the United States and Canada with a larger supply of low-priced labour. As a consequence, Mexico will be able to provide a home for a greater share of those footloose industries that are able to supply the expanding North American market and are attracted by low wages.

What is the likelihood of barriers to imports from the Western Pacific being raised by these blocs? In the case of Western Europe, strengthened internal competition will impose structural adjustment pressures on numerous industries. The better organised of those industries (including textiles and motor vehicles) may well be successful in seeking protection from the full force of the adjustment pressures. And insofar as Eastern European producers are insulated via association agreements from such increased protection, most of the burden will fall on East Asia. In the case of North America, since it is a free-trade area rather than a customs union, the main fear is a rise in US external barriers, including through strict interpretations of rules of origin.[12] Whether US trade barriers rise depends in part on how well the United States perceives it is being treated by its trading partners, a point to which attention is now turned.

Aggressive unilateralism

The past decade is full of examples of cases where America has blamed declining US competitiveness on external factors. The introduction of NAFTA during a recession has added a further reason for US protectionists to demand higher external trade barriers, and for battling US exporters to demand more use of aggressive unilateral tactics to obtain greater market access overseas, most notably in the trade-surplus economies of East Asia.

Japan is an especially obvious target for unilateral action under Section 301 and Super 301 of the US trade acts. Not only does Japan have an overall trade surplus but it also has a strong bilateral trade surplus with the United States. Moreover, as noted on p. 24 (part (iii) of table 2.3), Japan's trade-to-GDP ratio has grown very little relative to that of other industrial countries, leaving it vulnerable to the criticism that it has been opening up its markets less than have other countries. Japan may well claim that the share of GDP traded extra-regionally is no different for Japan than for North America or Western Europe (see table 2.4), but such claims are likely to have much less impact in improving US perceptions of Japanese trade policies than would increases in import penetration ratios. That fact, unfortunately, has led to calls for the setting by the United States of quantitative import targets to be achieved by Japan, with failure to do so triggering punitive restrictions on imports by the United States of Japanese goods. The possibility of US policy moving further down this path of managed trade is justifiably worrying not just for Japan but for all supporters of a non-discriminatory, open, rules-based multilateral trading system (Bhagwati and Patrick, 1991).[13] This is especially so because US demands are typically for more access not to imports in general (for example, of cellular phones or beef) under freer trade but to imports of US products in particular (for example, Motorola phones and grain-fed beef) under quantitatively managed trade.

Even if the enhanced dispute settlement mechanism of the WTO helps to reduce the frequency and severity of US unilateral actions of this type (although note the sobering assessment by Geoff Raby in chapter 3 in this volume on this point), there are at least two other worrying aspects of US trade policy trends to watch. One is the possibility of the United States signing 'free'-trade agreements with other countries, Chile being the most likely candidate in the medium term. That hub-and-spoke development is likely to be much less beneficial or more harmful to excluded economies than a clean customs union or multi-country free-trade area, for the reasons mentioned earlier (see Snape *et al.*, 1993). Even the idea of a discriminatory Asia Pacific free trade arrangement that has been promoted by the United States recently is still inferior economically to the idea of open regionalism characterised by unilateral or regional trade liberalisation on a most-favoured-nation (Mfn) basis. And the other worrying aspect of US policy is the interest in putting social issues, such as environmental and labour standards, on the WTO's already overcrowded work agenda, despite the fact that the countries of Latin America, Asia and Africa would rather see those issues debated elsewhere than in the WTO.

How should East Asia respond?

Just as there are three levels of trade challenges facing East Asia (multilateral, regional and unilateral), so too are there opportunities to act and react at these three levels. The ratified WTO came into being at the beginning of 1995 and has already begun to deal with not only its enlarged routine work programme but also the potentially damaging threats to it from the promotion of regionalism, environmentalism, labour standards and aggressive unilateralism. The staff is being increased to cope with (a) the growing workload of the Trade Policy Review Body and others charged with monitoring the implementation of the Uruguay Round agreements, (b) the backlog of disputes postponed during the Round, and the testing of the new rules under the enhanced dispute settlement mechanism, (c) the flood of applications for WTO member-ship, particularly from the former centrally planned economies, and (d) the need for more legal and economic research on the new agenda items mentioned above plus others such as competition policy.[14] With respect to research on the trade/environment and trade/labour standards issues, it is especially important for the trade-policy community to become immediately active, for not to do so runs the risk that open trading regimes and the WTO will be made scapegoats for perceived problems whose causes, and hence solutions, lie elsewhere. More research is needed on the effects both of liberalising trade in products and capital on the environment and workers, and of raising environmental and labour standards on trade and economic welfare in poor as well as in rich coun-tries.

To the more specific issue of the proliferation of regional integration agreements in Europe and America, the excluded economies of East Asia and Australasia could respond in one or more ways. One response is simply to continue to search imaginatively for ways to circumvent these blocs' import barriers and to meet the rules of origin associated with direct foreign investment within the blocs. NTBs to trade have been found to be porous in the past (Yoffie, 1983), and they are likely to continue to be so in the future. A second obvious response is to invest more both in lobbying for better market access and in actual manufacturing within Western Europe and North America. A more radical third possibility is to take up former President Bush's offer to seek membership of NAFTA or a free-trade area with the United States – although it might be more desirable for North American and East Asian countries to join ANZCERTA since the latter is a much 'cleaner', less-distorting agreement!

Outsiders are also likely to consider forming closer links, and perhaps even new regional integration agreements, with other excluded economies. Within the Western Pacific in recent years integration has deep-ened among the economies of mainland China, Hong Kong and Taiwan (Chia and Lee, 1993; Jones *et al.*, 1993), the ASEAN free-trade agreement was signed, the East Asian Economic Caucus (EAEC) was proposed, and various attempts made to give more life to the Asia Pacific Economic Cooperation (APEC) concept. The hope is that all of these initiatives will lead to a strengthening of the unconditional open regionalism that has characterised the East Asian region in recent decades and set it apart from the more discriminatory regionalism elsewhere (Young, 1993).

Certainly it is not in the economic interests of East Asia to form an inward-looking trading bloc, because of the risks of losses not only from trade diversion but also from retaliatory closure of export markets outside the region. Nor is it likely that an entire East Asian, Western Pacific, or broader Pacific rim free-trade area will form. First, the smaller East Asian countries would be unlikely to form a trade bloc with Japan alone for fear of Japanese domination in the absence of a North American counter-weight. And for domestic political reasons it is unlikely North America would be able to join such a bloc in the near future – after all, much of US trade policy during the past two decades has been aimed at reducing imports from East Asia and Australasia. Similarly, governments in Northeast Asia have found it difficult politically to reduce their barriers to agricultural and other processed primary products from North America or even just from Australasia. In short, the high degree of potential (as distinct from actual) trade complementarity that would exist between freely trading resource-rich and resource-poor Pacific rim countries works against the political feasibility of creating a free-trade area in the region (Drysdale and Garnaut, 1989).

Instead, the interests of Western Pacific economies will continue to be served best by the maintenance and strengthening of an open multilateral trading system under the WTO. That can be facilitated in various ways. One is by promoting trade liberalisation in the Asia Pacific region itself. Fortuitously, even if this is done on a non-discriminatory, Mfn basis as discussed in APEC circles, most of the benefits would be reaped within the region because of strong intra-regional trade bias (for reasons of economic and cultural proximity) and strong (and potentially much stronger) trade complementarity among the economies of the region.

Finally, one other way for APEC countries to strengthen the multilateral trading system is to play a leading role in shaping the debate on trade policy and the new issues on the WTO's agenda. The APEC region comprises a rich variety of economies (rich, poor, resource-abundant, resource-scarce). And yet there is a great deal of goodwill among them, so the chances of examining these issues calmly is much greater in an APEC than in the larger WTO forum. The challenge will be to convince the wider world community that trade liberalisation can be consistent not only with economic growth but also with sustainable development, improved labour and environmental standards, and even improved political freedom and other human rights.

NOTES

1. This is not to say those complaints are fully justified. For discussions on the extent to which the trade-to-GDP ratio for one country relative to the rest of the world can be used as a measure of openness, and in particular on the extent to which it indicates the degree of openness of the Japanese economy, see, for example, Leamer (1988), Srinivasan (1991) and Lawrence (1992).
2. These data refer only to merchandise trade; the increase would be even greater if services trade were to be included.
3. The Japanese might call them *tama-mushi* agreements, after the *tama-mushi* beetle which has translucent wings that appear as different colours depending on the angle of the viewer and the sunlight.
4. For more discussion of this issue see the volume of papers prepared as background for the special coverage of this topic by the GATT Secretariat (Anderson and Blackhurst 1993).
5. For more discussion of this issue, see the 1992 GATT *Annual Report* and the volume of papers prepared as background for the special coverage of this topic in that report (GATT, 1992a; Anderson and Blackhurst, 1992a).
6. Since the services of the natural environment are normal (and possibly superior) goods in the sense that more of them is demanded as incomes rise, and since the supply of many of those services is limited to differing extents across countries depending on population density, the degree of enforcement of property rights, etc. it is not surprising that environmental standards differ across countries and change at different rates over time (Anderson, 1993a).
7. For more on the phenomenon of capture of proponents of these issues by traditional protectionists, see Anderson and Blackhurst (1992, chapters 10 and 11).
8. The history is patchy but goes back a hundred years (Charnovitz, 1987).
9. France has also been encouraged to seek the addition of this issue to the WTO's agenda following its qualified success in getting a 'social charter' signed by EU member governments at Maastricht.
10. This section draws on Anderson (1991) and Anderson and Snape (1994).
11. An important caveat to keep in mind with *ex ante* empirical studies, however, is that typically they ignore the rules of origin and anti-dumping and countervailing duty provisions to be applied within the bloc, the effects of which (a dampening of intra-regional trade and GDP growth) become clear only well after the agreement has been passed into law.
12. On the risk of rules of origin effectively raising an integrating region's external trade barriers to the highest tariff equivalent in the region, see Krueger (1992).
13. Motivation for US unilateral trade policy action is unfortunately not restricted to claims of unfair trading practices. It has also been triggered by, for example, concerns about human rights especially in China, leading to threats to withdraw China's Mfn status as an exporter to the United States; by concerns about lack of progress on resolving missing-in-action cases in Vietnam, which until

this year had prevented trade and investment by Americans in Vietnam; and by Norway's decision to resume some limited whaling in the light of evidence presented to the International Whaling Convention that Minky whale numbers are no longer endangered, in response to which the United States is threatening to violate its GATT obligations to provide market access for Norwegian fish. The latter is similar to, but less subtle (more-obviously GATT-illegal), than the unilateral action the United States took against Mexico in its dispute over the use of dolphin-unfriendly tuna nets.

14. The research challenges include looking for ways to harness the energy of groups seeking higher environmental and labour standards such that they support, rather than oppose, trade liberalisation. The cases of coal and food trade liberalisation were mentioned above as examples which are likely to be environmentally friendly (Anderson and Blackhurst, 1992, chapter 8). But convincing agnostics and sceptics is sure to require much more quantitative economic/environmental modelling, a task that will make conventional economic modelling appear simple (Powell, 1993; Anderson and Strutt, 1994).

3

The new world trade order and OECD

GEOFF RABY

Even before the ink was dry on the Uruguay Round Final Act, commentators were questioning aspects of the new rules and their expected effectiveness. Why is it that a multilateral agreement, negotiated over seven years, signed by over 120 countries and producing benefits for just about all concerned, is subject to such scepticism? The central policy concerns from an OECD perspective appear to be whether the multilateral trading system after the Uruguay Round is more fragile than it was before and what, if any, the implications are for policy makers in both OECD and non-OECD areas.

A communiqué from the OECD Ministerial Meeting in June 1994 laid out clearly the opportunities and challenges presented by the successful conclusion of the Round.

> OECD Members celebrate the signing of the Uruguay Round Final Act and the establishment of a World Trade Organisation . . . as historic events which mark an important step towards a universal trading system, and will enhance world trade leading to new opportunities for employment. The agreements concluded will substantially advance trade liberalisation, expand and strengthen the multilateral rules and disciplines governing international trade, and promote further non-inflationary growth in accordance with the objective of sustainable world-wide development.

It is something of a paradox, however, that what was almost universally hailed as a triumph of good sense and international cooperation over antagonistic, narrow and sectional interests, akin to the original decision to establish the GATT, was accompanied by grave warnings about the future health of the multilateral system (OECD, 1994c).

Since the conclusion of the Uruguay Round it has been remarked that the 'devil is in the detail'. And in such a massive volume of detail, there is much work for the devil to do. With that perhaps in mind, OECD Ministers in their statement moved straight from the celebration to the sober realities of ratification and implementation – as if the hangover came before the last drink! They urged speedy ratification, avoidance of any measures that would contradict the letter or spirit of the new rules and disciplines, or were inconsistent with the principles of free trade: steps they had agreed to take only two months earlier in Marrakesh.

Does this suggest that despite being an outcome for everyman, everyman may not be content with the results of the Round? For OECD Ministers, at least, there would seem to be a degree of apprehension about the resilience of the agreements, and perhaps the entire multilateral trading system itself. A tension is evident between the genuine, and well deserved, enthusiasm for the outcome of the Round and concern that the multilateral system will come under pressures that could be intolerable.

Bearing in mind these continuing uncertainties, a number of the main results from the Round will be reviewed in an attempt to indicate strengths and weaknesses in the agreements and in the transition to the new world trading system.

Trade liberalisation

Tariffs

Before the Uruguay Round began, average tariffs on a trade-weighted basis were already quite low for OECD countries as a result of commitments under earlier Rounds and regional trade arrangements. Autonomous trade liberalisation became a distinctive feature of the global economy during the course of the Uruguay Round negotiations. While developing economies set the pace for autonomous trade liberalisation, under pressures of export-oriented growth strategies and then continuing high rates of economic growth, developed economies continued to lower border barriers, largely in the context of expanding or deepening regional trade arrangements. The transition economies, too, had moved for their own domestic economic and political reasons to cut state interventions in the trading system and to liberalise their trading regimes. Momentum consequently gathered behind trade liberalisation, despite mounting protectionist pressures within some of the older industrialised economies.

Possibly because of these trends, tariff reductions agreed exceeded the expectations that were held at the beginning of the Round. For the developed OECD countries, trade-weighted average tariffs on industrial products will be reduced after the Round from 6.3 per cent to 3.9 per cent, a reduction of 39 per cent (table 3.1). After the Round, the highest trade-weighted average tariffs among the developed economies for industrial products will be South Africa and Australia, with 17.3 per cent and 12.2 per

Table 3.1. *Western Pacific concessions under the Uruguay Round, percentages*

	Tariff averages		Bindings		Duty-free imports	
	before	after	before	after	before	after
Hong Kong	0.0	0.0	1.0	23.0	100.0	100.0
Indonesia	20.4	36.9	30.0	92.0	16.0	2.0
Korea	18.0	8.3	24.0	89.0	4.0	26.0
Macau	0.0	0.0	0.0	10.0	100.0	100
Malaysia	10.0	9.1	1.0	78.0	19.0	23.0
Philippines	23.9	22.5	9.0	67.0	0.0	0.0
Singapore	0.4	5.1	0.0	73.0	97.0	46.0
Thailand	35.8	28.1	10.0	70.0	6.0	1.0
All developing	15.3	12.3	15.0	58.0	52.0	49.0
Australia	20.1	12.2	36.0	96.0	8.0	16.0

Note:
The post-Uruguay Round decrease in the percentage of duty-free imports of developing countries is attributable to ceiling bindings offered on tariff lines with zero base duties.
Source: A. Hoda, in OECD (1994c, pp. 47–52).

cent, respectively. The lowest industrial tariffs will be levied by Switzerland and Japan, with 1.5 per cent and 1.7 per cent, respectively (Hoda, in OECD, 1994c).

Tariff cuts from developing countries in the Round will be smaller, but these were, of course, from a much higher base in nearly all cases. It is worth recalling that in terms of the economic impact of tariff cuts, the absolute size of the cut is the most important consideration because of its effect on the price of the product in the importing market. In the Round, trade-weighted tariff averages on industrial goods for developing countries as a single group (based on the GATT definition which includes the four 'tigers') were cut by 20 per cent. The biggest cuts were made by India and South Korea, 55 and 54 per cent, respectively. Apart from Hong Kong and Macau, which are duty-free (Singapore is in the same category but chose to bind its tariffs above zero in the Uruguay Round), the trade-weighted tariff averages of Singapore, South Korea and Malaysia will be among the lowest for 'developing' countries, at 5.1, 8.3 and 9.1 per cent, respectively.

One innovation introduced in the Round was 'zero-for-zero' tariff cuts negotiated between the major OECD countries ('Quad' countries – EU, United States, Canada, and Japan). This set an important precedent, not least because it was effective in some sectors where tariffs had remained an important source of protection. The share of duty-free imports also increased substantially in the developed countries (table 3.1).

An important achievement of the Round was the big increase in the number of tariff lines that are to be bound by developing countries; before the Round bindings were generally low in these countries (see chapter 9 in this volume). For the developed countries, some 99 per cent of tariffs will be bound compared with 94 per cent before the Round, and for developing countries 58 per cent will be bound compared with 15 per cent before the Round. While many of the bindings are at high rates, and often substantially more than the current applied rates, binding nevertheless introduces a degree of predictability into the system. Bindings also provide a clear starting point for future negotiations on tariff reductions.

The reduced tariff averages conceal marked divergences in tariffs between countries and sectors. Tariff escalation remains an important issue and tariff peaks still prevail in many developed and developing countries. Tariff peaks, defined as *ad valorem* duties above 15 per cent, will be reduced in certain sectors, but remain important in others. For example, textiles and clothing will have average tariff peaks in developed countries of 28 per cent after the Round, compared with 35 per cent before. Although tariffication of non-tariff barriers (NTBs) in agriculture was a major breakthrough in the Round, it has left some very high tariff peaks. Tariff peaks and escalation will remain to be addressed in future multilateral trade negotiations.

Non-tariff barriers

At the outset of the Uruguay Round negotiations, it was intended to deal with NTBs by tariff-line, which would have allowed a fine comb to have been passed through these pervasive impediments to trade. In the event, this did not happen and less was achieved than expected. Before the Round, the main barriers to market access in this category were quantitative restrictions (QRs). In developed countries these included voluntary export restraints (VERs), price-fixing arrangements, QRs on imports and exports under the Multifibre Agreement (MFA). Among developing countries, QRs and import licensing for balance of payments reasons were widespread. Negotiating efforts were directed at strengthening the general rules relating to NTBs.

Developed countries impose QRs mainly through the use of 'grey-area' measures, such as VERs or the restrictions imposed under the MFA. These have been addressed in the Agreement on Safeguards which explicitly bans grey-area measures and the agreement on textiles and clothing which will phase out the twenty-year-old MFA. The agreements on agriculture, sanitary and phytosanitary measures (SPS), and technical barriers to trade each address major NTBs. With regard to QRs applied by developing countries, these were covered under the balance of payments provisions; in the transitional economies, the relevant provisions were included in the understanding on Article XVII of GATT. The agreement on import licensing, as well as new agreements on pre-shipment inspection and rules of origin, address other aspects of non-tariff measures. The plurilateral agreement on government procurement also removed a major barrier to trade for those countries that have signed it: non-military public procurement, for example, is estimated to be up to 10 per cent of the EU's GDP – more than twice the size of the Communities' agricultural sector (Messerlin, in OECD, 1994c).

The Multifibre Arrangement

The decision to phase out the MFA contributes both to encouraging trade liberalisation and to strengthening the integrity of the system by accepting that textiles and clothing will be treated like any other manufactured good.

Consumers in developed countries will be the major beneficiaries since they had supported the cost of this protection by paying high prices. Most developing countries will gain as well. It is estimated that the benefits, in terms of world net welfare from liberalisation of both quotas and tariffs on textiles and clothing, will be $US23.4 billion, with big net gains to China ($US1.8 billion), Korea ($US1.6 billion) and Taiwan ($US1.2 billion) (Trela and Whalley, 1990). About a third of estimated total global net welfare gain would go to developing countries as group. These estimates will need to be revised to allow for changes in world textile and clothing markets and the actual agreements, but they are indicative of the expected orders of magnitude and the distribution of the benefits.

The phasing out of the MFA will take ten years and will be supervised by the Textiles Monitoring Body. The bulk of quotas, however, do not have to be removed until the end of the ten-year period. At the same time, transitional safeguards may be applied if injury or threat of it can be demonstrated. These measures can only be applied for a maximum of three years and must be phased out over their duration. Some anti-circumvention measures are specified.

The agreement on textiles and clothing raises expectations, which will cause disappointment and frustration if the spirit of the Round is not implemented. For example, some developing countries are sceptical about how the MFA will be dismantled, and concern has been expressed that potential exists for a change in the protection regime by, for example, a series of dumping investigations. There is also concern that the growth rate provided for quotas will be insufficient over the transition period to eliminate quotas in ten years, which will mean that the agreement will be effectively non-binding. Product sequencing, whereby products are gradually removed from MFA restrictions, is another area of potential difficulty. Initially, most of the imports liberalised will be selected from non-binding quotas, which will delay domestic adjustments. Uncertainty exists also over the functioning of the safeguard provision in the Agreement, which could provide another avenue for delaying or minimising adjustment in developed countries' industries and markets. Inevitably, these practices will raise doubts about the political will and good faith of developed countries to meet their commitments to eliminate restrictions on trade in textiles and clothing (Whalley, in OECD, 1994c).

It is worth recalling what led developing countries to adopt the MFA in the first place. The reason offered was that without that arrangement, the trade regime would have been far more restrictive. This 'threat-driven' approach to negotiation has not really changed, as demonstrated by the way the MFA is to be phased out. Developing countries have received a pledge from developed countries that after ten years trade restrictions applied under the MFA will be terminated, but no commitment has been made that other instruments will not be used to continue to protect textile and clothing industries.

WTO rules and dispute settlement

The welfare benefits accruing from a rules-based multilateral trading system depend on the extent to which trade liberalisation is reliable and its results enforceable. In recent years, remedies sought outside the framework of the multilateral system have been eroding it. East Asia has directly felt the consequences of weak rules as it has often been the target of grey-area measures, such as VERs, and GATT-consistent actions, such as anti-dumping. Attempts have been made to clarify the anti-dumping rules since the Kennedy Round. A more far-reaching attempt was made in the Uruguay Round negotiations to put an end to grey-area measures. At the same time, much was done to strengthen dispute settlement procedures in the future WTO.

Safeguards

For a well functioning system, it is important that adequate means exist to defend industries against sudden surges in imports or to manage the pace of adjustment in an industry arising from obligations entered into under the GATT. Article XIX was intended to provide such safeguards, but the conditions in Article XIX discouraged governments from using it. Other means of protection, such as VERs, were more popular. The growth of grey-area measures was seen as having the potential seriously to weaken the multilateral system.

The Agreement on Safeguards tightens the disciplines for recourse to Article XX. All grey-area measures are to be eliminated within four years, with only a few exceptions. All existing safeguard measures are to be eliminated within five–eight years. The serious injury test has been tightened for new safeguard measures, and their application must be notified immediately to the GATT Committee on Safeguards. Safeguards are to be limited in duration and must be progressively liberalised throughout their duration. Flexibility has been enhanced by permitting discrimination in their application and easing the compensation provisions. Special provisions have been made for less developed countries (LDCs), including extending the period for which they may be applied, allowing for the possibility of reimposing measures, and in some cases exempting LDCs from safeguard action.

It remains to be seen how governments will respond. The new disciplines in this area are much stronger and are likely to see the removal of VERs as formal government-to-government agreements. One concern is that the new flexibility which has been introduced to encourage governments to act within the system could lead to a proliferation of safeguard actions. Whether, ultimately, there will be more or less protection as a result of changes cannot be foreseen. But a key question is whether the Safeguards Agreement will put an end to the expansion of grey-area measures or whether they will just take on other guises. In particular, there is a danger that the stronger rules and disciplines may drive such measures underground, making them potentially more harmful than formal transparent agreements. One of the powerful attractions of VERs is that they create cartels which provide rents for both importers and exporters. Incentives will remain for new cartel arrangements, while the effectiveness of VERs as a form of protection is likely to remain attractive to governments.

Grey-area measures could spread underground in a variety of ways. Governments may encourage firms to enter into cartel-type arrangements by not enforcing, or weakly enforcing, their domestic competition laws. To the extent that government restraints could be replaced by industry-to-industry arrangements, there may be a role for competition authorities if these practices lead to anti-competitive behaviour. In part, the expansion of such collusive agreements could be checked by the GATT's Trade Policy Review Mechanism (TPRM). This will become an increasingly important instrument to ensure that the Round's agreements are implemented in both the spirit and the letter. In time, may be, competition rules could be elaborated to make the GATT dispute settlement system applicable to such practices. Given these uncertainties, it has been suggested that rather than driving out VERs, aspects of them could be 'legalised' in order to keep them open and transparent (Deardorff, in OECD, 1994c).

The reform of Article XIX and attempts to ban VERs will put more pressure on anti-dumping measures as contingent protection (Robertson, 1992). The Agreement on implementation of Article VI (Anti-dumping) was the most difficult to negotiate. Although the Round has tightened some regulations on anti-dumping, the extent to which national anti-dumping laws and practices can be challenged by the multilateral authority is limited to whether an assessment of the facts of a case are 'unbiased and objective'. At this stage, it is difficult to gauge what effect the revisions to Article VI will have in practice. Early assessments suggest that little has changed, national anti-dumping authorities are likely to continue to enjoy the extensive freedoms they have had in the past to take action (Hindley, in OECD, 1994c).

If indeed the rules have not been strengthened sufficiently to prevent widespread abuse of the anti-dumping instrument, this may diminish gains made elsewhere in the Uruguay Round liberalisation and in GATT rules. There may be greater recourse to anti-dumping for textiles and clothing with the phasing-out of the MFA and the outlawing of grey-area measures. This could have important implications for East Asia. More countries are beginning to use anti-dumping and it is becoming more widely embodied in developing countries' trade legislation. This will increase the burden on WTO panels, because many countries which could have recourse to anti-dumping measures lack the resources to conduct satisfactory investigations of dumping complaints.

Subsidies and countervailing duties

The agreement on subsidies and countervailing duties sought to clarify the rules on which subsidies were actionable and which were non-actionable. By defining subsidies, the Agreement has identified which subsidies can be countervailed. Agricultural subsidies are excluded. The new agreement defines three categories of subsidies under the so-called 'traffic light' approach. One category contains permissible subsidies (green light), those for research and development, for regional aid and for adaptation to environmental standards. The second category contains actionable subsidies (amber light), where countries needed to prove injury, impairment of GATT rights or serious prejudice before taking countervailing action. The third category includes prohibited subsidies (red light), for which countervailing action may be automatic.

In seeking to remove the ambiguity that has surrounded subsidies and the application of countervailing duties, the Uruguay Round may have left governments with less defence against domestic pressures for subsidies than in the previous, more ambiguous situation. Substantial derogations are available to developing countries which may encourage them to use subsidies in their economic development strategies. Against these concerns, the attempt at clarifying the definitions of subsidies should go some way to remove trade frictions. It still remains to be seen whether the definitions are in fact clearer when tested.

Dispute settlement

A strong and efficient dispute settlement system is crucial for the credibility of trade agreements. The integrated dispute settlement procedure agreed in the Uruguay Round Final Act is intended to ensure procedural and interpretative consistency in dispute settlement practices across all issues. Its main features are the automatic establishment of a dispute settlement panel if bilateral consultations fail, adoption of reports by dispute settlement panels, and the right of retaliation for non-compliance with panel findings. Significantly, adoption of panel reports is now virtually guaranteed under a 'consensus to reject' rule, compared with the old 'consensus to accept'. These and other reforms in dispute settlement together mark a major strengthening of the system.

While there was a need to make the dispute settlement procedures stronger and more credible than under the old GATT, care is needed not to push it too far too soon. It could be harmful for the new dispute settlement procedures if they were to step too far in front of the political acceptance of such systems within national administrations. The acceptance of the new dispute settlement procedure will depend heavily on the quality of the panels and on the commitment by major players to respect panel decisions.

A question remains whether the disciplines will be sufficiently strong to restrain contracting parties from taking actions outside the system. While it is possible that, occasionally, countries could 'escape' from the system, this need not necessarily undermine the system itself. On the other hand, more systematic and sustained failures would have serious consequences. The removal of veto power over adoption of reports and over retaliation should make it embarrassing for governments to defy the system, and that may create some pressure to comply with panel reports.

New areas

One of the difficulties at Punta del Este in 1986, when the terms for the new GATT Round of negotiations were drawn up, was reaching agreement on new areas of trade that should be covered. During the negotiations positions changed over these new areas. The final outcomes, however, show important progress from the negotiations.

Services

The establishment of the GATS framework represents a major achievement in view of the initial reluctance of several developing countries to engage in multilateral negotiations in this area and the wide range of services to be covered. Reflecting divergent negotiating positions among major players and across sectors, the advocates of reaching an agreement on a sectoral basis, as opposed to binding obligations for all services sectors, prevailed (Hoekman, in OECD, 1994c).

The GATS addressed issues of establishment and regulatory regimes which are fundamental for trade in services. It was against that background that a set of trade principles emerged for services, a number of which differed markedly from trade principles applied in the GATT to merchandise trade. The GATT is a general agreement, while the GATS is a specific agreement which is applied to specific sectors.

The GATS incorporates the most-favoured-nation (Mfn) principle as a general obligation for services, but members have the option to exempt specific sectors from that obligation for a period of up to ten years. It is an open question whether the long list of exemptions will be phased-out by the end of that transition period. In contrast to the GATT, national treatment was addressed not as a general obligation under the GATS, but only applied in sectors subject to specific commitments. Furthermore, national treatment only applies to measures which have not been excluded by members. Members' schedules of commitments are structured on the basis of a positive list to which the GATS disciplines apply. This may create an incentive to offer fewer commitments on the cross-border movement of services. An alternative to the sector-specific approach would be to provide for complete free trade for all services and modes of supply unless specifically excluded in schedules (Snape, in OECD, 1994c). This was the approach adopted in the NAFTA and the Australia–New Zealand Closer Economic Relations Trade Agreement (ANZCERTA).

The negotiation of an Agreement on Services was a major and complex task that was made all the more difficult by the lack of experience in negotiating on services. While the GATS may fall short of expectations in a number of respects, it is worthy of at least two cheers for making an important start and for providing a basis for future negotiations. Negotiations on basic telecommunications, financial services and maritime transport are continuing which, if successfully concluded, would extend the sectoral coverage. Meanwhile, recognition of the need for more comprehensive rules and disciplines for trade in services will increase interest in some of the newly emerging regional economic arrangements, such as AFTA and APEC.

Intellectual property

The Agreement on trade-related aspects of intellectual property rights (TRIPs) was one of the major achievements of the Round, far exceeding initial expectations. The Agreement has integrated the substance of the existing international property rights conventions into the WTO, with legally enforceable obligations under the uniform dispute settlement procedures. This has enhanced the substance and effectiveness of existing conventions. GATT principles, such as national treatment and non-discrimination, will now be applied to intellectual property.

Areas in which minimum standards of protection have been established include copyright, trade marks, patents, geographical indications, industrial design, layout designs for integrated circuits and company secrets. Provisions are available to ensure that intellectual property rights can be enforced effectively by foreign rights holders, as well as by a country's own nationals. The TRIPs agreement includes a ten-year derogation for developing countries – with a few exceptions – and the possibility of excluding from patents some bio-technological inventions, which raise contentious ethical and environmental issues.

The new Agreement will diminish discrepancies between national property rights, limit unilateral action and should stimulate technology transfer (Knutrud, in OECD, 1994c). Among other things, further work on intellectual property rights will need to address the competition issues. Intellectual property rights that restrain competition may have adverse effects on trade and impede the transfer and dissemination of technology.

Trade-related investment measures

The negotiations on trade-related investment measures (TRIMs) achieved only modest results, which suggests that future progress towards multilateral investment rules may be difficult. The Agreement confirmed that GATT Articles III and XI should apply to certain trade-related measures, such as local content requirements, import content restrictions and export requirements, which represents a useful strengthening of GATT rules.

Some practices are not covered explicitly by the Agreement, such as technology transfer, other requirements on investors and investment protection. But for the first time, GATT rules have been applied to trade relating to investment. Changes in developing countries' attitudes made the TRIMs agreement possible. Work under way in the OECD on a multilateral investment code will help to maintain momentum on a multilateral agreement on investment. The TRIMS agreement has formally established that trade and investment are interrelated.

Policy considerations

Ultimately, the benefits of the Uruguay Round outline depend on the implementation of the agreements and the changes that are made in domestic policy and practices: whether the undertakings made are followed in both the letter and the spirit. The implementation of the agreements will take place over many years, which will require continuing commitments by governments, possibly through several swings in business and political cycles.

To identify some of the challenges which confront the multilateral trading system after the Round is not to diminish the achievement. In many respects, it is a measure of the magnitude of that achievement that the system will be tested. It may also lead some to ask questions about the basic architecture: how useful is the GATT 1947 approach when agreements are moving well beyond traditional trade in goods to areas such as services, investment and intellectual property? Moreover, with declining use of traditional forms of protection and increasing globalisation of business, more attention will be given to the relationship between trade and a raft of domestic policies, such as environment and competition policies. Some areas, most notably labour standards, but also environmental issues and trade in high-technology products, where the issues are not well defined, could easily become vehicles for protectionist pressures which deny evolving comparative advantage.

The linkage of such issues with trade instruments could lead to divisions within the WTO, particularly on North–South lines. This would be an unfortunate prospect, not least because some of the most successful and innovative results from the Round came in areas where developed and developing Contracting Parties discovered new common interests. Future progress in strengthening and extending the multilateral system will depend on cooperation in such areas.

Where agreements lack precision because politically it was not possible to be precise, definitions will need to be provided by dispute settlement procedures. It is important to consider how robust these procedures will be and whether there is a risk that the system could become overburdened – not just in terms of resources, but also in terms of legal authority. The Uruguay Round Final Act takes the WTO further into dispute settlement than any other international organisation. It will, therefore, be important to avoid complex early challenges on legal and political issues. There will need to be a continuation of the GATT-negotiated solutions, rather than an exclusively juridical approach. The new dispute settlement procedures must build credibility by fairness, sound argument and good process (Jackson, in OECD, 1994c). This will require the international community to devote adequate resources towards this goal. Care must be taken that the institution is not required to bear the strain of the new agreements and extension of multilateral rules into new areas too quickly.

The establishment of WTO provides a wide agenda for multilateral trade negotiations, which has encouraged other interest groups – protectionists, human rights activists or environmentalists – to seek links between trade remedies and other social–political issues. There is a risk that the new trade agenda, with its widening range of new trade-related issues, might become politicised. Pressure may arise for the use of trade measures to make up for a perceived lack of adequate multilateral rules of the game in fields such as environment, labour and monetary policies (Robertson, 1994).

It is also necessary to be careful not to dissipate energies needed to implement the agreements by working within existing multilateral frameworks. Efforts to promote regional arrangements, for example, while not necessarily incompatible with strengthening the multilateral system, risk suggesting that the achievements of the Uruguay Round are unsatisfactory, which could weaken public resolve to implement the undertakings fully. The capacity to conduct further negotiations at the multilateral level may also be jeopardised by regionalism. Financial resources and, critically, high-level direct government and bureaucratic attention, may be diverted from settling down and developing the multilateral system further. This will be particularly so for smaller countries which already have difficulties adequately servicing their interests in the many international and regional forums that exist. The competition for high-quality political and bureaucratic resources will become more pronounced as the more litigious WTO, compared with GATT 1947, places new demands on Members.

The small results in some of the key areas where pressure from global-isation is leading to heavy demands for strengthened rules and disciplines – particularly investment and services – could encourage interest in regional arrangements. It may be less costly for potential participants in these arrangements to negotiate more comprehensive and stronger agree-ments to liberalise rules on investment and services, for example, than to wait for a possibly more uncertain outcome in future multilateral negotia-tions. This could discourage efforts to address these issues at the multi-lateral level.

The outcome of the Uruguay Round in terms of trade liberalisation and breadth of coverage is an historic event akin to the establishment of the GATT. It is incumbent on governments not to allow the achievements of the Round to be the undoing of the multilateral system. The search for new rules and disciplines in response to globalisation of economic activity has already placed a great strain on existing approaches (Wellenstein, in OECD, 1994c). Governments must exercise restraint in their trade policies and refrain from testing the new rules and procedures before the system is well equipped to handle such demands, lest the system be overburdened. Crucially, governments also need to resist the temptation of seeking to extend multilateral trade rules in new areas before there is adequate inter-national consensus on what the problems are and what rules are required to address them.

NOTE

The views expressed in this chapter are personal, and should not be attributed to the OECD or its Member countries.

(Asia)

4

The Multifibre Arrangement in practice: challenging the competitive framework

F13

ठ19

KALA KRISHNA AND LING HUI TAN

F14

L67

The Multifibre Arrangement (MFA), is one of the most important non-tariff trade barriers (NTBs) facing developing countries today. It has particular relevance to developing East Asian economies, which account for a large share of world exports of textiles and apparel. It was established in 1973 to

> achieve the expansion of trade, the reduction of barriers to such trade and the progressive liberalisation of world trade in textile products, while at the same time ensuring the orderly and equitable development of this trade and avoidance of disruptive effects in individual markets and on individual lines of production in both importing and exporting countries. (GATT, 1974, p. 6)

It sanctions a structure of country- and product-specific quotas on apparel and textiles exported by developing to industrial countries. These quotas are implemented by the exporting countries and the presumption is that they obtain the quota licence rents that ensue. These rents, it is often thought, cause developing countries to prefer the MFA quotas to the alternative of GATT-compatible tariffs.

Instead of furthering the economic and social development of these countries however, the MFA acts as a major stumbling block to industrialisation (Faini *et al.*, 1992). Standard paradigms of economic development have countries progressing through phases of industrialisation, starting from light manufactures such as textiles and apparel, and graduating to more capital- and skill-intensive industries such as iron and steel. Critics claim that by cutting access to their major export markets for textiles and apparel, the MFA effectively short-circuits the industrialisation process for many developing countries at an early stage.

The MFA has its origins in the voluntary export restraint (VER) on cotton textile products that the United States negotiated with Japan in 1957. This restraint succeeded in curbing Japanese cotton goods exports, but its side-effect was a huge increase in US imports from new entrants to the industry, notably Hong Kong, Portugal, Egypt and India. In its quest for a more comprehensive solution to control cotton imports, the United States initiated multilateral discussions, held under the auspices of the GATT, which eventually led to the Short Term Cotton Textile Arrangement. This was in operation for a year, starting from 1961. It was succeeded in 1962 by the Long Term Arrangement on Cotton Textiles (LTA). The LTA worked in restricting the supply of cotton textile exports to the United States, but its side-effect was an increase in US imports of man-made fibre textiles and apparel. The five-year LTA was twice extended. Eventually the United States sought to extend it to include wool and man-made fibre textile and apparel products, and the MFA was born.

Despite being initially conceived as a temporary measure, the MFA has persisted for more than twenty years (Keesing and Wolf, 1980; Hamilton, 1990). Since its inception in 1973, the MFA has been through four successive negotiations, with each round encompassing a wider range of products and countries. By the end of the negotiations for MFA II, the United States had succeeded in bringing more than 80 per cent of its total imports of textile and apparel products under restraints using bilateral quotas with twenty supplying countries, and agreements with consultative mechanisms with eleven other countries. Subsequent negotiations widened the country coverage to include many emerging suppliers such as Bangladesh and the Maldives. In the negotiations for MFA III, the United States also extended its fibre coverage to include silk blends and other vegetable fibres. The United States currently has some 147 individual textile and apparel categories under restraint, some of which are further divided into sub-categories. There are presently nine industrial countries and thirty-three developing countries participating in MFA IV, which was twice extended and remained effective until the end of 1994.

The Uruguay Round Final Act includes an agreement for the elimination of the MFA. The phase-out is based on 1990 import volumes and is to occur gradually in four stages over a ten-year transitional period, with the adjustments heavily loaded toward the end of the period. Transitional safeguards will be permitted only on products not yet integrated into the MFA, and may include restricted and unrestricted products. The safeguards may be applied selectively on particular exporters, but only for a maximum of three years.

The MFA has been widely studied and much attention has been devoted to its welfare consequences (Hamilton, 1990). For example, Morkre (1984) estimates that US quotas on clothing imports from Hong Kong in 1980 generated quota rents of US$218 million, or 23 per cent of the total value of clothing imports from Hong Kong; Hamilton (1986) calculates the tariff equivalent rate of import quotas on textile and apparel imports from Hong Kong to be 9 per cent in 1981 and 37 per cent in 1982; and Trela and Whalley (1990) suggest global gains from the elimination of quotas and tariffs of more than US$17 billion (of which US$11 billion would accrue to developing countries) and gains to the United States from the removal of quotas as US$3 billion.

Studies of the effects of the MFA tend to take the simple static competitive model as the basis for empirical and policy analysis. Little effort has been made to establish whether this is the appropriate model to use, or what the implications of alternative assumptions might be. The assumption of competitive markets is usually defended on the grounds that there are a large number of producers in the textile and apparel market. Yet rent-sharing could arise if, for example, importers have some degree of buying power which enables them to bargain for a share of the quota rent. In fact, Goto (1989, p. 218) claims that

> [a]lthough governments of exporting countries under the MFA often allocate export licences in a manner that helps exporters capture the quota rent, many of these exporters face large importing enterprises that can negotiate prices that capture some of the rent for themselves.

Khanna (1991, p. 171) concludes from his survey of thirty-five textile and apparel exporting firms in India that

> for consignments where an exporter has to buy quotas, the importer bears about half the burden of the quota prices with the remainder being borne by the exporter whose profitability goes down.

Such considerations are important for policy purposes, as the welfare consequences of the MFA and its reform are affected by such variations in the underlying models.

In addition, since exporting countries administer their MFA quotas in very different ways, one might expect a large part of the work on the MFA to focus on how differences in implementation procedures result in different outcomes with regard to the size and distribution of quota rents. Yet there is little analytical work on this issue. While descriptions exist of quota allocation schemes in different countries (Morkre, 1979; Hamilton, 1990; Trela and Whalley, 1991), there is insufficient theoretical analysis of these schemes and even less of an attempt at empirical work on this issue. The amount of effort required first to model the institutional differences, and then to undertake some cross-country comparisons, is daunting.

Some rough data from various MFA-restricted exporting countries is available for analysis which seems to be at odds with the standard perfectly competitive model. An attempt will be made here to assess where the MFA quota rents seem to be going. Are they appropriated by the exporting country, as is usually assumed? Or do exporting countries receive less of these rents than the standard static models would suggest?

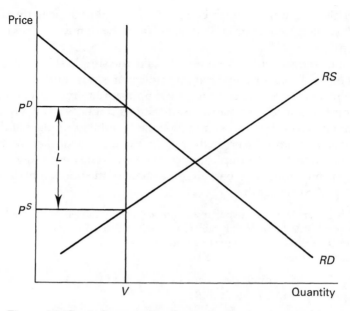

Figure 4.1 Quota licence price determination in a competitive market

Following this, a descriptive summary is provided of some theoretical and empirical work by Krishna and Tan on the MFA.

Where rents go, and why: some suggestive evidence

The first question is whether MFA quota rents actually accrue to exporting countries. The standard depiction of quota licence price determination in a competitive market is shown in figure 4.1. Let RD represent excess demand in the importing country, and RS excess supply in the exporting country. If V is the size of the quota, then P^S denotes the price in the exporting country (including tariffs and transport costs) and P^D represents the price in the importing country. If the market for licences is competitive, then the licence price should equal the difference between P^D and P^S. Thus, if the quota licences are allocated to agents in the exporting country, then all the quota rents will be retained in the exporting country if P^S+L (the adjusted import price) equals P^D. On the other hand, if the actual licence price does not reflect the potential licence price because, say, some part of the quota rent is appropriated by the importers (who are often large players in the market), then the above equality need not hold.

A rough idea of cross-country differences in the behaviour of P^S+L and

P^D, is given by plotting adjusted export prices against the US prices, for eight supplying countries (figure 4.2): Hong Kong, Korea, Indonesia, Thailand, India, Pakistan, Bangladesh and Italy. Wide differences are apparent. For Hong Kong and Korea, two of the world's most established apparel exporters, the points lie roughly on the 45 degree line. In the case of Italy, the points lie above the diagonal, an observation which is consistent with the country's reputation as a high-fashion exporter. For the remaining countries there is a rough upward slope, but the points lie generally below the diagonal.

All the correlation coefficients are positive (table 4.1), implying that all the prices tend to move in the same direction. However, the correlation of the adjusted export price with the US price is very different across countries: it is highest for Italy, the unrestrained country, followed by Korea and Hong Kong; in between are Thailand and Indonesia, with Pakistan, India and Bangladesh at the bottom.

What could be behind these large differences in price correlations? The evidence suggests that the adjusted prices of apparel exported from the countries in the Indian subcontinent are more insulated from the prices of US-made apparel than is the case for the other countries. One explanation could be that these apparel exports are not close substitutes for domestically-produced apparel. This would be consistent with the usual perception that countries in the Indian subcontinent produce poorer quality goods which do not compete with those made in the United States. If this explanation is correct, the adjusted export prices of these three countries should be moving together. In other words, their price correlations should be high. Furthermore, the correlation between their prices should be higher than the correlation with the US price. In fact, the correlation between the adjusted prices of Indian exports and Pakistani exports is only 0.6940 (table 4.1), although it is slightly higher than the correlation with the US price. The correlation between the adjusted prices of Bangladesh exports and Indian exports is lower than the correlation of either of these export prices with the US price. The same is true for the adjusted prices of Bangladesh exports and Pakistani exports. Therefore, quality differences cannot fully explain the patterns observed.

An alternative explanation for the low correlation with the US price, for India, Pakistan and Bangladesh, might be that these countries have a large bureaucracy which creates many hidden costs for exporters. However, such costs should simply reduce the licence price, leaving the 'free-on-board' (f.o.b.) price unaffected. This explanation does not seem entirely satisfactory either.

A third explanation is that the MFA quota rents are not being captured

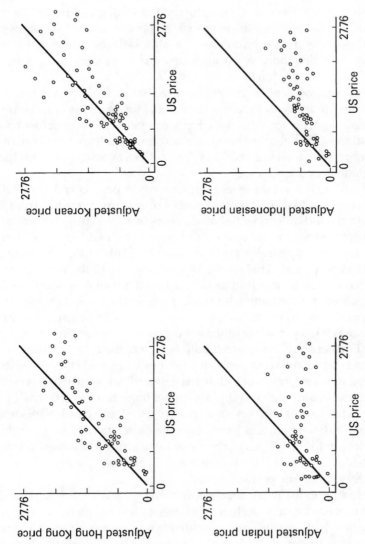

Figure 4.2 Adjusted export prices against US prices for eight supplying countries, price per unit, US$, apparel groups 1–10, 1981–8

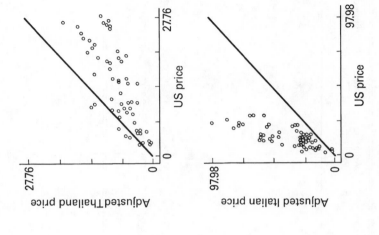

Figure 4.2 cont.

Table 4.1. *Price correlations, adjusted export prices and US prices, 1981–8*

	US price	Adjusted HK price	Adjusted Korean price	Adjusted Indian price	Adjusted Indonesian price	Adjusted Pakistan price	Adjusted Thailand price	Adjusted Bangladesh price	Adjusted Italian price
US price	1.0000								
Adjusted HK price	0.8657	1.0000							
Adjusted Korean price	0.8795	0.9359	1.0000						
Adjusted Indian price	0.5454	0.6554	0.6017	1.0000					
Adjusted Indonesian price	0.7911	0.7173	0.7014	0.5966	1.0000				
Adjusted Pakistan price	0.6403	0.7137	0.6313	0.6940	0.6751	1.0000			
Adjusted Thailand price	0.8267	0.7946	0.7900	0.6160	0.7537	0.7843	1.0000		
Adjusted Bangladesh price	0.4118	0.3746	0.3107	0.2515	0.6026	0.3944	0.3363	1.0000	
Adjusted Italian price	0.9102	0.7107	0.7614	0.4371	0.8253	0.5695	0.7816	0.4629	1.0000

by the exporters. If that is the case, and if all rents are appropriated by the importers, then the 'f.o.b.' price of the exports could actually track cost conditions in the exporting country rather than the US price. To the extent that higher costs are likely to make countries move into the high-quality end of the product market (an empirical regularity few will dispute), export prices will tend to rise with costs. Unless quality effects can be disentangled from cost effects, therefore, this approach is not fruitful. Given the lack of disaggregated data, such decompositions are not possible using the standard quality index procedures.

In addition, some of the quota allocation rules in these exporting countries could be responsible for their adjusted export prices falling below the US price. For example, official practices such as allocating some quota licences free of charge on a 'first-come-first-served' basis to exporting firms with proof of orders could erode the bargaining power of these firms *vis à vis* their US buyers. During price negotiations between importers and exporters, it is common practice for the buyer to ask whether the supplier had to pay for his or her quota – if not, the offered price would usually not include the licence price. As a result, the rents from the 'free' quotas could accrue to the importers. This is likely to be true since markets for quota licences are not well established (and sometimes illegal), and property rights are weak. Many countries impose penalties for non-utilisation of licences, in the form of reductions in future allocations. This could reduce the price at which exporters are willing to sell their apparel, particularly towards the end of the quota year. Several countries also place restrictions on the transferability of the quota licences. Given the maze of regulations for different types of quotas in each country, it is difficult to make any predictions.

A final possibility is that the bureaucratic jungle, together with other obstacles associated with production in developing countries, makes exporting from such locations an uncertain activity. This could hinder their appropriation of the potential quota rents. For example, these uncertainties may impose costs on the importers, such as the inconvenience of not always being guaranteed delivery dates and quantities in advance, which may reduce the attractiveness of exports from these countries. However, a unitary correlation coefficient is also perfectly consistent with differences in price which are 'fixed' in nature, so this is not an entirely satisfactory reason for the failure of prices to move together. In any case, whether the cause is rent-sharing, or costs to importers which make the exported product less competitive, the idea that these countries are somehow receiving less rent from the MFA than the static model might suggest cannot be dismissed.

Table 4.2. *Quota utilisation rates for seven countries, 1981–9*

Year	Hong Kong	Korea	Thailand	Indonesia	India	Pakistan	Bangladesh
1981	0.9610	0.9458	0.6287		0.6966	0.6311	
	(21)	(19)	(29)		(31)	(13)	
1982	0.9449	0.9668	0.6596	1.0000	0.6592	0.6137	
	(20)	(20)	(29)	(2)	(30)	(5)	
1983	0.9923	0.9737	0.8029	0.9919	0.9834	0.5510	
	(28)	(28)	(12)	(4)	(6)	(4)	
1984	0.9532	0.8018	0.8422	0.9695	0.9978	0.8257	
	(30)	(29)	(15)	(9)	(8)	(8)	
1985	0.9238	0.9582	0.6975	0.7936	0.9564	0.8569	
	(30)	(31)	(16)	(18)	(8)	(7)	
1986	0.9845	0.9737	0.7334	0.9819	0.9840	0.8688	0.9658
	(30)	(30)	(17)	(22)	(7)	(7)	(8)
1987	0.9899	0.9612	0.7194	0.9444	0.9821	0.9516	0.9612
	(30)	(30)	(20)	(20)	(10)	(21)	(13)
1988	0.9892	0.9009	0.6774	0.9676	0.9707	0.8754	0.9196
	(30)	(30)	(20)	(20)	(10)	(22)	(13)
1989	0.9608	0.9480	0.9748	0.9869	0.9571	0.9005	0.9353
	(29)	(31)	(6)	(20)	(10)	(20)	(13)

Source: World Bank data.

The pattern of quota utilisation in the various countries may shed some light on the price correlations that have been observed. Changes in the degree of quota utilisation and the number of categories under quota over time are shown in table 4.2. Hong Kong and Korea were early exporters to the United States and they exhibit high quota utilisation rates throughout the sample period of 1981–9. Also, the number of apparel categories subject to quota in these countries increased over the period, from around twenty to around thirty at the end of the decade. The same pattern is apparent for Indonesia, which consistently recorded utilisation rates of more than 90 per cent (with the exception of 1985), and which experienced a substantial increase in the number of products brought under restraint. The correlations between the adjusted export prices and the US price for 1981–2 are given in table 4.3(a). The price correlations for 1983–8 are in table 4.3(b). In the case of Hong Kong, Korea and Indonesia, the correlation between their adjusted export price and the US price was higher in 1981–2 when there were fewer categories under quota. This is difficult to explain, as quality upgrading over time (towards the US quality level) would suggest the opposite. These countries have, by and large, higher price correlations with other countries in the later years, which is more or less consistent with quality upgrading by the other countries.

India and Pakistan had a large number of categories under restraint in

Table 4.3. *Price correlations, adjusted export prices and US price, 1981–2 and 1983–8*

(a) 1981–2

	United States	Italy	Hong Kong	Korea	Thailand	Indonesia	India	Pakistan	Bangladesh
United States	1.0000								
Italy	0.9710	1.0000							
Hong Kong	0.9677	0.9396	1.0000						
Korea	0.9491	0.9327	0.9867	1.0000					
Thailand	0.9501	0.9297	0.8756	0.8804	1.0000				
Indonesia	0.9428	0.8751	0.8936	0.8425	0.8621	1.0000			
India	0.4265	0.2512	0.5215	0.4931	0.3132	0.5061	1.0000		
Pakistan	0.9048	0.8049	0.8869	0.8349	0.8268	0.8822	0.5927	1.0000	
Bangladesh	0.5791	0.4970	0.4012	0.3361	0.6018	0.7304	0.0768	0.5687	1.0000

(b) 1983–8

	United States	Italy	Hong Kong	Korea	Thailand	Indonesia	India	Pakistan	Bangladesh
United States	1.0000								
Italy	0.9148	1.0000							
Hong Kong	0.8448	0.7085	1.0000						
Korea	0.8802	0.7869	0.9285	1.0000					
Thailand	0.8319	0.8394	0.7850	0.7761	1.0000				
Indonesia	0.7926	0.8138	0.7592	0.7710	0.8766	1.0000			
India	0.5850	0.5401	0.6870	0.6240	0.6738	0.7108	1.0000		
Pakistan	0.6001	0.5752	0.6807	0.5886	0.7790	0.7113	0.7125	1.0000	
Bangladesh	0.3891	0.4380	0.4467	0.3883	0.3788	0.4913	0.4061	0.4338	1.0000

Source: US Annual Import Trade Tapes (IA245).

the early years, when quotas were under-utilised. In India, the quotas for these under-utilised categories were eventually dropped and replaced with a less restrictive consultative arrangement. This caused the quota utilisation rate for India to rise in 1983. As the utilisation rate rose, additional categories were brought under quota; hence the number of categories under quota and the utilisation rate rose for Pakistan in 1984. There were no MFA quotas imposed on Bangladesh until it reached a threshold presence in 1986. After that, the number of categories brought under restraint increased as its quotas exports rose.

For India, Pakistan and Bangladesh, the correlation of their adjusted export prices with US and world prices was higher in the period 1981–4, than in the period 1985–8 (table 4.4(a) and 4.4(b)). This could be due to a greater degree of economic development and integration with world markets, or quality improvements (making their goods closer substitutes for US goods), or growth in the level of rent retention by exporters, or even learning by importers of how to deal with the regulated environment.

Thailand exhibits no clear pattern in the number of apparel categories under quota. In 1981–2, there was a large number of restrained categories which were not fully utilised. In 1983, quotas were lifted for the under-utilised categories, and this raised the overall utilisation rate. Over time, however, additional quotas were imposed despite low utilisation rates of around 70 per cent in the mid-1980s. Thailand's adjusted export prices were more highly correlated with US prices in 1981–4, but they were more highly correlated with the adjusted export prices of India, Pakistan, Indonesia and Bangladesh in 1985–8. This suggests that over the last decade, Thailand's apparel exports became less competitive with US products, and more competitive with those of India, Pakistan, Bangladesh and Indonesia.

In contrast, Italy's price correlation with the United States remained consistently high over the sample period. Its price correlation with Hong Kong and Korea fell slightly during the 1980s, but its price correlation with India, Pakistan, Bangladesh and Indonesia rose. This is consistent with quality upgrading on the part of these developing countries.

Countries whose adjusted export prices had a high correlation with US prices were also the ones with relatively transparent quota implementation systems. Countries such as those in the Indian subcontinent, which had low price correlations with the United States, had strong bureaucratic quota administration.

These loose price correlations suggest that circumstances change so frequently that no clear pattern can emerge. Exporting countries face different quotas from year to year, the quality of their exports changes over time, and institutional changes occur frequently. There is no single explanation

Table 4.4. *Price correlations, adjusted export prices and US and world prices, 1981–4 and 1983–8*

(a) 1981–4

	United States	Italy	Hong Kong	Korea	Thailand	Indonesia	India	Pakistan	Bangladesh
United States	1.0000								
Italy	0.9197	1.0000							
Hong Kong	0.9071	0.8111	1.0000						
Korea	0.9200	0.8334	0.9655	1.0000					
Thailand	0.9137	0.8419	0.8660	0.8421	1.0000				
Indonesia	0.7101	0.7656	0.6737	0.6329	0.5845	1.0000			
India	0.3655	0.2414	0.5197	0.4675	0.2972	0.4997	1.0000		
Pakistan	0.5834	0.4581	0.7587	0.6133	0.6440	0.5873	0.6576	1.0000	
Bangladesh	0.3471	0.3795	0.3398	0.2896	0.3878	0.6029	0.1805	0.4296	1.0000

(b) 1983–8

	United States	Italy	Hong Kong	Korea	Thailand	Indonesia	India	Pakistan	Bangladesh
United States	1.0000								
Italy	0.9178	1.0000							
Hong Kong	0.8449	0.6988	1.0000						
Korea	0.8790	0.7804	0.9267	1.0000					
Thailand	0.8528	0.8845	0.7884	0.7828	1.0000				
Indonesia	0.8647	0.8829	0.7857	0.7929	0.9462	1.0000			
India	0.6986	0.6691	0.7477	0.6784	0.7604	0.7320	1.0000		
Pakistan	0.7035	0.7224	0.7038	0.6362	0.8491	0.7953	0.7056	1.0000	
Bangladesh	0.7716	0.7713	0.7861	0.7016	0.8013	0.8385	0.7989	0.8027	1.0000

Source: US Annual Import Trade Tapes (IA245)

to account for the empirical observations. The preliminary evidence suggests that empirical observations are not consistent with the basic competitive model often used in studies of the MFA. Quota implementation, market structures and the institutional arrangements play a significant role in the determination of market outcomes.

Theoretical issues

The theoretical analysis described below focuses on three main aspects of quota implementation. First, what are the effects of transferability versus non-transferability of quota licences on exports? Second, what is the effect on the prices of transferable licences of having a portion of the total quota available free of charge (free quota)? Third, is there a theoretical case to be made for the exporting country to sub-categorise its quotas beyond the level imposed by the MFA agreement? This section draws on some earlier analysis of these issues (Krishna and Tan, 1993a).

Transferability

There is significant variation between exporting-country participants in the MFA in the degree of quota transferability permitted. For example, quotas may be traded relatively freely between firms on either a permanent or temporary basis in Hong Kong, whereas in other countries, only a portion of quotas may be transferred, and those only subject to official regulation (for example, in Korea), or only permanently (for example, in India, Pakistan and Bangladesh). The usual presumption is that transferable licences will always go to agents who value them the most, and this will result in a higher licence price. Moreover, since transferable licences will be allocated 'properly' by the market under perfect competition while non-transferable ones need not be, welfare in the exporting country, defined as the sum of licence revenue and surplus, will necessarily be higher under transferability.

However, allowing licence transfers might actually reduce the licence price and, if revenue is an important consideration, this would be less desirable than an outright ban on licence trades. In contrast to the existing work on this issue, which compares transferable and non-transferable licences taking the quota allocations as given, the outcomes of the two systems should also be examined when the quota allocations are endogenously determined. Of course, the two systems are different only if there is some uncertainty in final valuations, so that there exists a potential for trades after the initial allocation has taken place.

In a simple two-period example, suppose that licences are not transferable, and that all agents face an identical distribution of valuations. Then, as long as the quota is binding, the price for a licence will equal the licence's expected value. This is independent of the size of the quota. If transferability is allowed, then the price of a licence in the first period, when the valuations are uncertain, is tied to the price in the second period, when the valuations are realised. In the second period, the value of a licence depends on the size of the quota, as the agents' valuations differ *ex post*. If the quota is small, the second-period price will be high, and the price of the transferable licence will exceed that of a non-transferable licence. If the quota is large, the second-period price will be low, and the price of the transferable licence will be less than that of a non-transferable licence.

Free quota

A common practice among MFA-exporting countries is to allocate a portion of the total quota free of charge on a 'first-come-first-served' basis to agents with proof of an order. Hong Kong, India and Bangladesh, among other countries, have this 'free' quota scheme. The rationale for this scheme is to facilitate entry by new firms which are not eligible for past performance quota allocations and may otherwise have to purchase quotas from existing licence holders. Free quotas, once allocated, are usually not transferable. However, they could affect the price of the remaining licences which are transferable. Clearly, the size of the free quota is relevant. On the one hand, a large amount of free quota may lower the price of the tradeable licences since each agent stands a good chance of obtaining his quota without charge. On the other hand, a large amount of free quota may raise the price of the tradeable licences for two reasons: first, because the more licences are allocated free of charge, the fewer will be the available licences for sale; and second because more people will apply for the free quota, thereby lowering the expected gain from this course of action.

Sub-categorisation

Another aspect of quota implementation is sub-categorisation, practised in the Indian system of MFA quota allocation. Even though MFA categories are quite detailed (by fabric and garment type, in the case of exports to the United States), the Indian authorities often further divide them into sub-categories, for example knitted, hand-loomed and mill-made or power-loomed garments, with the entitlements calculated separately. The standard argument (Khanna, 1991) is that sub-categorisation raises the effective restrictiveness of the total quota, since it can lead to situations where the quota is not binding in some sub-category, and very binding in others. However, theoretically, a case could be made for sub-categorisation of MFA quotas by price and to exert monopoly power. This would explain the practice in India. Clearly, if the country is a 'large' exporter, its first-best welfare-optimising policy would be to restrict exports of a particular MFA category to the 'optimal quota' level (that is, the quantity associated with the optimal tariff) and then divide this amount optimally between the various sub-categories. The bottom line, however, is that even if the country faces an exogenously fixed overall quota for that category, there may still be room for sub-categorisation. For example, if the given overall quota is larger than the 'optimal quota', the authorities could create an unusable 'dummy' sub-category in order to achieve the optimal quota result. The information requirements probably make quota sub-categorisation unmanageable.

Empirical issues

Krishna and Tan's first approach to assessing whether all the MFA quota rents were being captured by the exporting countries was to develop 'rent-sharing equations'. This follows from the standard presentation of quota licence price determination under perfect competition (figure 4.1). The licence price, L, should equal $P^D - P^S$ if there is perfect competition throughout. In other words, the adjusted export price, $P^S + L$, should equal P^D under these circumstances. Other considerations should not affect this equality as long as the product market is competitive. For example, if production costs rise in the exporting country, its supply price will also increase, and competitive market forces will result in the licence price falling with the cost increase; the equality between the adjusted import price and the domestic price would be maintained. As long as all markets are competitive, factors such as the quota size and utilisation rate, and the distribution of licence holdings, should have no effect on the licence price or the above equality.

This is the concept underlying the basic rent-sharing equations. Using 'f.o.b.' import prices (which include the licence price), adjusted for tariffs and transport costs, the empirical analogue of $P^S + L$ is obtained. By regressing this against P^D (the price of US-produced goods) and other factors such as licence-holding concentration, and the quota level and utilisation rate, as well as dummy variables for year and MFA category, the null hypothesis of no rent-sharing would predict the coefficient on P^D to be unity, and those on the other variables to be zero.

Ideally, a narrowly defined homogeneous product should be tracked to check if actual licence prices reflect the potential rents identified by the standard static model. However, this is not possible. Not only do the exporting and importing countries employ different (and frequently changing) methods of data classification, but even the MFA categories are not standardised for all the importing countries. For this reason, attention is restricted to MFA exports to the United States and a concordance for this trade was developed, with a focus on a selected number of countries which export to the United States: Hong Kong (which is widely thought to have the best administered quota system), Korea, Indonesia, Thailand, Bangladesh, Pakistan, India, Mexico and, as an unrestricted country, Italy.

The data from the exporting countries is classified according to MFA categories, and US data is indexed by SIC codes. In order to achieve some degree of comparability between the two sources of data, data are aggregated into larger apparel groups. This creates ten apparel groups: dresses, skirts, playsuits, sweaters, trousers, men's coats, women's coats, knitted shirts, woven shirts, and underwear. For many countries in the sample, not all the categories in each apparel group are under quota. In such cases, other variables of interest could not be defined clearly, such as quota utilisation rates by apparel group.

The rent-sharing regressions for Hong Kong (in Krishna *et al.*, 1994) and Korea (in Krishna and Tan, 1993b), show that $P^S + L$ fell significantly short of P^D. A \$1 increase in the US price is associated with only a US\$0.54 increase in the Hong Kong price, and a US\$0.63 increase in the Korean price. Furthermore, other regressors such as the quota level, the quota utilisation rate, and the degree of concentration in licence holdings, are found to have explanatory power. These results are inconsistent with the perfectly competitive model.

The adjusted export price and the domestic price need not be the same and the coefficient of P^D need not equal unity if imports and domestically produced apparel are different. This raises the question of comparing the price of apples with that of oranges! There are several reasons why this could be the case. US-made apparel may be of a higher (or lower) quality than imported apparel. Second, US-made apparel may be simply different (not necessarily better or worse) than imported apparel. Third the data aggregations undertaken – as the ten aggregated apparel groups were broadly defined – could contain compositional differences in the make-up of the domestic and imported apparel groups.

Quality differences over time are allowed for by introducing category-specific dummy variables and a time trend into the rent-sharing equation.

The results, however, remain qualitatively unchanged. In the case of Hong Kong, (Krishna *et al.*, 1991), a method is devised to test for compositional differences. Although the tests are hampered by the limited sample size and the results are not clear, these compositional differences are not significant on the whole.

The question of (horizontal) product differentiation is dealt with by looking at the effects of exchange rate changes in the exporting country. If the inequality between the price of imports and US-produced goods are due to different brands of apparel being produced in the two countries, a coefficient different from unity need not reflect rent-sharing. However, even in this general model, exogenous supply shocks such as exchange rate changes should be compensated for by changes in the licence price, leaving P^D unaffected. Consider an appreciation of the US dollar relative to the exporting country's currency. If the price axis in figure 4.1 is measured in terms of US dollars, this appreciation should have no effect on excess demand, RD, which is a function of the dollar prices of US-produced and imported apparel, among other variables. However, excess supply, RS, is a function of price measured in the exporting country's currency, which can be expressed in terms of the dollar export price and the exchange rate. Hence, for a given dollar export price, an appreciation of the US dollar *vis à vis* the exporting country's currency would swivel RS up. With V and P^D unchanged, however, the appreciation results only in an increase in the licence price so that $P^S + L$ is still equal to P^D. This hypothesis was examined in Krishna and Tan (1993b), using data on Korean exports to the United States, because Korea had a flexible exchange rate *vis à vis* the United States. Again, evidence was contrary to the standard model: exchange rate changes did seem to affect the adjusted import price significantly despite the quota, with an appreciation of the dollar actually lowering the dollar price of Korean exports!

Another perspective on price differentials is to be found in Bannister's (1992) work on Mexico. In Mexico, only certain apparel groups are bound by the quota restrictions, while others are not. For the unbound group, accounting for quality differences seemed to go much further in explaining US–Mexico price differentials than was the case for the bound group, suggesting that the quotas themselves may lead to price differentials.

Finally, the data for apparel exports from an unrestricted country, Italy are examined. In Krishna and Tan (1993b) the relationship between the adjusted Italian import price and the domestic price appeared quite different from that for most constrained countries. In fact, in the case of Italian apparel exports to the United States, the hypothesis that quality differences alone account for price differences could not be rejected!

Conclusion

The MFA is due to be phased-out over the next ten years and attention will focus on the consequences of its elimination. The evidence presented in this chapter suggests that the standard competitive framework may be inadequate for analysing the welfare effects of the MFA. Details of quota implementation and possible market imperfections affect the degree of quota-rent appropriation by exporting countries, and should be taken into account to obtain a clear understanding of how the MFA affects welfare in supplying countries. The theoretical and empirical difficulties are considerable. However, by taking many different approaches to the issue, and finding ways to resolve data and analytical problems at least partially, a number of answers as well as a larger number of new and provocative questions have been identified which should help to shape future research.

5

U.S.,
(Asia)

Financial deregulation and trade expansion

SUIWAH LEUNG

One of the little recognised Declarations in the Marrakesh Agreement (April 1994) concerns the enhanced contribution that the World Trade Organisation (WTO) is called upon to make to bring more coherence to global economic policy making. In recognising the contribution that liberal trading policies make to their own economies and developments in the world economy, Trade Ministers called for greater cooperation with other policy areas. The Declaration notes that more orderly economic and financial conditions should contribute to the expansion of trade and economic development, and the correction of external imbalances. While difficulties that arise from causes outside the trade field cannot be redressed through trade measures alone, there are important linkages between different aspects of economic policy. Greater exchange rate stability, based on more orderly underlying economic and financial conditions, would contribute to reducing uncertainties around trade and investment decisions and provide more confidence in a dynamic and open trading system. Similarly, an increased flow of concessional and non-concessional financial and investment resources to developing countries would help them to overcome debt problems and improve their development prospects. The Declaration, therefore, called on the WTO to increase its cooperation with the international agencies responsible for monetary and financial affairs.

Links between exchange rate stability and international trade have been a recurrent theme in the literature over the past twenty years, since the fixed exchange rate regime began to decay. A decade ago short-run exchange rate fluctuations were the focus of interest. Now the worries about longer-term current account imbalances are associated with exchange rate misalignments under a generalised floating regime. The 1981–5 real appreciation of the US dollar has been blamed for the loss of about 1 million jobs in US manufacturing (Branson and Lowe, 1987; Bergsten and Williamson, 1983; McKinnon, 1993). This type of structural unemployment leads to generally protectionist sentiments in the United States which is detrimental to an open trading system. The IMF has

Table 5.1. *Exchange rate arrangements and capital controls for selected Asia Pacific countries, 1975–91*

	Pegged to US$	Pegged to other currency or composite	Other flexible arrangement	Managed flexibility	Independent floaters	Capital Controls		
						Substantial	Limited	None
1975	3	5	1	2	1	9	2	1
1976	3	4	1	3	1	9	2	1
1977	3	4	1	3	1	9	2	1
1978	2	4	1	4	1	9	1	2
1979	1	4	1	5	1	8	2	2
1980	0	4	1	6	1	8	2	2
1981	0	3	1	7	1	8	2	2
1982	0	3	1	7	1	8	2	2
1983	0	3	1	7	1	6	3	3
1984	0	3	1	5	3	6	2	4
1985	0	4	0	4	4	5	3	4
1986	0	3	0	5	4	5	3	4
1987	0	3	0	5	4	4	4	4
1988	0	3	0	5	4	4	4	4
1989	0	3	0	5	4	4	4	4
1990	0	3	0	5	4	4	4	4
1991	0	3	0	5	4	4	4	4

Note:
Numerals refer to number of countries. The countries are Australia, China, Hong Kong, Indonesia, Japan, Korea, Malaysia, New Zealand, Philippines, Singapore, Taiwan and Thailand. The 'independent floaters' are Australia, New Zealand, Japan and the Philippines, but the Philippines has substantial capital controls.
Sources: IMF (1976–8, 1979–83).

announced that it will undertake 'a study of the possible ways to introduce a higher degree of discipline in the present exchange rate system' (joint press conference of Philippe Maystadt, Chairman, Interim Committee and Michel Camdessus, Managing Director, IMF, 25 April, 1994).

In the Asia Pacific countries outward-looking growth policies resulted in strong export growth throughout the 1980s, in spite of increased short-term exchange rate fluctuations and misalignments amongst the world's major currencies. There is some evidence that the period of US dollar appreciation experienced in the first half of the 1980s enabled the Asian newly industrialising economies (NIEs) to establish their exports to the United States (McKibbin and Sundberg, 1993). Many Asian countries moved away from pegging strictly to the US dollar to pegging to currency baskets, often with either a 'crawling' or 'managed' flexibility (table 5.1). Singapore, Indonesia and Malaysia shifted the weight of their currency baskets away from the US dollar and increased the weights of the yen and deutschmark during the periods of US dollar appreciation. This insulated their competitive position *vis à vis* other countries and enhanced their competitiveness in the US market (Frankel, 1992). The effect of misalignments on trade-led growth appeared to work both ways.

A re-examination of the arguments and evidence that links exchange rate volatility to trade is relevant to economic development in the Asia Pacific region in the post-Uruguay Round trade order. That exchange rate fluctuations can affect trade flows is acknowledged in the Uruguay Round Statement on policy cohesion. The pattern of trade, as well as the total volume of trade is influenced by financial deregulation and the development of hedging instruments in coping with short-term exchange rate fluctuations. The relationship between domestic macroeconomic policies and current account imbalances will affect opportunities to stabilise exchange rates.

Short-term exchange rate volatility and trade

Short-term exchange rate volatility has increased under the generalised floating regime, and that includes the twelve Asia Pacific countries (table 5.1). Japan, Australia and New Zealand have floated their currencies independently since the mid-1980s with very few capital controls. The remaining nine currencies have been either pegged to, or otherwise strongly influenced by, movements in the US dollar (Frankel, 1992). Exchange rate variability of these nine currencies occurs both as a result of volatility of the US dollar *vis à vis* other currencies, and variability in the weights each country assigns to the US dollar. Both types of variability increased substantially in the 1980s compared with previous decades.

Nominal exchange rate volatility among the major world currencies has increased sharply since the generalised float in 1973, and there has been no tendency for this volatility to diminish over time (Crockett, 1984, Frenkel and Goldstein, 1989). The average of monthly and quarterly changes in nominal exchange rates (weighted by trade shares) increased sixfold between the period 1961–70 and 1974–83. The weighted average of real rates (similarly weighted) increased by 2.5 to 3 times for the corresponding period.

The average monthly changes in bilateral exchange rate between the Asia Pacific currencies and the US dollar showed increased variability in the 1980s compared with the previous decade, except for the Hong Kong dollar and the Malaysian ringgit (table 5.2). Late in the 1970s and early in the 1980s, the Hong Kong dollar was loosely pegged to the US dollar. The imminent merger with China and the need for stability induced the Hong

Table 5.2. *Average monthly
bilateral exchange rates,
domestic currency/US$, 1970–9
and 1980–93, percentage change*

	1970–9	1980–93
Australia	0.87	1.80
New Zealand	1.09	1.94
Japan	1.44	2.27
Hong Kong	1.19	0.58
Indonesia	0.68	0.83
Korea	0.41	0.63
Malaysia	0.89	0.81
Philippines	0.69	1.22
Singapore	0.84	0.88
Thailand	0.05	0.49
China	1.20	1.75

Note:
Data on Taiwan is not collected by
the IMF.
Source: IMF (1970–93).

Kong authorities to tighten the peg after 1985, bringing it very close to one during the period 1987–1992. At the start of the 1980s, the Malaysian ringgit was pegged to a diversified basket of currencies in which the yen featured to some extent. The large weight given to the dollar fluctuated throughout the 1980s between 0.64 and 0.90, being lower at times when the dollar was perceived to be over-valued (Frankel, 1992).

Trends in real exchange rates are less clear than for nominal rates. Prior to the generalised float in 1973, when a country experienced persistent inflation, the real exchange rate appreciated until a devaluation was effected, at which time the real exchange rate was restored close to previous levels. In theory, the volatility in the real exchange rate should be reduced once the nominal rate became more flexible, provided the nominal rate adjusted to long-run equilibrium in a smooth manner. However, international capital mobility means that nominal exchange rates become strongly influenced by short-run interest differentials and show tendencies to 'over-shoot'. Provided there is sufficient wage–price flexibility, real exchange rates need not over-shoot. However, with the possible exception of Hong Kong, most Asia Pacific economies did not have a high degree of wage–price flexibility, so real exchange rate variability followed the variability of nominal rates.

For the Asia Pacific countries, the volatility in their nominal exchange rates definitely increased during the 1980s, and their real exchange rate variability also increased. How did this increased exchange rate volatility affect the trade of the Asian economies?

Traditional arguments link exchange rate volatility to trade. Exchange rate volatility affects trade negatively by increasing the costs of uncertainty. In the short term, uncertainty occurs in the domestic price of imports. In the case of exports being invoiced in foreign currencies, uncertainty affects the domestic currency returns to producers. In this sense, it is short-term fluctuations in nominal bilateral exchange rates that are important. Much of the short-term uncertainty can, of course, be hedged, at a price (see below). Other things being unchanged, this will raise the price of traded relative to non-traded goods. Over time, there would be a tendency for the traded goods sector to contract, biasing industrial structures away from trade.

In the longer term, uncertainty in the foreign sales price and in domestic production costs also matters, in addition to uncertainty generated by nominal exchange rate fluctuations. Uncertainty in real exchange rates and, in the case of multilateral trade, uncertainty in real effective exchange rates, are the significant variables.

Whilst uncertainty arising from nominal exchange rate fluctuations can, in principle, be hedged, there are macroeconomic effects that cannot be hedged. In an open economy, exchange rate depreciation raises the domestic price level. To the extent that prices are subject to a ratchet effect, they will rise more easily and will be 'sticky' downwards in response to exchange rate appreciations, and an increase in exchange rate fluctuations will result in a rise in inflationary levels that could adversely affect economic growth, and hence trade.

More recent theoretical literature points to a much less negative view about the impact of exchange rate volatility on trade. Franke (1991) argues that there are entry and exit costs for a firm exporting to foreign markets. A depreciated currency below long-term equilibrium may make it profitable for the firm to overcome tariffs, transport and other transactions costs to enter a foreign market. Once established, the firm is likely to endure unprofitable times due to upswings of domestic currency in the belief that these would be temporary, and because of the potential costs of re-entering the market. Far from discouraging trade, therefore, exchange rate volatility increases the length of time on average during which firms do engage in trade, while the number of firms actively engaged in trade also increases. This argument is consistent with the increased incidence of 'dumping' since the generalised float, being a manifestation of firms' willingness to stay in a foreign market. Anti-dumping duties, quotas and other non-tariff barriers (NTBs) provide more effective protection than tariffs from foreign competition under a situation of variable exchange rates.

With such conflicting theoretical viewpoints, it is not surprising that most empirical studies of the impact of exchange rate variability on the volume of international trade are unable to establish a systematically significant link between measured variability and the volume of aggregate or bilateral international trade. (The literature published in the 1980s is surveyed in Crockett, 1984; Willett, 1986; Franke, 1991). It is worth reviewing the evidence used in two of the most recent empirical studies on this subject (Qian and Varangis, 1992; Frankel, 1992).

First, the impact of exchange rate volatility on the volume of bilateral trade is very much smaller than the impact of the country's size as measured by its GNP, the stage of its economic development as measured by GNP *per capita*, and the distance from its trading partner. Using 1980 data, the relative sizes of the coefficients are -0.008 for nominal exchange rate volatility and -0.010 for real exchange rate volatility, compared with $+0.73$ for GNP, $+0.27$ for GNP *per capita*, and -0.56 for distance (Frankel, 1992). This suggests that transport costs pose a stronger impediment to bilateral trade than exchange rate uncertainty and the associated costs of hedging.

Second, using a small data set and a different estimation method, Qian and Varangis (1992) find that exchange rate volatility affects export volumes negatively in the case of Japan, Canada and Australia, but positively in the case of the Netherlands, the United Kingdom and Sweden, (statistically significant only for Sweden). The authors argue that in the case of Japan, Canada and Australia, significant proportions of exports are invoiced in US dollars so that exporters bear the costs of exchange rate fluctuations, often by cutting profit margins. In the case of Sweden, whose exports are, to a large extent, invoiced in kroner, the importers bear the exchange rate risk. Importers, however, find it easier to pass on price changes to the final consumers who have various means of absorbing them. The negative impact on trade would be stronger if exports were invoiced in foreign currencies. This is particularly relevant for the Asia Pacific economies whose exports are, to a large extent, invoiced in US dollars and yen; yen invoices are still low but increasing in recent years (Tavlas and Ozeki, 1991). This is consistent with these countries' attempts to stabilise their currencies *vis à vis* the US dollar.

Third, when a firm is exporting to different countries, increased volatility *vis à vis* the currency of a particular country could induce the firm to increase its exports to another country whose currency forms a natural hedge. Therefore, exchange rate volatility may affect the pattern rather

84   *Suiwah Leung*

Table 5.3. *Global markets for selected derivative securities, US$ billion, 1986–91*

	1986	1987	1988	1989	1990	1991
Exchange-traded instruments						
Interest rate futures	370	488	895	1201	1454	2159
Interest rate options	146	122	279	387	600	1072
Currency futures	10	14	12	16	16	18
Currency options	3	23	38	66	88	132
Over-the-counter instruments						
Interest rate swaps	400	683	1010	1503	2312	3065
Currency swaps	100	184	320	449	578	807

Source: Extracted from Glen (1993).

than the volume of trade. The impact of exchange rate volatility on export volumes is much smaller in the case of multilateral than bilateral exports (Qian and Varangis, 1992). In the case of Japan's bilateral exports to the United States, the coefficient for exchange rate volatility is four times higher than for Japan's multilateral exports. Likewise, both the size and significance of the exchange rate volatility coefficient are larger for Canada's bilateral exports to the United States than for its multilateral exports.

Finally, the impact of exchange rate volatility on bilateral trade changed over time, from being statistically significant and negative in 1980 to zero in 1985, and then to statistically significant and positive in 1990 (Frankel, 1992). Increased use of currency hedging is offered as an explanation for the change in the direction of this effect.

In summary, both earlier and recent empirical work has failed to find any consistently significant relationship between exchange rate volatility and the volume of trade. Even in periods when there appeared to be a significant relationship, the actual size of the impact is very much smaller than other factors such as transport costs. There is some evidence to suggest that the pattern of trade could be affected by exchange rate volatility, that the currency used to invoice trade matters, but that currency hedging provides a reasonably satisfactory solution to the problems of exchange rate fluctuations. How can financial hedging be made cheaper and more accessible for Asia Pacific countries? Financial hedging instruments traded on international exchanges and among financial institutions around the world increased rapidly from 1986 to 1991 (table 5.3). There is some evidence also that the costs of hedging have been decreasing, particularly with the introduction of electronic trading which has made financial futures trading increasingly international in nature (Slayter and Carew, 1993).

However, for countries in the Asia Pacific region that have substantial capital controls (China, South Korea, Philippines), access to the international exchanges is difficult. This is particularly the case when knowledge of financial hedging is limited so that officials administering capital controls are unable to distinguish between speculative capital movements and genuine requirements on the part of domestic firms to undertake financial hedging. Limited knowledge on the part of firms would also mean that they would not gain access to international exchanges even when capital control regulations are 'porous'. More familiarity with hedging instruments, as well as liberalisation of the external capital account, would enable firms in the region to gain access to financial hedging in a cost-effective manner.

International exchanges, however, provide hedging in major world currencies, but firms in many Asian countries lack instruments to manage the risks they face in their own currencies. This points to the desirability of developing regional or in-country financial centres or exchanges.

Rapid growth in trade and investment in the Asia Pacific region during the 1980s has led to increased demands on foreign exchange markets, while on-going financial deregulation in these countries has enabled the markets to blossom. The foreign exchange turnover between 1989 and 1992 increased strongly (table 5.4). The regional centres of Hong Kong, Singapore and Tokyo recorded the highest levels of activity. China, on the other hand, only recently abandoned its dual exchange rate system, and little activity occurs in its formal foreign exchange market. Given the proximity of southern China to Hong Kong, informal channels have been built up, but no data are available. Korea, Indonesia and Thailand embarked on financial deregulation in the mid-1980s, and foreign exchange turnovers expanded rapidly. In the Philippines, with its combination of macroeconomic instability and low growth, the process of financial liberalisation itself is threatened. Australia and New Zealand deregulated their financial sectors early in the 1980s, and their foreign exchange markets expanded rapidly. Between 1989 and 1992, however, foreign exchange turnovers recorded little growth because of economic recession.

Currency futures traded on the exchanges of the region are limited (table 5.5), being traded in only four of the five most financially liberalised countries. Singapore is the Asia Pacific's major financial centre and has the largest range of currency futures, but there are no US$/East Asian currency futures traded. The countries' pegged exchange rate regimes, with heavy weights given to the US dollar, have discouraged the development

Table 5.4. *Foreign exchange average daily turnover, US$ billion, 1989 and 1992*

	1989	1992
Australia	29.7	29.8
New Zealand	5.2	4.2
Japan	115.0	126.1
Singapore	55.0	75.9
Hong Kong	49.0	60.9
Korea*	0.30	0.96
Taiwan*	. . .	n.a.
Indonesia*	. . .	0.28
Malaysia*	. . .	. . .
Philippines*	0.05	0.04
Thailand*	0.08	0.35

Notes:
Data for countries with an asterisk are for years 1985 and 1991.
. . . = Nil or negligible. n.a. = Not available or not applicable.
Sources: Bank for International Settlements (1993); New Zealand Reserve Bank (1993); Asian Development Bank (1993); World Bank (1994d).

Table 5.5. *Currency futures traded on exchanges of the Asia Pacific region*

Tokyo	US$/yen
Sydney	US$/AUS$
New Zealand	US$/NZ$
Singapore	US$/yen
	US$/deutschmark
	US$/sterling

Sources: Park and Schoenfeld (1992); Slayter and Carew (1993).

Table 5.6. *Summary features of forward exchange systems in selected Asia Pacific countries, 1992*

	Cover by private sector		Cover provided by official agencies to:			Forward cover provided by or through banks
	Unregulated rates	Regulated rates	Banks	Traders	Debtors	
Australia	Yes	No	No	No	No	Yes
New Zealand	Yes	No	No	No	No	Yes
Japan	Yes	No	No	No	No	Yes
Singapore	Yes	No	No	No	No	Yes
Indonesia	Yes	No	Yes	No	No	Yes
Korea	Yes	No	Yes	No	No	Yes
Malaysia	Yes	No	Yes	No	No	Yes
Philippines	Yes	No	Yes	No	Yes	No
Thailand	Yes	No	Yes	No	No	Yes
China	No	Yes	No	No	No	Yes

Note:
Data on Hong Kong and Taiwan not available from IMF sources.
Sources: IMF (1979–93); Quirk *et al.* (1988).

of this section of the market. Malaysia is planning to extend its commodity futures exchange into currency futures. Taiwan and South Korea are also studying schemes for their own financial futures markets (Asian Development Bank 1993).

Financial deregulation results in the development of forward exchange markets because of the direct relationship between domestic interest rates, the spot and the forward rates. This relationship results from the activities of international traders and investors who wish to hedge their foreign transactions, international interest arbitragers and currency speculators, who willingly take on exchange risks in the expectation of making profits from currency fluctuations. In a financially deregulated environment, financial intermediaries (mostly commercial banks) would be able to set market-clearing forward rates once the domestic interest rates and spot exchange rates were determined in the market. Exchange rate risks are borne by currency speculators. If domestic interest rates and/or spot rates are highly regulated, then exchange rate risks are borne by the central bank, either directly through providing cover for international traders and debtors, or indirectly through the central bank providing cover for commercial banks.

Features of forward exchange rate systems in selected countries in the Asia Pacific region are shown in table 5.6. Countries with fully deregulated financial sectors have domestic interest rates, spot rates and forward rates determined in the market. Their central banks do not provide cover for international transactions. Countries that are in the process of deregulating their domestic and/or external financial markets still rely on their central banks to cover the commercial banks and hence assume the exchange rate risks. Highly regulated countries, such as China, have central banks setting forward rates as well.

The Philippines in the mid-1980s was an example where strong government intervention not only hampered the development of forward exchange markets, but impeded both trade and economic growth. The combination of increased exchange rate volatility and over-valued spot exchange rate meant that the central bank was exposed to large currency risks, and consequently suffered losses (up to 3.1 per cent of GDP in 1986) through the forward cover that it provided to corporate debtors with US$-denominated debts, as well as through its foreign currency swaps with the commercial banks. At the same time, the budgetary implications of these large losses from the central bank's foreign exchange operations delayed devaluations of the spot rate, leading to a loss of competitiveness in the real economy (especially the manufacturing sector). Ultimately, the losses were realised and monetised, resulting in inflation levels of 50.3 per cent in 1984 and 23.1 per cent in 1985, much higher than other ASEAN countries (World Bank, 1992). The Philippines has since placed greater reliance on the free market determination of forward rates (Quirk *et al.*, 1988).

The Indonesian government swap mechanism is yet another example of how government intervention can hamper the development of forward currency markets. Since 1971, Indonesia has had an open external capital account. In order to encourage foreign investment, the Indonesian government sought to reduce exchange rate risk by having its central bank guarantee investors that they could take the same amount of foreign exchange out of the country as they had brought in, and at the same exchange rate. In return, the central bank charged a swap margin. However, this meant that whenever the domestic interest rate rose above the Eurodollar rate by more than the swap margin, there were profits to be made by investors without any risk of capital loss through depreciation of the rupiah. This resulted in large periodic demands for swaps with the central bank, exposing the bank to substantial exchange risks. In 1989, the government decided to adopt the covered interest parity condition for pricing swap arrangements, and chose to set the swap margin equal to the difference between the dollar deposit rate in international banks in Singapore and the deposit rate for the rupiah in Indonesian banks. Unfortunately, this arrangement was one-sided in the sense that, although a foreign investor would be indifferent as to whether the funds were placed in Indonesia or in Singapore, there was a positive incentive for Indonesian firms to borrow funds from abroad since the interest rate spread (the difference between lending and deposit rates) in Indonesia was much higher than that in Singapore. The large interest rate spread in Indonesia was a direct result of inefficiencies in the banking system, particularly amongst the large state banks. It was shown that the difference between the interest rate spread in Indonesia and in Singapore resulted in a swap subsidy to Indonesian firms borrowing from abroad, funded by the government (Woo and Hirayama, 1994). This subsidised swap system hindered the growth of the private hedge market, which showed very little growth until 1991, even though financial liberalisation had begun in 1983, but it showed rapid growth after November 1991 when the government-subsidised swap system was abolished.

It is clear therefore that the financial environment is crucial to the development of markets for financial hedging. In a relatively deregulated environment, where interest rates and spot rates are market-determined, forward exchange markets and other derivative markets will grow to meet the needs of firms to manage the risks associated with international trade and investments. All the export-oriented countries in the Asia Pacific region have already embarked on financial deregulation, albeit some having gone further than others. Admittedly, issues of prudential supervision and deposit insurance need to be addressed (Leung, 1993). However, continued financial liberalisation in the region should enable financial hedging to be a more accessible and cost-effective tool for managing short-term exchange rate fluctuations.

Exchange rate 'misalignments' and trade

Since the advent of flexible exchange rates, claims of currency misalignments have been blamed for widening trade imbalances, especially with respect to Japan. Have currency misalignments had serious effects on trade?

The bilateral current account balances between the United States and Japan and the yen/dollar exchange rate for the period 1970–92 show that the US current account underwent large deficits for much of the 1980s, peaking in 1987, and that large deficits have re-emerged since 1992 (figures 5.1 and 5.2). At the same time, the yen has appreciated steadily against the dollar, with a reversal of this trend between 1981 and 1985, and then a sharp appreciation of the yen from 1985 to 1988. Strictly speaking, exchange rate misalignments are defined as deviations from the fundamental effective

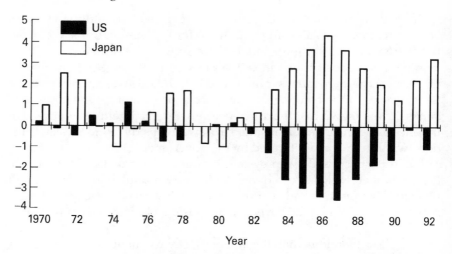

Figure 5.1 Current account balance, as percentage of GDP, 1970–92

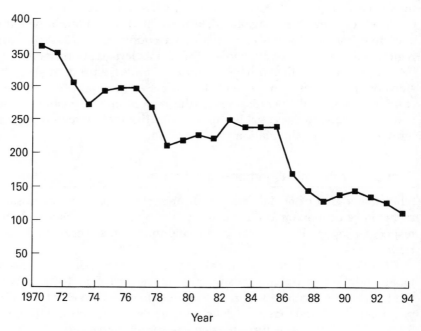

Figure 5.2 Exchange rates, yen per US$, 1970–94

exchange rate of a country (FEER). However, measurement of the FEER depends on definitions of internal and external balance over time. The latter, in particular, is dependent on some notion of a 'sustainable' current account balance of which there is no generally agreed method of measurement (Williamson, 1992). The protracted periods of US current account deficit and the associated current account surplus in Japan have therefore been taken loosely as indications that the yen/dollar exchange rate has been in long-term disequilibrium or 'misaligned'.

Misalignments of exchange rates may lead to structural unemployment and increased protectionism in countries with large current account deficits (Bergsten and Williamson, 1983; Williamson, 1985). The real appreciation of the US dollar between 1981 and 1985 is estimated to have cost about 1 million jobs in US manufacturing, after allowing for other causes of unemployment, and that this strengthened protectionist pressures in the United States (Branson and Lowe, 1987). Furthermore, since exchange rate variability reduces the effectiveness of tariff protection to domestic producers, the new forms of protection take the form of voluntary export restraints (VERs) and other non-tariff barriers (NTBs) which are more certain to reduce imports than tariffs and other market measures. Between 1981 and 1986, the proportion of non-petroleum imports of OECD countries affected by such 'hard-core' NTBs rose from 15.1 per cent to 17.7 per cent. Further disaggregation shows that the rise in NTBs has been the highest in the United States, from 11.4 per cent of imports in 1981 to 17.3 per cent in 1986 (McKinnon and Fung, 1993). One solution to this new protectionism would be to stabilise or otherwise 'manage' the exchange rates of the major currencies.

At the same time, there are sound theoretical and empirical arguments to suggest that the appreciation of the US dollar between 1981 and 1985 resulted from the US fiscal expansion (McKinnon, 1993). There is econometric evidence to support the argument that increases in the US fiscal deficit in the early 1980s led to increases in US interest rates relative to Japanese and German rates. Investors demanded US dollar financial assets, thereby appreciating the US dollar (McKibbin and Sundberg, 1993).

Experiences of developing countries, on the other hand, tell a different story. Developing countries are much more likely to use trade restrictions to correct their current account imbalances if they are unable to use exchange rate flexibility to do the job (Corden, 1993). Stabilising exchange rates, therefore, would lead to more trade restrictions in these countries. In any case, whether the increased protectionism in US trade policy should be tackled by stabilising exchange rates or by confronting the NTBs directly depends, to a large extent, on the causes of the misalignments. If exchange rate behaviour is erratic and/or simply based on extrapolation of existing trends in exchange rates, then there may be a *prima facie* case for stabilising the rates. On the other hand, if exchange rate behaviour is strongly influenced by 'fundamentals' relating to government policies, then stabilising exchange rates *per se* may not solve the problem unless the fundamentals can be changed.

There is a large literature on whether the foreign exchange market is efficient (MacDonald and Taylor, 1991). Until recently, tests of exchange market efficiency depended on a joint hypothesis of the existence of rational expectations and exchange risk premium in the foreign exchange market (Bilson, 1981). In order to test for rational expectations, the researcher had to assume risk neutrality, and vice versa. In recent years, the existence of exchange rate expectations surveys has made it possible to measure expectational errors and exchange risk premium separately (Froot and Frankel, 1989; Leung, 1992). The conclusions so far point to the existence both of expectational errors and the existence of a time-varying risk premium, and that the risk premium seems to be rather small. The foreign exchange market does not appear to be efficient.

A consensus that combines the 'chartist' approach (that is, simple extrapolation of trends) with a fundamentalist view of the foreign exchange market offers a more realistic model of the workings of that market (MacDonald and Taylor, 1991). Given the relatively recent availability of exchange rate expectations surveys, a great deal more needs to be done both in measuring the extent of the exchange risk premium as well as the failure of rational expectations in the foreign exchange market. It would be premature to conclude that the evidence points to a *prima facie* case for stabilising exchange rates. Furthermore, evidence in support of fundamentals would raise the question whether a more stable exchange rate regime can influence the fundamentals in the desired direction, and at what cost.

Williamson (1985), in his initial discussions on the 'target zone' exchange rate regime, recognised the need to control fiscal expenditures independently. Later proponents of the 'target zone' claimed that membership in the European Monetary System (EMS) made France exercise more fiscal restraint in the early 1980s than it would otherwise have done. The fiscal performance of other European countries later in that decade did not bear this out (Frenkel and Goldstein, 1989). Furthermore, the experience of ten developing countries that switched from fixed to flexible exchange rate regimes showed no general evidence that the regime change was associated with changes in inflation rates, and hence in their fiscal and monetary policy stance.

Asian countries, in particular, have had low inflation not because of their fixed exchange rates, but because their policymakers were heavily committed to low inflation as a fundamental policy objective. (Little *et al.*, 1993)

Further evidence is obviously needed to support exchange rate stabilisation as far as its effect on fundamentals is concerned. On the other hand, what are the possible costs associated with stabilising the exchange rate?

First, if a lax fiscal policy places too much weight on monetary policy, and if adherence to a target zone means that monetary policy is forced to be loose, inflation will ensue, with detrimental effects on trade and growth. More importantly, if monetary policy is used to keep exchange rates within the target zone, then there would only be three possible instruments left for internal stabilisation: namely, fiscal policy, labour market policy and sterilised intervention. Fiscal policy on its own is too inflexible as an instrument for short-term stabilisation (Frenkel and Goldstein, 1989). Short-term unemployment cannot be overcome in most economies without major structural reforms of the labour market. Whilst Williamson (1993) asserts that recent empirical work points to the relative success of sterilised intervention, this work also attributes the success to the market taking exchange rate intervention as a 'signal' that monetary policy will be changed (Dominguez and Frankel, 1990; Froot and Frankel, 1989; Leung, 1992). This gives monetary policy the burden of trying to achieve both external and internal balance. In these circumstances, political commitment to remain within the target zone can be seriously tested, and attempts by authorities to defend exchange rates would prove very costly (for example, the experience of Britain and other European countries during 1992 in their efforts to contain domestic unemployment and to remain within the EMS at the same time). The coexistence of exchange rate stability, free movement of international capital, and monetary autonomy has been dubbed (Fischer and Reisen 1993) the 'impossible trinity'!

It has been claimed that

The success of East Asian countries in achieving the impossible trinity challenges . . . the Mundell-Fleming framework on which most macroeconomic analysis of the open (or opening of the) capital account is based. (Fischer and Reisen, 1993, pp. 76–7)

Belief in such 'exceptions' has led some economists to propose that industrialised countries with deregulated financial sectors (such as Australia), should consider a pegged exchange rate regime while maintaining free international capital flows along the lines of Singapore (Garnaut, 1994).

Recent research has suggested that, far from being 'exceptions', the experiences of Singapore, Malaysia and Indonesia confirm rather than refute the 'impossible trinity' (Woo and Hirayama, 1994). In Singapore early in the 1980s, real wages were rising (by about 60 per cent in US dollars between 1980 and 1984). Singapore was losing its international competitiveness, and in 1985 it registered its first negative growth rate since independence in 1965. The market expected a depreciation of the Singapore dollar, and took positions accordingly. But the government chose to lower wage costs by cutting payroll taxes and social security contributions, and used its ample foreign exchange reserves to intervene and to appreciate the Singapore dollar, to 'cane the speculators'. This shrank the money supply and compromised monetary autonomy; the success came from the government's ability to make rapid changes to the fundamentals (that is, cut wage costs to improve competitiveness), which removed the reason for speculation against the Singapore dollar.

The second episode relates to heavy foreign capital inflows into Malaysia during 1993 and early 1994, which threatened to appreciate the Malaysian ringgit. The government was able to stop the speculation by requiring banks to pay a lower (and at times, zero) interest rate on foreign deposits. This was a form of capital control, and enabled the government to maintain monetary autonomy. Beating the speculators, in this instance, required direct intervention in the form of capital controls.

The third episode relates to Indonesia in 1987 and 1991. In both years, the government was able to stop capital outflows by ordering state enterprises to withdraw substantial amounts of their funds from the banking system to purchase central bank certificates. Monetary autonomy was clearly compromised to maintain the pegged exchange rate regime.

The lesson to be drawn from these episodes is that there is no escape from the loss of monetary autonomy for a country that maintains a pegged exchange rate regime and free capital flows. The apparent success of East Asian economies in maintaining pegged exchange rates in the face of speculative capital flows lies in their institutional wage settings, the control over state-owned enterprises, and the ability and willingness to enforce short-term capital controls. Proposals to stabilise exchange rates for industrialised countries with deregulated capital markets should therefore take full account of the institutional settings of the East Asian countries. These permit changes to fundamentals when they conflict with the exchange rate objective.

International economic 'policy coherence'?

With the current gaps in knowledge about the determinants of misalignments (chartists versus fundamentalists), the size of exchange risk premia, and the appropriate 'equilibrium' real exchange rate (purchasing power parity versus Williamson's fundamental equilibrium exchange rate), it is not surprising that international monetary cooperation has a mixed record. Lack of fiscal discipline was an important determinant of misalignments in the 1980s, and monetary cooperation to influence exchange rates did nothing to address this problem. Indeed, the concentration on exchange rates rather than fiscal policy could have entailed a loss of credibility (Currie, 1993).

McKinnon's proposal for the United States and Japan to cooperate in their monetary policies so as to bring about purchasing power parity falls into the same category (McKinnon, 1988, 1993). It is generally agreed that the price of tradeables ought to be used in measuring purchasing power parities. This means that the consumer price indices should not be used because they incorporate prices of non-tradeables, which would tend to rise as a country engages in export-led growth. The price of tradeables, on the other hand, would tend to fall since these goods are subject to international competition (the 'Balassa effect'). However, it is not always easy to find a price index that measures the price of tradeables; normally the wholesale price index or the manufacturing price index are used. Not only is purchasing power parity a difficult concept to measure, there is no consensus that it provides an appropriate 'equilibrium' exchange rate (Williamson, 1992). Even if these problems were overcome, the McKinnon proposal still does nothing to address the fiscal problem.

The neglect of fiscal policy in international economic policy coordination is understandable. The fiscal powers of individual countries are jealously guarded and not easily open to international coordination (Currie, 1993). The fiscal powers of the US Congress, for instance, severely limit the Administration's ability to control the US fiscal deficit. In Germany, fiscal policy was used to ease the problems of re-unification. The constraints on fiscal policy lead to many questions about the benefits of international economic policy coordination (Feldstein, 1988).

The gaps in current knowledge, the potential costs in terms of the disruptions to the payments system if political commitment to defend a pegged rate is put to the test, and the difficulties experienced with fiscal policy coordination explain the failure so far to achieve exchange rate stability and macroeconomic coordination. The World Trade Organisation (WTO) may be able to contribute to greater economic policy coherence by introducing more disciplines into trade policy and eliminating some of the impediments to international economic transactions. By curbing access to contingency protection and other GATT escape clauses that allow trade protection to be used for balance of payments reasons, the WTO will introduce more order into international economic policies.

Continuing research into the macroeconomy of East Asian countries could disclose the institutional factors, and the possible costs involved, in maintaining exchange rate stability. Global macroeconometric research along the lines of McKibbin and Sundberg (1993) would underpin the importance of domestic US fiscal policy for the trade and growth of the entire Asia Pacific region.

Conclusion

The adoption of schemes to stabilise world exchange rates on the grounds of promoting trade, as suggested in the Marrakesh Declaration on policy coherence, is premature. Such a move cannot be justified on the grounds of short-run exchange rate volatility. Empirical evidence has failed to show any systematic link between short-term exchange rate volatility and the volume of bilateral and multilateral trade. Even in periods when a negative relationship between exchange rate volatility and bilateral trade existed, the actual impact was much smaller than other factors that affected trade, for example, the level of economic development and transport costs. Some evidence suggests that the pattern of trade could be affected by exchange rate volatility: that currency invoicing of trade matters. But currency hedging provides a reasonably cost-effective way of managing exchange rate volatility. Future growth of trade in the Asia Pacific with continuing financial deregulation will permit the development of financial hedging in the region.

Attempting to stabilise exchange rates to counter protectionism resulting from longer-term imbalances or 'misalignments' would be premature. First, gaps in our knowledge about the causes of the imbalances, about the long-term 'equilibrium' exchange rate, and about the way in which sterilised intervention could be made to work (whether through the 'signalling' of future monetary policy stance or through portfolio effects) make any such strategy risky. Secondly, external imbalances in the 1980s were attributed to inappropriate fiscal policy. Concentrating on exchange rates and monetary policy coordination may do nothing to change fiscal policy, and could undermine the credibility of coordination programmes, there would be very real risks of disruption to the payments system if political commitments to a pegged exchange rate regime were put to the test. The adoption of sound fiscal and monetary policies in the United States would contribute a great deal to trade and growth in the Asia Pacific region.

Coordination of work done in the WTO with that of the IMF and the World Bank has been enhanced by regular meetings of senior staff from the three institutions and by the participation of the Director-General of the WTO in the meetings of the IMF Interim Committee and IMF/World Bank Development Committee. WTO links to the UNCTAD have also been strengthened. This institutional cooperation should establish coordinated research into the whole range of economic and monetary policies, and shed some light on their interdependence.

II

Modelling the Uruguay Round outcome

(global) /01 - 30
Fo2 F13 Q17

The Uruguay Round: a global general equilibrium assessment

D 58
F43
F47

JOSEPH F. FRANCOIS, BRADLEY McDONALD AND
HÅKAN NORDSTRÖM

An assessment of the likely effects of the Uruguay Round on trade and welfare is a complex and uncertain exercise. Using a fifteen-sector, nine-region computable general equilibrium (CGE) model of the world economy, an attempt will be made to quantify the effects of the Uruguay Round. While those aspects of the Final Act dealing with tariffs and direct government subsidies are readily subjected to quantitative analysis, other aspects of the agreements, such as those dealing with non-tariff barriers (NTBs) and indirect government support, can be only roughly quantified. Still other aspects of the Round are beyond meaningful quantitative analysis, including the effects of implementing a strengthened and extended set of rules and procedures, and the long-run effects on investor confidence, investment and growth.

Three aspects of the Uruguay Round results are considered here. First, improved market access for goods resulting from tariff reductions are analysed using the CGE model. Secondly, the effects of eliminating GATT exceptions for quantitative restrictions (QRs) on industrial products are assessed, particularly the agreement to bring textiles and clothing back under normal GATT rules. This agreement calls for a ten-year phase-out of the multifibre arrangement (MFA). Similarly, the effects of phasing-out quotas (voluntary export restraints or VERs) on Japanese cars in the EU market are analysed. Finally, an attempt is made to measure the effects of the agreement on agriculture, which includes a conversion of NTBs to tariff equivalents combined with some cuts in the rates, and a reduction of trade-distortive export and production subsidies.

The analysis and estimates presented here are based on the final offers made in the Uruguay Round negotiations. The model structure is modified to take account of imperfect competition and scale economies. Previous assessments, with the exception of Haaland and Tollefsen (1994) and Yang (1994a), have used models built on the assumption of perfect competition and constant returns to scale. Specifically, sectors for which evidence of scale economies are available are characterised either by Marshallian 'external'-scale economies and perfect competition (Panagariya, 1981), or by Chamberlinian 'internal'-scale economies and large-group monopolistic competition (Dixit and Norman, 1980; Krugman, 1980; Helpman, 1981; Ethier, 1982). This implies cross-border spillover of the effects of liberalisation (Francois, 1992, 1994a). The latter specification has important ramifications for the results, in particular for developing countries. Allowance is also made for the medium-run dynamic effects of trade liberalisation (Smith, 1976, 1977; Baldwin, 1989, 1992). It is assumed that a share of the static income gains is saved and invested in new production capacity, compounding the initial impact over time.[1]

The Uruguay Round results are estimated in a set of counterfactual simulation experiments. Given the structure of the world economy in the 1990 benchmark data set, what would the economy have looked like if the Round's agreements on tariffs, industrial quotas, and agriculture had been in place? This exercise is meant to offer some sense of the isolated impact of these limited aspects of the agreements. It does not constitute a forecast of the global economy. Other 'shocks' to the system – exogenous technological changes, changes in the taste of consumers, unilateral policy reforms in developing economies, continued rapid growth and industrialisation in East Asia, the new market-orientation of transition economies – will all independently shift the pattern of global production and trade. None of these effects are captured this study.

The assessment of the efficiency gains is that, had the accounted market access provisions of the Round agreements been in place in 1990, global GDP might have been US$291 billion higher.[2] Based on OECD and World Bank regional growth projections, the market access provisions by the year 2005, when the Uruguay Round agreement is supposed to be fully implemented, may contribute US$510 billion annually to global GDP (measured in 1990 dollars). The efficiency gains result from specialisation and trade based on comparative advantage and scale economies. These welfare gains are supported by an estimated increase in world merchandise trade of between 8 and 23 per cent (above where it would otherwise be). The welfare gains are relatively broad-based among the regions defined in our model, which follows, in part, from the inclusion of scale economies, imperfect competition in industrial markets, and income–investment dynamics. Overlooking these aspects of the global economy can lead to significant under-estimation of the impact of the Uruguay Round.

Background: tariffs, textiles and clothing, and agriculture

In contrast to previous GATT rounds, the Uruguay Round was born largely out of concerns about non-tariff measures. The successful

reductions of tariffs in the first seven rounds – particularly those on industrial goods in the industrial countries, which were reduced from 40 per
cent in 1947 to 5 per cent today – had made traditional, non-discriminatory
(most-favoured-nation or Mfn) tariff protection a relatively minor issue
between industrial countries. These hard-fought gains were, however,
gradually being eroded by less transparent trade barriers that had
emerged, or otherwise become more evident as tariffs were reduced. For
many sectors, protection had shifted to modes not covered by Mfn tariff
bindings. The relative decline of tariff barriers merited a shift in the focus
to more pressing areas for reforms: NTBs; GATT rules (including the procedures for settling trade disputes and providing contingent protection);
specific sectoral exemptions from general GATT rules (such as textiles,
clothing and agriculture); trade-related investment measures (TRIMs);
trade-related aspects of intellectual property rights (TRIPs); and trade in
services (GATS).[3] While still important, tariffs were one of many areas that
called for attention in the Uruguay Round.

Tariffs

The main tariff issues addressed in the Uruguay Round can be grouped
under five headings: (i) tariff peaks, (ii) nuisance tariffs (defined as tariffs
less than 5 per cent), (iii) differences in tariff bindings, (iv) credits for
autonomous liberalisation, and (v) tariff escalation. The Ministerial
Declaration at Punta del Este[4] mandated that

> negotiations shall aim, by appropriate methods, to reduce or, as appropriate,
> eliminate tariffs including the reduction or elimination of high tariffs and tariff
> escalation. The emphasis shall be given to the expansion of the scope of tariff
> concessions among all participants.

The Mid-term Ministerial Meeting in Toronto at the end of 1988 specified
an overall target for tariff reductions 'at least as ambitious as that achieved
by the formula participants in the Tokyo Round', that is, a reduction of 33
per cent on a trade-weighted basis.[5] The target for the developing countries was set at 24 per cent.

The Ministerial Declaration called for tariff concessions by all parties,
including the developing countries. Developing countries had not been
required fully to reciprocate the tariff cuts (or other liberalisation efforts)
of the industrial countries in previous Rounds. They were granted special
and differential treatment, with obligations commensurate to their perceived development needs. Lacking the incentive and peer pressure to
liberalise, many developing countries have for decades been stuck with
high and costly levels of protection. These levels have only recently started

Table 6.1. *Tariff bindings on industrial and agricultural products, percentages*

Country groups	Percentage of tariff lines bound		Percentage of imports under bound rates	
	Pre-UR[b]	Post-UR	Pre-UR	Post-UR
	Industrial products			
Industrial	78	99	94	99
Developing	22	72	14	59
Transitional	73	98	74	96
	Agricultural products			
Industrial[a]	58	100	81	100
Developing	18	100	25	100
Transitional	54	100	54	100

Notes:
[a]The major exceptions are the tariffs on rice in Japan and Korea, which are still unbound.
[b]UR=Uruguay Round.
Source: GATT Integrated Data base (IDB).

to come down as outward-oriented development strategies have won ground over inward-oriented ones, stimulating countries to embark either on unilateral liberalisation sponsored by the World Bank and the IMF, or on liberalisation in the context of regional trade agreements.

One of the most important results of the tariff negotiations is that many developing countries have 'locked in' their recent unilateral liberalisations by binding a majority of their tariffs, although in some cases at levels above (sometimes far above) currently applied rates.[6] On industrial products, tariff bindings of the developing economies increased from 22 per cent of the tariff lines to 72 per cent, for transition economies from 73 to 98 per cent, and for industrial economies from 78 to 99 per cent. The progress in tariff bindings has been even more dramatic in agricultural products. For the first time, bindings cover a broader share of agricultural than industrial product trade. Indeed, bindings will now cover almost 100 per cent of agricultural trade (Japanese and Korean rice being a notable exception), including tariffs that resulted from the tariffication process of NTBs (table 6.1).[7] In addition to binding most of the tariff lines, the data point to a tariff reduction of some 27 per cent on average for the developing countries, including the autonomous trade liberalisation undertaken during the course of the negotiations. Hence, it appears that the developing countries as a group, if not individually, reached the 24 per cent target set out for developing countries in the Uruguay Round. Reductions of the average tariffs of industrial countries are clustered around the 33 per cent target, as shown in table 6.2.[8]

Table 6.2. Pre- and Post-Uruguay Round Mfn tariff rates on non-agricultural products

	Australia and New Zealand			Canada			United States			Japan		
	Old	New	Cut	Old	New	Cut	Old	New	Cut	Old	New	Cut
Fishery products	0.7	0.5	28.3	3.2	2.1	34.4	1.2	0.9	20.6	5.7	4.1	28.6
Forestry products	0.2	0.2	0.0	0.0	0.0	34.3	0.3	0.0	100.0	0.0	0.0	30.2
Mining	1.5	1.1	31.5	2.6	1.3	49.3	1.3	0.8	36.4	1.3	0.6	56.3
Textiles	24.6	14.5	41.1	18.6	11.7	36.8	10.5	7.5	29.0	7.4	6.0	19.5
Clothing	50.5	34.8	31.0	22.9	16.6	27.7	16.7	15.2	9.1	13.0	10.2	21.9
Primary steel	9.7	1.6	83.5	7.4	0.4	95.2	4.5	0.2	95.2	3.9	0.6	84.6
Primary non-ferrous metals	11.2	6.4	42.8	4.9	2.7	44.4	2.9	2.6	7.2	4.1	2.4	41.7
Fabricated metal products	17.1	12.7	25.9	9.7	6.0	37.8	4.7	2.8	41.1	3.4	0.9	74.3
Chemicals and rubber	11.9	7.5	37.0	10.3	5.3	48.4	5.0	3.0	39.7	4.1	1.6	60.9
Transport equipment	25.7	19.4	24.8	8.1	5.4	34.1	4.8	4.6	4.5	1.5	0.0	100.0
Other manufactures	11.6	7.6	34.5	6.3	2.9	54.3	3.5	1.5	56.5	2.0	0.9	52.1
Total merchandise	14.2	9.5	32.9	7.4	4.2	43.9	4.6	3.2	30.1	4.4	2.7	38.2

Table 6.2 cont.

	EU			EFTA			Dev/trans			Dev/trans excl. Hong Kong		
	Old	New	Cut	Old	New	Cut	Old	New	Cut	Old	New	Cut
Fishery products	12.9	10.7	17.4	1.7	1.4	17.9	35.2	8.1	76.9	35.2	8.1	76.9
Forestry products	0.0	0.0	100.0	0.2	0.1	48.0	0.1	0.1	14.3	5.8	5.0	14.3
Mining	1.1	0.8	27.3	1.0	0.8	23.2	11.5	9.5	17.6	11.5	9.5	17.6
Textiles	9.0	6.8	25.0	12.2	8.0	34.3	30.3	20.3	33.0	30.5	20.4	33.0
Clothing	12.6	10.9	13.2	17.0	11.4	33.1	14.6	10.8	25.9	20.2	15.0	25.9
Primary steel	5.3	0.5	90.8	4.1	0.6	85.7	8.7	6.1	30.7	16.9	11.7	30.7
Primary non-ferrous metals	7.2	5.9	17.9	4.0	2.9	26.4	2.7	2.1	20.7	17.3	13.8	20.6
Fabricated metal products	5.7	3.1	46.4	5.3	3.0	43.1	8.5	6.9	18.9	20.7	16.8	18.8
Chemicals and rubber	7.7	4.2	44.8	5.8	3.0	48.9	19.1	13.2	30.7	19.2	13.3	30.7
Transport equipment	6.9	6.0	13.0	7.5	6.3	16.2	27.2	17.3	36.6	29.5	18.7	36.6
Other manufactures	5.5	2.5	54.7	4.3	2.3	46.9	18.0	13.3	26.1	18.0	13.3	26.1
Total merchandise	5.3	3.2	39.7	6.2	3.9	36.4	13.5	9.8	27.4	18.2	13.2	27.5

Note:
Dev/trans=Developing and transitional.

The tariffs of the industrial countries are normally below 5 per cent (10 per cent in the case of Australia/New Zealand), textiles and clothing being an exception with tariffs in the range 10–30 per cent being imposed in addition to MFA quotas. The tariffs of developing countries are generally higher, but with no apparent tariff peaks. However, this is an artifact of the high level of aggregation; tariff peaks are masked by averaging over a large number of commodities (tariff lines) that composes a sector, and over a large number of countries that composes the 'region' of developing and transitional economies. In the real world, national tariff schedules range from being virtually flat (like that of Chile) to having rather dramatic peaks and troughs. This is true for industrial and developing countries alike.

The reported tariff rates do not include customs surcharges that are common in developing countries in particular. Customs surcharges and fees are tariffs under another name (but with a different justification), and can add substantially to protection; indeed, examples exist where surcharges add 50 per cent or more to the basic tariff rates. Unfortunately, comprehensive data on custom surcharges and related fees are not available, so these are not incorporated in the model. The data used, therefore, under-state the effective tariff distortions for countries which complement base tariffs with custom surcharges. The underlying level of protection is also under-stated because of lack of data on contingent protection. For the present, data on contingent protection are limited to anti-dumping actions reported to the GATT secretariat until mid-1992. The most recent round of dumping actions in the industrialised countries is missed, as is the spread of anti-dumping regimes to developing countries. A similar downward bias originates from the high level of sectoral and regional aggregations that hide the tariff peaks of the real world. Based on Magee (1972), comparing two sectors (regions) that are identical in all aspects except for the intra-sector (intra-region) variance in tariffs, a uniform tariff cut would give a higher welfare boost in the sector (region) with the higher tariff variance. This is not captured in the model, where tariff cuts are effectively treated as if all products in a sector (region) face identical rates. For the above reasons, the welfare estimates of the Uruguay Round tariff cuts are conservative.

Textiles and clothing

The aim of integrating textiles and clothing into the normal GATT rules and disciplines was explicitly stated in the Punta del Este Declaration.[9] This sector had previously been treated as a special case with its own regulatory framework. Like the preceding arrangements (see chapter 12), the

Table 6.3. *Estimated MFA quota price wedges*

Importers/Exporters	China	Taiwan	Dev/trans	China	Taiwan	Dev/trans
		Textiles			*Clothing*	
Canada	23.2	14.2	15.0	42.0	28.7	30.0
United States	18.4	12.2	12.0	40.3	29.0	35.0
EFTA	13.5	8.5	7.5	18.0	16.5	17.5
EU	27.4	17.5	15.0	36.1	33.5	35.0

Note:
Dev/trans=Developing and transitional economies.

MFA provides rules for the imposition of quotas, either through bilateral agreements or unilateral actions, when surges of imports cause or threaten market disruption in importing countries. In recent years, six industrial participants have been applying quotas under the MFA (EU, United States, Canada, Norway, Finland and Austria), almost exclusively on imports from developing countries.[10]

The restrictiveness of the applied MFA quotas varies from product to product, and from supplier to supplier, and aggregate measures are highly uncertain. Measures of the aggregate, bilateral restrictiveness of the MFA quotas that are used in this study are derived from the estimated MFA quota price wedges reported by Yang (1992, 1994b), Whalley (1992), and the US International Trade Commission (1991,1993). These estimates are detailed in table 6.3, the estimated quota price wedges are approximately 8 to 27 per cent for textiles and 17 to 42 per cent for clothing.

The Uruguay Round Agreement on Textiles and Clothing requires a gradual phase-out of the quota restrictions carried over from the MFA regime. The integration of the products covered by the agreement is to be achieved in three stages under a ten-year transition period (table 6.4). Each importing country is free to choose the products it will integrate at each stage, the only constraint being that they shall encompass products from each of the four groupings: tops and yarn, fabrics, made-up textile products and clothing. At the end of the ten-year transition period, all remaining QRs (carried over from the MFA regime) are to be terminated. From this point onward, import restrictions must be sought under normal GATT rules (Article XIX).[11]

Agriculture

Agriculture has always been a special case within the GATT framework, with generous scope for government interventions (Stewart, 1993;

Table 6.4. *Integration scheme for textiles and clothing, 1995–2005*

	Integration (Base: 1990 import volume of the products listed in annex)		Growth rate of residual quotas (Base: Previously agreed annual MFA growth rates of quotas)
Stage I (1 January 1995)	16 %		16% higher growth rate than initially (Ex: 3%–3.48%)
Stage II (1 January 1998)	Further 17%	(Total 33%)	Increase by 25% (Ex: 3.48%–4.35%)
Stage III (1 January 2002)	Further 18%	(Total 51%)	Increase by 27% (Ex: 4.35%–5.52)
End of the ten-year transition period	Remaining 49%	(Total 100%)	

Note:
Ex=Example.

Anderson, 1994a; Tangermann, 1994). In the absence of international disciplines, the normal market forces of supply and demand have given way to a policy cocktail of subsidies, tariffs and quantitative measures with considerable side-effects on the world trading system.

The decision to break with the past and incorporate agriculture into the Uruguay Round negotiations was made because agricultural policies were draining government budgets and had become a constant source of trade friction among the Contracting Parties (total transfers from consumers and taxpayers to farmers in the OECD countries were in 1990 approximately US$300 billion, OECD, 1991, or about US$1400 for an average family of four). The Ministerial Declaration at Punta del Este stated that there was an

> urgent need to bring more discipline and predictability to world agricultural trade by correcting and preventing restrictions and distortions including those related to structural surpluses so as to reduce the uncertainty, imbalance, and instability in world agricultural markets.

The negotiation mandate aimed at (i) improving market access through reduction of import barriers; (ii) improving the competitive environment by increasing discipline on the use of all direct and indirect subsidies and other measures affecting agricultural trade; and (iii) minimising the trade-distortive effects of sanitary and phytosanitary (SPS) regulations.

The starting point for the negotiations was a GATT regime with several special provisions for agriculture. For instance, the ban on export subsidies under Article XVI did not apply to primary products, provided that the subsidy did not give the user more than an equitable share of the world market in a particular product. This qualification has failed to discipline the use of export subsidies in agricultural trade. It is estimated that over 55 million tons of wheat, or more than half of world trade, is being exported under various subsidy schemes (Wolter, 1994). Similar trade distortions are commonplace in products like coarse grain (including corn, barley, oats, etc.), beef, butter, margarine and skim milk powder.

Agricultural trade was also exempted from the ban on quantitative import restrictions under Article XI, provided that such restrictions were necessary to the enforcement of government measures that operate to control the domestic production or marketing of like products. This provision was invoked to justify an array of quantitative import restrictions, from import licensing to effectively zero import quotas. Some countries have pointed to the so-called Section 22 waiver granted to the United States, which allowed the imposition of import quotas on sugar, peanuts, tobacco, and manufactured dairy products,[12] as a justification for their own import quotas. VERs were also used, an example being the EU agreement with Thailand limiting cassava imports.

Another characteristic in the protection of agriculture was the use of variable levies in addition to base tariffs. The variable levy is normally determined by the difference between the world market price and domestic target price of the product. A reduction of the world market price is automatically offset by a higher levy to keep the domestic price of the imported good constant at the desired level. Variable levies are often combined with a similar instrument on the export side. For instance, the Common Agricultural Policy (CAP) of the EU combines variable import levies with variable export restitution payments. The export restitution is effectively a variable export subsidy which depends on the difference between the domestic target price and the world market price. The combination of variable import levies and variable export subsidies shields domestic farmers and consumers from price fluctuations. This may benefit the home country but at the same time such actions tend to exacerbate the price fluctuations in the world market,[13] pushing the burden of adjustments onto other parties (Bigman, 1987). Domestic agents have no incentive to take part in the normal equilibrating demand and supply responses that dampen price fluctuations. Variable levies and export subsidies have, therefore, an additional beggar-thy-neighbour dimension, or 'destabilise thy neighbour', as Bigman (1987) put it, by imposing the adjustment costs on others. This aspect cannot be captured by non-stochastic models.

Imports have also been restricted on health and sanitary grounds. Such measures can be invoked under Article XX of the GATT, if necessary to protect human, animal or plant life or health. SPS regulations may

Table 6.5. *Summary of the Agreement on Agriculture*

		Market access (Base: 1986–8)	Export subsidies (Base: 1986–90)	Domestic support (Base: 1986–8)
Value	i	Tariffication of NTBs	i 36 (24)% cut in budget outlay	Cut of AMS by 20 (13.3)%[a] 'Green Box' measures exempt
	ii	36 (24)% average tariff cut including converted NTBs		EU 16.8% (special)[a]
	iii	15 (10)% minimum tariff cut per tariff-line		
Volume	i	Minimum market access of 3% rising to 5%	i 21 (14)% cut in subsidised export quantity	

Note:
[a]Developing country provisions are in parenthesis. The least industrial countries are exempted.
Source: GATT Secretariat.

discourage exports from developing countries in particular, because compliance requires a scientific infrastructure currently lacking in many developing countries.

Finally, besides providing the regulatory framework, governments were often themselves directly involved in the agricultural sector through marketing boards and state trading enterprises. For instance, it is estimated that 90 per cent of the international trade in wheat and 70 per cent of the trade in coarse grains flows through state trading enterprises (Hathaway, 1987). The operation of these entities may distort trade, as explicitly noted in Article XVI of the GATT, because government agencies are often required to take other than market concerns into account when making decisions. For example in Japan, the Food Control law designates the Japanese Food Agency as the sole authorised importer of rice. Rice imports are only allowed for specific purposes, such as a special grade of rice needed to brew a type of alcoholic beverage called *Awameri* (GATT, 1992b). The Republic of Korea operates a similar scheme through the Grain Management Fund, which sets domestic intervention prices for rice and barley with a view to maintaining the self-sufficiency of these products. The agency is typically not authorised to import any rice or barley as long as domestic production is sufficient to satisfy the domestic demand (GATT, 1992c).

The Uruguay Round Agreement on Agriculture is clearly a break with the past, although not a clean break. The main features are summarised in table 6.5.

Table 6.6. *Estimated base protection in agriculture, budget outlays, 1990 US$
million, rates in percentages*

	Production subsidies				Export subsidies				Tariffs and NTBs	
	Grains ($)	(%)	Other ($)	(%)	Grains ($)	(%)	Other ($)	(%)	Grains (%)	Other (%)
Canada	688	11	844	4	366	11	60	2	13	8
United States	16,553	32	4,489	3	644	6	43	0	5	8
EFTA	3,071	49	4,219	15	650	206	893	88	247	117
EU	2,115	18	45,800	40	4,105	132	1,320	16	70	55
A and NZ	59	1	0	0	0	0	134	2	0	6
Japan	1,868	5	12,814	18	0	0	0	0	470	84
Dev/ trans	n.a.	n.a.	n.a.	n.a.	1,356	33	871	2	27	42

Notes:
n.a.=Not available.
Dev/trans=Developing and transitional.

The data on agricultural protection are drawn from OECD and US Department of Agriculture estimates of agricultural support (OECD, 1990, 1993; US Department of Agriculture, 1990), and from the submitted schedules of commitments. The latter need substantial data processing before they become readily available. For instance, comprehensive data are not available on the *ad valorem* tariff rates that resulted from the tariffication of NTBs in agriculture. Many countries converted their NTBs into specific rather than *ad valorem* tariffs, and the specific tariffs must somehow be converted into *ad valorem* equivalents before they can be aggregated into broad agricultural categories like grains and other agricultural products defined in the model. In this model, therefore, formula tariff cuts are applied to the base level of border protection, where the latter is deduced from data underlying the OECD and US Department of Agriculture estimates.

Estimates of the base level of agricultural protection are detailed in table 6.6. The budget outlays on domestic subsidies and export subsidies, and the implied subsidy rates for grains and other agricultural products are also given. In addition, the estimated base level of border protection is given (tariffs and NTBs). The rates are low for land-abundant countries with a comparative advantage in agricultural production (United States, Australia/New Zealand and many developing and transitional countries), while high-cost producers in Japan and Europe are heavily protected.

Benchmark social accounting data

The model is benchmarked to 1990, meaning that the unknown parameters of the model are chosen so that the model generates the observed market data for 1990 as an initial market equilibrium; 1990 is taken as a representative year for the world economy preceding the Uruguay Round agreement, while still being sufficiently close to the various Uruguay Round base periods for liberalisation provisions, normally 1986–90.

The benchmark data are organised as a social accounting matrix (SAM). The SAM provides a comprehensive and consistent record of national income accounting relationships between different sectors and regions.[14] An initial SAM was drawn from an eight-region, fifteen sector aggregation of the Global Trade Analysis Project (GTAP) 1990 data set. The GTAP SAM was then augmented by separating the (pre-1995) EFTA countries into a single region in order to avoid mixing industrial countries with developing and transitional economies (Jomini *et al.*, 1991; Hambley, 1995; Hertel and Tsigas, forthcoming). The Rest of World region comprises developing and transitional economies, as currently defined by the GATT.

A number of patterns are evident from the social accounting data (tables available on request). The economic structure of OECD and non-OECD countries is quite different. In the OECD countries, agricultural and primary sector value-added make up 5–10 per cent of GDP, compared to 25 per cent in the aggregate of developing and transitional economies. The GDP share of manufacturing is in the range 20–30 per cent in the OECD countries, compared to around 30 per cent in non-OECD economies. The opposite relation holds true in services, which in the OECD countries make up 65–75 per cent of GDP, compared to 45 per cent in developing and transitional economies. Within the OECD block, Australia and New Zealand have a relatively large share of agriculture and primary production, while Japan has a relatively large share of manufacturing.

Exports of OECD countries are generally concentrated in manufactured goods, which range from 40 per cent of the total exports of Australia and New Zealand to 75 per cent of the total exports of Japan. Imports of OECD countries are also concentrated in manufactures, implying a high degree of intra-industry trade (IIT) in addition to inter-industry trade. Japan, being relatively scarce in natural resources, imports relatively more primary products and fewer manufactures, while the opposite is the case for Australia and New Zealand, one-third of whose exports are composed of agricultural and primary products. Data on trade in services are still rather undeveloped, and are frequently unreliable. However, available data indicate that the share of services in exports ranges from 15 to 30 per cent for the OECD countries. The generally higher export shares than import shares suggest that the OECD countries are net exporters of services to developing and transitional economies.

Exports of developing and transitional economies are made up of roughly one-third agricultural and primary products, one-half manufactured products and one-sixth services. The export composition of manufactured products differs from that of the industrial countries. The export share of clothing and textiles is generally larger, and so is the share of natural resource-based manufacturing; note the high share of textiles and clothing in China's exports (25 per cent). Imports of developing and transitional economies are concentrated in services and manufacturing, which together make up more than 90 per cent of imports, and are divided in about equal shares. Note the low share of services in the imports of China and Chinese Taipei (Taiwan), services constitute less than 5 per cent of their total imports, compared to some 45 per cent for other developing and transition economies.

Trade intensity, as measured by the share of output that is exported or the share of demand that is imported, is generally higher for small than for large countries. It is not uncommon, for instance, for small Western European countries to export more than two-thirds of production, or import more than two-thirds of consumption, of a particular product. Note also that, controlling for size, the trade intensity of industrial countries seems larger than that of developing countries.

The model

The formal analysis is based on a fifteen-sector, nine-region computable general equilibrium (CGE) model of the world economy. A central feature of CGE models is the input–output structure, which links industries together in a value-added chain from primary goods, over continuously higher stages of intermediate processing, to the final assembling of consumption goods for households and governments. The link between sectors may be direct, like the input of steel in the production of transport equipment, or indirect, via the intermediate use in other sectors. An example of the latter is the indirect link between steel and agriculture through production of steel-intensive equipment like tractors and ploughs. Sectors are also linked through various economy-wide constraints. For instance, firms in different sectors may compete for the same production factors: labour, capital and land. Given a fixed supply of these factors, expansion of one sector must then be accompanied by a contraction of another sector, except when the expansion is driven by technological improvements that economise on the use of scarce production factors.

The general equilibrium structure recognises that all parts of the world economy hinge together in a network of direct and indirect linkages. This means that any change in any part of the system will, in principle, have repercussions throughout the entire world (albeit often too small to be noticed, let alone measured). The effect will normally be greatest in the sector and country where the policy change is initiated. It will then spread through forward and backward production and consumption linkages to adjacent sectors at home and in the markets of trading partners.

The CGE model used in this assessment of the Uruguay Round has three versions. The basic version has constant returns to scale technologies in all sectors. Firms employ domestic production factors (capital, labour and land) and intermediate inputs from domestic and foreign sources to produce outputs in the most cost-efficient way that technology allows. There is a single representative, composite household in each region, with expenditures allocated in fixed shares over personal consumption, government consumption and savings (future consumption). The composite household owns endowments of the factors of production and receives income by selling them to firms. It also receives income from the receipt of tariff revenue and rents from the sale of import/export quota licences (when applicable). Part of the income is distributed as subsidy payments to some sectors, primarily agriculture. Prices on goods and factors adjust until all markets are simultaneously in (general) equilibrium. Quotas are modelled explicitly through a Leontief specification where imports cannot exceed the quota allocation (Rutherford, 1994a, 1994b). The effective size of the bilateral quotas are calibrated from initial price wedges.[15] The changes in international capital flows induced by the Uruguay Round are not modelled; rather, the capital market closure involves fixed net capital inflows and outflows. Factor markets are competitive, with labour and capital being mobile between sectors but not between countries. A third factor, land, is used only in two agricultural sectors of the model.

The second version of the model allows for industry-wide national (regional) scale economies that are external to individual firms. These scale economies relate production costs to the aggregate activity level of the industry. The larger the aggregate activity level of the industry, the lower the production cost of each individual firm. External scale economies may, for instance, arise because of the dissemination of production experience (knowledge) among the firms in an industry, or because a larger industry is able to support production of a wider variety of intermediate,

116   *Joseph F. Francois, Bradley McDonald and Håkan Nordström*

specialised inputs that boost the productivity of the industry. (The latter interpretation is explicit in the third, monopolistic competition version.) The firms in the industry are small in that they perceive themselves as having no influence over industry-wide scale economies. External scale economies are therefore consistent with the assumption of perfect competition between price taking firms. The constant-returns and external scale economy versions incorporate the so-called Armington assumption (1969a), meaning that goods are differentiated by their region of origin. Japanese and American cars are hence imperfect substitutes in the eyes of consumers.

The third version of the model incorporates imperfect competition and scale economies that are *internal* to each firm, depending on the firm's own production level rather than the aggregate level of the industry. In particular, for sectors where estimates of scale elasticities are available, they are modelled as being characterised by Chamberlin's large-group monopolistic competition. An important property of the monopolistic competition model is that increased specialisation at intermediate stages of production yields returns due to specialisation, where the sector as a whole becomes more productive the broader the range of specialised inputs. These gains are realised through two-way trade in specialised goods (Brown, 1994; Ethier, 1982; Krugman, 1980). The scale economy sectors are mining, textiles, clothing, chemicals, steel, non-ferrous metals, fabricated metal products, transport equipment and other manufactures. The mining sector is not modelled as being monopolistically competitive, but rather as a sector subject to external scale economies. Given the pervasiveness of state ownership, cartel pricing and state trade in this sector, the assumptions of free entry and exit and average cost pricing that underlie monopolistic competition seemed particularly inappropriate. The other sectors (grains, other agriculture, forestry, fishery, trade and transport services, and other services) are assumed to operate with constant return to scale technologies.

The model also includes a simple dynamic link, whereby the static or direct efficiency (income) gains from trade liberalisation induce additional savings and investment, which compound output and welfare effects over the medium run. The dynamic link is a general equilibrium version of the Baldwin (1989, 1992) multiplier, which was used in assessments of the medium-run impact of the EC1992 programme. Given the parameters in the model, the income–investment linkage adds about 60 per cent to the static welfare effects. (Details of the model are available as a technical appendix from the authors or the National Centre for Development Studies, Australian National University.)

Simulation results

The results are divided into trade effects and income effects, and based on the commitments outlined in the previous sections. The actual equilibrium in the benchmark year (1990) is used with a counterfactual 1990 equilibrium. Some of the income results are translated into 2005 estimates using OECD and World Bank regional growth projections. This is done to facilitate comparisons to other studies, such as the World Bank–OECD (Goldin *et al.*, 1993) and OECD (1993).[16] (The 2005-based tables are available as a technical appendix from the authors or the National Centre for Development Studies, Australian National University.)

In the simulations, the agreement on agriculture is taken at face value. Some would argue that this is too optimistic: for example, it is still unclear how closely the outcome of the tariffication process has matched existing protection. The calculus is complicated by the fact that many countries covert NTBs into specific rather than *ad valorem* tariffs. It is also complicated by evidence of 'dirty tariffication', meaning the introduction of tariffs yielding higher protection than the NTB that is being replaced (International Agricultural Trade Research Consortium, 1994). In addition, it is debatable whether the domestic support provision identifies any real cuts. The calculation of the base Aggregate Measure of Support (AMS), to which the cuts apply, is based on outlays during the period 1986–8, which was characterised by relatively low world market prices for agricultural goods and therefore high outlays of domestic support programmes to farmers. Because of a combination of higher world market prices and domestic reforms, the new commitments may not, initially, entail any further real cuts in domestic support. However, we believe that the agreement will lead to some liberalisation over time as inflation erodes the real value of nominal (dollar) commitments. For the interested reader, a minimal liberalisation scenario with zero cuts in tariffs and domestic support is simulated in Francois *et al.* (1995). The specification of either a 'fair value' or a minimal scenario has important implications for the distribution of gains between industrial and developing regions. Less liberalisation in agriculture shifts overall estimated gains towards developing regions.

Trade effects

Once the Uruguay Round has been implemented, shifts will occur in the global pattern of production and trade. While new trading opportunities will arise for exporting firms, competitive pressures will be increased on

Table 6.7. *World export volume, percentage change*

	Dynamic specification		
	CRTS PC	IRTS PC	IRTS MC
Grains	4.1	4.4	4.6
Other agricultural products	21.1	21.0	22.1
Fishery products	13.0	12.9	13.5
Forestry products	3.7	4.1	5.6
Mining	1.6	1.8	3.1
Textiles	17.5	18.6	72.5
Clothing	69.4	87.1	191.6
Primary steel	8.3	8.4	25.5
Primary non-ferrous metals	3.6	3.9	14.2
Fabricated metal products	5.3	5.4	16.0
Chemicals and rubber	5.2	5.4	21.4
Transport equipment	11.7	13.6	30.1
Other manufactures	4.7	4.7	12.7
Total merchandise	8.6	9.6	23.5

Note:
CRTS=Constant returns to scale.
PC=Perfect competition.
IRTS=Increasing returns to scale.
MC=Monopolistic (imperfect) competition.

import-competing firms in protected home markets. The associated efficiency gains and pro-competitive effects will impact on incomes and demand, magnifying initial trade effects. The estimated aggregate effects on world trade are given in table 6.7. Estimated trade expansion (measured from the export side) is sensitive to the model specification, ranging from 8.6 per cent in the perfect competition (PC) constant returns to scale (CRTS) version to 23.5 per cent in the monopolistic competition (MC), increasing returns to scale (IRTS) model. Not surprisingly, the Armington specifications of the model, which feature a geographic anchor placed on the location of production, yield the smallest trade effects. External scale economies, by magnifying the efficiency gains associated with resource reallocation somewhat, provide some additional incentives for specialisation and trade. The monopolistic competition framework, which emphasises firm- rather than location-based product differentiation, is more akin to factor intensity models of trade in terms of the determinants of the location of production. Even this specification, however, entails some geographic preference through the CES share parameters.

The small differences in trade expansion between the two PC versions of the model (a 9.6 per cent increase in merchandise exports compared to 8.6 per cent) are largely due to their shared national product differentiation assumption. Under this assumption, intra-industry trade (IIT) results from the assumption that products are differentiated by country of origin. German automobiles are therefore treated as different from US automobiles, and as a result Germany and the United States will trade with each other.

If the assumption of regional product differentiation is dropped, a much more dramatic realignment of production and trade patterns occurs. The increase in merchandise trade jumps from around 10 per cent to over 20 per cent when this assumption is relaxed. There are at least two reasons for the jump in trade. First, the national or regional anchor provided by the national product differentiation assumption is relaxed. Secondly, variety *per se* is valued in this specification of the model, implying that any increased production also increases the incentives for trade, even between similar countries. Consumers like to wear different types of clothing, for instance, while producers become more productive following improved access to more highly specialised machinery and related inputs. These gains are realised through increased IIT. Indeed, as shown in table 6.7, it is the imperfectly competitive sectors of the model – chemicals, steel, non-ferrous metals, metal products, transport equipment, textiles, clothing and other manufactures – where the jump in trade between the two different demand specifications is concentrated.

The estimated changes in real exports of various sectors and regions (as simulated in the two polar versions of the model: (CRTS, PC) and (IRTS, MC)), are shown in tables 6.8a and 6.8b. The results indicate a realignment of production and trade pattern in accordance with (current) comparative advantages. Developing countries are estimated to expand production and export of labour-intensive clothing, textiles (which are relatively more capital-intensive than clothing) and other (presumably light) manufactures, while industrial countries are estimated to expand production of capital- and technology-intensive industrial products, including transport equipment. Moreover, countries that are well endowed with arable land – United States, Canada, Australia, New Zealand and many developing countries – are estimated to increase their exports of agricultural products, due to the reduced presence of export-subsidised competition, and improved access to foreign markets.

On a regional basis, the merchandise trade of all regions is expected to expand, led by the trade of developing and transition economies. On a sectoral basis, under both model specifications the greatest increases in trade flows are in textiles and clothing from China, Taiwan, and the ROW aggregate of developing and transition economies. EU exports of grain fall

Table 6.8. *Real export effects at world prices (f.o.b.), billion 1990 dollars*

1990 (a) counterfactual, model: CRTS, PC, dynamic

	Canada	US	EFTA	EU	A and NZ	Japan	China	Taiwan	Dev/trans	Total (%)
Grains	0.3	1.0	-0.1	-0.7	0.3	0.0	0.1	0.0	0.2	1 (4)
Other agricultural products	0.6	3.6	0.0	1.1	0.6	0.2	0.7	0.1	12.3	19 (21)
Fishery products	0.1	0.3	0.8	0.4	0.1	0.1	0.0	0.1	1.1	3 (13)
Forestry products	0.0	0.1	0.0	0.0	0.0	0.0	0.0	0.0	0.2	0 (4)
Mining	0.2	0.4	0.8	0.6	0.2	0.0	-0.6	0.0	3.3	5 (2)
Textiles	0.1	1.1	0.2	3.5	0.3	1.0	1.3	1.1	7.7	16 (18)
Clothing	0.0	0.2	-0.5	-0.1	0.0	-0.1	5.2	2.1	51.8	59 (69)
Primary steel	0.3	0.5	0.2	1.6	0.1	0.9	0.0	0.0	2.2	6 (8)
Primary non-ferrous metals	0.2	0.3	0.1	0.4	0.2	0.0	0.0	0.0	0.9	2 (4)
Fabricated metal products	0.2	0.5	0.3	0.9	0.0	0.1	-0.2	0.0	1.5	3 (5)
Chemicals and rubber	0.5	3.0	0.9	5.0	0.1	0.8	-0.2	0.1	2.8	13 (5)
Transport equipment	1.8	6.0	1.3	10.6	0.1	10.2	0.3	-0.1	2.3	33 (12)
Other manufactures	2.3	11.3	3.8	14.0	1.6	8.0	-1.5	-0.2	12.9	52 (5)
Total merchandise	6	28	8	37	4	21	5	3	99	213
(%)	(5)	(7)	(3)	(7)	(8)	(7)	(6)	(4)	(14)	(9)

1990 (b) counterfactual, model: IRTS, MC, dynamic

	Canada	US	EFTA	EU	A and NZ	Japan	China	Taiwan	Dev/trans	Total (%)
Grains	0.3	1.1	-0.1	-0.7	0.4	0.0	0.0	0.0	0.2	1 (5)
Other agricultural products	0.5	4.0	0.0	1.3	0.7	0.3	0.3	0.1	12.9	20 (22)
Fishery products	0.1	0.3	0.8	0.5	0.1	0.1	-0.1	0.1	1.3	3 (14)
Forestry products	0.0	0.2	0.0	0.0	0.0	0.0	0.0	0.0	0.3	1 (6)
Mining	0.4	0.7	0.9	0.5	0.3	0.0	-0.8	0.0	7.5	10 (3)
Textiles	-0.4	-2.2	-0.2	5.1	0.2	-0.4	9.9	10.6	44.5	67 (73)
Clothing	-0.2	-2.1	-2.5	-10.6	0.0	-0.4	21.5	5.8	150.1	162 (192)
Primary steel	1.4	1.6	-0.2	6.6	0.4	3.0	-0.2	-0.1	5.8	18 (26)
Primary non-ferrous metals	1.5	1.1	-0.2	0.5	1.4	-0.2	-0.2	-0.2	4.1	8 (14)
Fabricated metal products	0.6	1.9	0.5	2.9	0.2	0.2	-1.2	-0.8	5.6	10 (16)
Chemicals and rubber	1.1	17.3	3.9	21.9	0.3	2.1	-1.2	0.8	6.8	53 (21)
Transport equipment	8.4	18.7	2.7	23.5	0.0	33.3	1.8	-0.6	-3.9	84 (30)
Other manufactures	6.4	39.3	9.8	48.0	6.8	14.5	-7.8	-5.2	30.8	143 (23)
Total merchandise	20	82	15	99	11	52	22	10	266	579
(%)	(17)	(22)	(6)	(19)	(24)	(18)	(27)	(14)	(37)	(23)

Note:
Dev/trans = Developing and transitional.

under all model specifications, while grain exports from Canada, Australia and New Zealand, the United States, and the aggregate of developing and transitional economies, increase under all scenarios. Of these countries, the impact on grain exports in relative terms is greatest for Australia and New Zealand. In viewing these results, an important qualifier is called for. It is questionable whether sometimes dramatic changes in export volumes for particular sectors and particular markets, like clothing and textiles, can be accommodated by the industrial economies without triggering a defensive response of contingent protection actions or related interventions.

Income effects

The income effects, measured in terms of equivalent variation, of the Uruguay Round agreement are summarised in tables 6.9 and 6.10 (equivalent variation measures the income change at current prices that would be equivalent to the proposed Uruguay Round agreement in terms of its impact on welfare). Both the 1990 counterfactual simulations (table 6.9a, 6.10a), and corresponding 2005-based estimates (table 6.9b, 6.10b), are reported. Corresponding income effects as a percentage of GDP are also reported (table 6.10c). Tables 6.9 and 6.10 present a decomposition of effects, depending in part on model structure assumptions. As with the trade figures, the estimates of the welfare or income effects of the Uruguay Round agreement are sensitive to the model specification. Table 6.9 highlights the impact as a basic, static constant returns to scale model is modified to incorporate scale economies, imperfect competition, and dynamic investment–income linkages. In column (1) a simple, Armington-type model of trade with constant returns is used, similar to GTAP and RUNS-type analyses of the Round. Column (2) in these tables provides a partial transition to monopolistic competition, through the introduction of external (national) scale economies under perfect competition. Column (3) provides the full transition to a static monopolistic competition model. Finally, columns (4)–(6) provide the corresponding results in which investment–income dynamics have been incorporated.

With the static specification, the estimated annual income gain for the world in the 1990 counterfactual simulation ranges from US$65 to US$181 billion, while the steady-state dynamic specification shifts the range upwards some 60 per cent to between US$110 and US$291 billion. The corresponding estimated range for 2005, using the World Bank and OECD growth projections, is US$109–US$315 billion with the static specification, and US$184 to US$510 billion with the dynamic specification. Under the full model, with dynamic features and imperfect competition, these gains are well distributed, with all regions (except Japan) gaining at least 1 full

Table 6.9. *Income effects, 1990, counterfactual and 2005 estimated, billion 1990 dollars*

(a) 1990 counterfactual

	Static specifications			Dynamic specifications		
	CRTS PC (1)	IRTS PC (2)	IRTS MC (3)	CRTS PC (4)	IRTS PC (5)	IRTS MC (6)
Canada	1.4	1.9	4.9	2.3	3.1	7.6
United States	18.7	22.0	46.5	30.2	36.5	75.2
EFTA	6.2	8.2	14.2	10.8	11.0	20.6
EU	29.3	36.0	63.5	48.2	53.6	100.5
Australia and New Zealand	0.9	1.2	1.9	1.5	2.2	3.6
Japan	7.3	9.3	10.5	13.0	11.8	16.4
China	1.2	2.6	3.0	2.0	4.2	5.5
Chinese Taipei	1.1	2.1	2.0	2.2	3.7	4.5
Developing and transitional	−0.9	2.1	34.8	−0.4	1.3	57.5
Total	65	85	181	110	128	291

(b) 2005 estimated

	Static specifications			Dynamic specifications		
	CRTS PC (1)	IRTS PC (2)	IRTS MC (3)	CRTS PC (4)	IRTS PC (5)	IRTS MC (6)
Canada	2.3	3.0	8.0	3.8	5.0	12.4
United States	30.4	35.9	75.6	49.2	59.5	122.4
EFTA	10.1	13.4	23.1	17.5	18.0	33.5
EU	47.7	58.6	103.3	78.5	87.2	163.5
Australia and New Zealand	1.5	1.9	3.1	2.4	3.6	5.8
Japan	11.9	15.2	17.0	21.2	19.3	26.7
China	4.1	8.9	10.1	6.9	14.3	18.7
Chinese Taipei	2.6	4.7	4.5	5.1	8.4	10.2
Developing and transitional	−1.9	4.1	70.2	−0.7	2.7	116.1
Total	109	146	315	184	218	510

Note:
Estimates for 2005 are based on World Bank and OECD real growth projections, applied to the 1990 counterfactual effects.

Table 6.10. *Decomposition of welfare effects, 1990 counterfactual and 2005 estimates, billion 1990 dollars, and percentage of GDP*

(a) 1990 counterfactual

	CRTS, PC, Dynamic				IRTS, MC, Dynamic			
	Ind. tariffs	Ind. NTBs	Agri-culture	Total	Ind. tariffs	Ind. NTBs	Agri-culture	Total
Canada	−0.3	1.7	1.0	2.3	0.4	6.3	0.9	7.6
United States	4.3	23.6	2.3	30.2	8.4	62.9	3.9	75.2
EFTA	3.4	2.6	4.8	10.8	6.0	10.9	3.7	20.6
EU	10.4	26.4	11.5	48.2	20.8	70.7	9.0	100.5
Australia and New Zealand	0.3	0.2	1.1	1.5	1.9	0.4	1.3	3.6
Japan	6.2	−0.3	7.1	13.0	11.1	1.3	4.0	16.4
China	2.8	−1.0	0.2	2.0	3.4	1.6	0.5	5.5
Chinese Taipei	2.5	−0.6	0.2	2.2	3.4	0.9	0.2	4.5
Developing and transitional	0.1	−6.0	5.5	−0.4	16.5	33.9	7.1	57.5
Total	30	47	34	110	72	189	31	291
(% of total gain)	(27)	(42)	(31)		(25)	(65)	(10)	

(b) 2005 estimates

	CRTS, PC, Dynamic				IRTS, MC, Dynamic			
	Ind. tariffs	Ind. NTBs	Agri-culture	Total	Ind. tariffs	Ind. NTBs	Agri-culture	Total
Canada	−0.5	2.7	1.6	3.8	0.7	10.2	1.5	12.4
United States	7.0	38.4	3.8	49.2	13.7	102.3	6.3	122.4
EFTA	5.5	4.2	7.7	17.5	9.8	17.7	6.0	33.5
EU	16.8	42.9	18.7	78.5	33.8	115.1	14.6	163.5
Australia and New Zealand	0.4	0.3	1.7	2.4	3.1	0.6	2.1	5.8
Japan	10.1	−0.4	11.5	21.2	18.1	2.1	6.5	26.7
China	9.5	−3.5	0.8	6.9	11.6	5.4	1.7	18.7
Chinese Taipei	5.9	−1.3	0.5	5.1	7.7	2.1	0.4	10.2
Developing and transitional	0.3	−12.2	11.2	−0.7	33.4	68.4	14.3	116.1
Total	55	71	58	184	132	324	53	510
(% of total gain)	(30)	(39)	(31)		(26)	(64)	(10)	

Table 6.10. *contd.*

(c) Percentage of GDP	CRTS, PC, Dynamic				IRTS, MC, Dynamic			
	Ind. tariffs	Ind. NTBs	Agri- culture	Total	Ind. tariffs	Ind. NTBs	Agri- culture	Total
Canada	−0.05	0.29	0.17	0.40	0.08	1.09	0.16	1.32
United States	0.08	0.42	0.04	0.54	0.15	1.13	0.07	1.35
EFTA	0.39	0.30	0.55	1.24	0.70	1.25	0.42	2.37
EU	0.18	0.46	0.20	0.83	0.36	1.22	0.16	1.73
Australia and New Zealand	0.08	0.05	0.31	0.44	0.57	0.11	0.38	1.07
Japan	0.21	−0.01	0.24	0.45	0.38	0.05	0.14	0.57
China	1.04	−0.38	0.09	0.75	1.26	0.58	0.19	2.03
Chinese Taipei	1.71	−0.37	0.16	1.49	2.26	0.61	0.12	2.99
Developing and transitional	0.00	−0.14	0.12	−0.01	0.37	0.76	0.16	1.29
Total	0.14	0.22	0.16	0.52	0.34	0.88	0.14	1.36
(% of total gain)	(27)	(42)	(31)		(25)	(65)	(10)	

per cent of GDP, as detailed in table 6.10c. In absolute terms, estimated gains are concentrated in the EU, the United States, and the group of developing and transitional economies.

The estimates for the prefect competition versions of the model are roughly in parity with previous estimates of the World Bank and OECD. This is as it should be, because of similarity in model specifications. The big difference, in contrast to previous studies, is the introduction of monopolistic competition. This addition captures the importance of intra-industry (two-way) trade in similar products. Compared to Armington-based specifications, trade liberalisation leads here not just to deeper exploitation of comparative advantages and scale economies, but it also enhances the variety of final and intermediate goods to the benefit of consumers and producers. This is why the trade and welfare effects loom so much larger in the monopolistic competition case, not least for developing countries that are net importers of industrial products produced under increasing returns to scale.

A rough decomposition of the welfare effects of the different parts of the Uruguay Round agreement is given in table 6.10a–6.10c. One element of the Uruguay Round after the other is introduced, starting with the tariff cuts on industrial goods, followed by the elimination of industrial quotas, and finally introducing the Agreement on Agriculture. Tables 6.10a–6.10c show the marginal contribution of each agreement for the two polar versions of the model: CRTS/PC and IRTS/MC.

According to these simulations, the most important overall source of gains from the Uruguay Round follows from the elimination of quotas on industrial products: the MFA quotas and the elimination of quotas on Japanese cars in the EU market. (There are a number of other industrial quotas that we have not been able to account for which would reinforce this conclusion.) The second most important aspect depends on the model: with a world characterised by constant returns to scale technologies in all industries, it is the Agreement on Agriculture. The agricultural reform provides up to 31 per cent of the income gains in this case. Industrial tariff cuts become relatively more important when scale and specialisation economies are at stake. In this case, the net complementarities implied by two-way trade, involving both pro-competitive effects and increased specialisation and variety, also yield cross-border spillovers of the benefits of liberalisation. These spillover effects, which prove particularly important for the group of developing and transitional economies, are missed in constant returns models.

One explanation for the low 'ranking' of the agricultural reforms is that agriculture makes up only a fraction of the OECD economies. Another explanation is that the model fails to capture the full gains from agricultural reform. When the model is 'calibrated' to fit the benchmark data set, prices and quantities are used to deduce what the underlying parameters in the model must be to generate the observed market outcome. In an Armington model, if a particular type of agricultural good is not imported initially, there will be no subsequent demand, even if the domestic price is lowered as a consequence of trade liberalisations. Starting from a 'corner solution' with effectively prohibitive trade barriers, the Armington specification may under-state the gains from the agricultural reforms because of under-stated preferences for imported agricultural products.

A major difference between the two polar versions of the model is the impact on the developing and transitional economies and on China and Chinese Taipei of the elimination of MFA quotas on clothing and textiles. While the constant returns to scale/perfect competition (CRTS/PC) model predicts a sizeable loss, the increasing returns to scale/imperfect competition (IRTS/MC) version predicts a substantial gain. How can this be the case?

Recall that the MFA quotas are administered through export licences that allow the 'quota rents' (scarcity premiums) to be captured by exporting countries. These quota rents will dissipate with the quotas, and the question is whether improved market access will compensate for lower prices. This is where the models disagree. According to the CRTS/PC model, with its inherent regional bias in consumer preference (the Armington assumption) and therefore low demand responsiveness to lower import prices, the answer is 'no'. According to the IRTS/MC model, which treats all varieties of a product as equally good (bad) substitutes, the answer is 'yes'. The IRTS/MC model predicts an export increase that is about three times larger than that of the CRTS/PC model, and this is sufficient to turn a potential loss into a sizeable gain (tables 6.8a and 6.8b).

Finally, countries gain not just from liberalisation in export markets but, and perhaps foremost, from their own liberalisations. For example, EU producers are not restricted by MFA quotas in their export markets, so they do not have a direct stake in the elimination of MFA quotas elsewhere. If anything, they will lose from other industrial countries' liberalisations in this sector, because of sharper competition in export markets from developing and transitional countries that were previously restricted by MFA quotas. Still, the simulations indicate a substantial gain to the EU as a whole from the elimination of industrial quotas. The positive force in this gain is the large benefit that EU consumers receive from the elimination of the EU import quotas. Consumers will gain from the lower prices and expanded variety of textiles and clothing that will follow the phase-out of the MFA, and car buyers will gain substantially from the price reductions and increased variety that should follow, as European quotas on Japanese cars are dismantled.

Conclusion

An attempt has been made to assess the possible trade and income effects of three key changes in market access arising from the Uruguay Round: reduced tariffs, the elimination of industrial quotas and agricultural reforms. As something of a reader's guide to empirical studies of the Round, the estimated effects of the Round have been decomposed along these lines, highlighting the impact of various assumptions about market structure and economic dynamics.

It is shown that assumptions about market structure and economic dynamics influence the results in systematic ways and in a manner consistent with the growing theoretical literature on market structure, dynamics and trade. Under constant returns, the estimated increase in world merchandise trade is about 10 per cent. The corresponding amount under monopolistic competition is over 20 per cent. With less agricultural liberalisation, trade effects would be correspondingly smaller (Francois *et al.*, 1995). Estimates based on perfect competition and constant returns to scale indicate global income gains in 2005 (when the Uruguay Round is supposed to be fully implemented) in the range of US$300 billion (in 1990 dollars). The estimated annual global income gains when monopolistic competition is considered in the model are US$510 billion. These differences indicate that assuming perfect competition may omit important aspects of the Uruguay Round.

These results are rough estimates of the three aspects of the Uruguay Round covered. While the text of the Final Agreement is no longer a moving target, the mechanics of implementation will continue to evolve through 2005, meaning that even for improved market access areas it is difficult to quantify the impact of the Round. Other key aspects of the Round remain unquantified, such as the partial liberalisation of services trade and strengthened multilateral trade rules. In addition, assessment of the potential impact of the Round on long-term economic growth has not been attempted, which is emphasised in the recent literature on international trade.

NOTES

The views expressed herein are strictly those of the authors, and should not be attributed to any institution with which they have been affiliated. Nothing contained in this document should be construed as being, in any way, representative of the views or opinions of the GATT's Secretariat or its Contracting Parties. The findings, interpretations, designations employed, the presentation of the material, or any maps, photographs, tables, charts, or diagrams used in this chapter are solely for the convenience of the reader and do not imply the expression of any opinion whatsoever concerning the legal status of any country, territory, city, area, or of its authorities, or concerning the delimitation of its boundaries, or national affiliations. Contents should only be used as directed. We are not responsible for any misuse. Any findings reported herein, empirical or otherwise, should not be attributed to institutions with which the authors are affiliated and should not be viewed as dispositive or otherwise indicative of possible findings or conclusions that might be made by such or similar institutions in an official capacity.

1. Note that no account is taken of the long-run linkages between trade and economic growth, which find plenty of support in the empirical literature. See Francois and Shiells (1993), and Francois, McDonald and Nordström (1993b) for a brief survey on the theoretical and empirical links between trade and economic growth.
2. Note that this estimate is not directly comparable with previous estimates in the range $213–$274 billion by the OECD/World Bank (Goldin *et. al.*, 1993; OECD, 1993). These studies involved moving the resource base forward to the end of the implementation period of the Uruguay Round using available growth projections for productivity, population and foreign capital flows. A given percentage welfare gain is then translated into a larger *nominal* amount because the economic base to which it is multiplied is larger in ten years than today. Here, we adopt the more straightforward procedure of comparing the actual equilibrium in the benchmark year (1990) with a counterfactual,

steady-state equilibrium. However, to facilitate comparisons, we also 'translate' some of our results into 2005 estimates, using OECD and World Bank regional growth projections.

3. Services have become the fastest-growing component in international trade; tables 6.7–6.8 show that services account for a large share of production and GDP, particularly in OECD countries.

4. The Uruguay Round of multilateral trade negotiations was formally launched in a ministerial meeting taking place in September 1986 in Punta del Este, Uruguay (GATT, 'Ministerial Declaration on the Uruguay Round'.)

5. The 'formula participants' of the Tokyo Round refer to a group consisting mostly of industrial countries that agreed to cut their tariffs according to a simple non-linear formula with the property that high tariff rates (tariff peaks) were cut by a greater percentage than low tariffs. The other participants used the traditional 'request–offer' procedure, detailing the duty reductions requested from another country and the concessions it was willing to offer in return.

6. Under the General Agreement, tariff rates are constrained only to the extent a country has made a specific 'tariff binding,' a commitment not to exceed the (ceiling) rate at which the tariff was bound. The applied rate may of course be lower, which is also commonplace.

7. While the progress on tariff bindings is extremely valuable, no attempts have been made in the simulations to account for the market-access-security aspects of the UR. Tariff bindings are particularly important for countries with a history of frequent policy reversals, and therefore in need of some institutional mechanism to make their trade regime more credible. Tariff bindings reduce the risk inherent in investing in distribution channels supporting trade or foreign direct investment (FDI) projects that are dependent on imported intermediate goods. They therefore have an important impact on trade, investment and welfare.

8. Table 6.2 reports the average Mfn tariff cuts for the sectors and regions defined in the model (except for China and Chinese Taipei, which did not formally participate in the Uruguay Round). The base (old) rate for each sector and region is calculated by averaging over the tariff-lines in the sector, and over the countries in the region, using trade shares as weights. The applied Mfn tariff rates are used as reported in GATT's Integrated Data Base (IDB). The base years are centred around 1988, ranging from 1986 to 1992, depending on data availability. The new rate is calculated by the same type of averaging using the offered rates for each tariff-line as input, except in cases where a country has offered to bind the tariff above the applied base rate. For tariff-lines where this is the case, we assume that no actual tariff cuts are being made.

9. The key part of the negotiation mandate given by trade ministers in the Punta del Este Declaration stated that

> Negotiations in the area of textiles and clothing shall aim to formulate modalities that would permit the eventual integration of this sector into GATT on the basis of strengthened GATT rules and disciplines, thereby also contributing to the objective of further liberalization of trade.

10. Sweden liberalised its textile and clothing regime in 1991 and withdrew from the MFA. (The MFA quotas may, however, be reintroduced temporarily with accession to the EU.) Two other developed country participants, Japan and Switzerland, have not imposed any MFA quotas. However, they have 'signalled' their readiness to do so by the mere act of being signatories to the MFA agreement, combined with (active) import surveillance. Indeed, as shown in Winters (1994), import surveillance can, at least in concentrated industries, induce a fall in import levels as producers are trying to forestall explicit quotas.

11. The Agreement contains a special transitional safeguard mechanism applicable in cases of import surges causing or threatening severe damage in products not yet integrated into GATT. It also contains provisions concerning the circumvention of quotas, the settlement of trade disputes, and special provisions for the least developed countries (GATT, 1994b).

12. The waiver refers to Section 22 of the Agricultural Adjustment Act, enacted in 1933 during the Great Depression. It authorised the US Department of Agriculture to impose import quotas on a wide range of agricultural products. The waiver was granted to the United States in the mid-1950s at a time when the US President's authority to enter into reciprocal trade agreements was conditioned on such agreements being applied in a manner consistent with the requirements of Section 22.

13. Sarris and Freebairn (1983), for instance, estimate that the variability of the world market price for wheat would decline by 35 per cent under free trade.

14. SAMs are based on a fundamental, general equilibrium principle of economics, namely that every income (receipt) has a corresponding expenditure (outlay). As opposed to the real-world records of economic activity, all accounts must add up in the world model (as they must do in reality). This necessitates various data adjustments to avoid statistical illusions like the apparent trade deficit that the world runs with itself (or perhaps the moon). The basic principles of SAMs, with application to trade policy modelling, are excellently summarised in Reinert and Roland-Holst (1995).

15. Sources of MFA quota price wedges were described above. The price effects of European restraints on Japanese cars are based on Flam and Nordström (1994).

16. As noted before, our 2005-based estimates are quite rough. We have only made the 2005-based projections to facilitate comparison of our results to other studies of the Round. Other studies have often involved moving the resource base forward to the end of the implementation period of the Uruguay Round, using available growth projections for world GDP, population, investment, etc. A given percentage welfare gain is then translated into a larger amount because the economic base to which it is multiplied is larger in ten years than today (given positive growth).

7

A general equilibrium assessment of the Uruguay Round with trade-related externalities

YONGZHENG YANG

H23

Research shows a link between export expansion and income growth (Edwards, 1993). Countries that record rapid export expansion also experience strong income growth. Being a component of GDP, exports naturally influence the growth of national income. However, the contribution of exports to income growth has been shown to go beyond the accounting relationship. By generating externalities, exports contribute to structural adjustment and dynamic changes that foster income growth (Feder, 1983).

By expanding world trade, the Uruguay Round trade liberalisation will generate externalities, which will in turn lead to productivity improvement in the world economy. This linkage between trade liberalisation and externalities has been incorporated in a computable general equilibrium (CGE) model to evaluate the impact of the Uruguay Round reform. While the model is simple, it enables one of the important gains from trade liberalisation to be assessed. It also captures a key element of the outward-oriented strategy now followed by an increasing number of developing Asian countries.

Trade and growth: theories and evidence

The superior growth performance of East Asian economies has generated interest in the relationship between growth and trade regimes. The dichotomy between outward- and inward-oriented strategies has focused research on comparisons of two competing policy paradigms.

At the theoretical level, the outward-oriented strategy has a number of advantages over the inward-oriented alternative. In static terms, export expansion allows a country to exploit its comparative advantage (Krueger 1985). This enables countries to achieve high economic efficiency in resource allocation, and hence a higher income level than would otherwise occur.

Export expansion also allows the exploitation of economies of scale which through specialisation reduce costs in many manufacturing activities. In a protected domestic market, especially a small one, there are often too many firms engaging in similar production. This has occurred, for example, in the iron and steel sector in China (Cao, 1992), bicycle production in Pakistan and automobile assembly in Venezuela (World Bank, 1991).

An important stimulus to growth comes from competition. If exports expand under an outward-oriented strategy, access to imports is at world prices. Competition from imports reduces monopoly in the domestic market in small countries, where the viable number of producers of a particular commodity tends to be small. While monopoly profits may be necessary for domestic firms to develop and to adopt new technologies, firms with monopolistic power tend to have little incentive to change. In contrast, competition forces domestic firms to improve their efficiency. The World Bank (1991) concludes that historical evidence shows that openness generally promotes technological progress.

An outward-oriented strategy exposes domestic firms to competition from the international market. To export successfully, firms have to innovate which means upgrading their technology and improving product quality. International competition provides them with opportunities to obtain the necessary technologies to survive competition. Firms engaged in export activities in product design, quality control, new products and processes and marketing (World Bank, 1987; Rhee *et al.*, 1984).

Export-oriented strategies are free from the foreign exchange shortages often associated with import-substitution strategies. The availability of foreign exchange enables domestic firms to buy necessary machinery, equipment and intermediate inputs at international quality and prices (Esfahani, 1991). Imports of these products often embody superior technologies that are not available in the domestic market at similar prices or quality. Some studies show that the use of specialised inputs permits faster growth (Backus, *et al.*, 1992; Kehoe, 1992).

One of the major advantages of the outward-oriented strategy is that it imposes constraints on government economic management (Krueger, 1980). Under the outward-oriented strategy, any mismanagement of the economy quickly affects the economy's export and growth performance, and the current account balance, for example, the unsuccessful promotion of heavy and chemical industry development in Korea in the late 1970s and the 'high-wage' policy adopted in Singapore in the mid-1980s. Such policies were abandoned quickly because the costs were highly visible in the open regimes of these two countries.

Thus, it is the set of policies imposed by outward-oriented strategies that leads to high growth, as well as efficient resource allocation. Exchange rates have to be realistic, fiscal and monetary policies have to be prudent, and effective protection has to be moderate to maintain the country's competitiveness in international markets. Once a favourable policy framework is in place, efficiency and rapid growth will follow; for example, foreign investment is more likely to be attracted to develop exports in line with comparative advantage. Even if foreign investment is aimed at the domestic market, production must be internationally competitive for it to be profitable. In contrast, under an inward-oriented strategy, foreign investment is more likely to be attracted to 'rents' provided by import restrictions, leading to net welfare losses to the host country (World Bank, 1991).

The evidence of superior economic performance from outward-oriented strategies are confined to the neo-classical framework. But it does not explain why a higher growth rate is sustained. Other reasons must be found to explain why technological progress in countries following the outward-oriented strategy is more rapid than with inward-oriented strategies. Empirical results show that differences in growth performance are determined by differing rates of technological change, although accumulation of both physical and human capital are also crucial (Belassa and Associates, 1982; Nishimizu and Robinson, 1984; World Bank, 1993). Competition is one explanation.

Recent developments in endogenous growth theories offer some new contributions on trade–growth links. In essence, these theories argue that output growth of a particular firm depends not only on the growth of capital and labour, but also on the accumulation of knowledge (Romer, 1987). Unlike the neo-classical growth models (Solow, 1957), production using knowledge as an input exhibits increasing returns to scale. The accumulation of knowledge itself depends on capital investment, learning-by-doing, deliberate activities of innovations, and research and development (Romer, 1990; Lucas, 1988, 1993, Grossman and Helpman, 1991). Thus, knowledge is endogenous and obtained in response to economic incentives. If such knowledge can be accessed exclusively by the firm or can be partly kept by the firm, this will give the firm a competitive edge. Such advantage allows the firm to specialise in production and to achieve economies of scale. Consumers' desire for variety, however, limits the power of any particular firm, leading to monopolistic competition.

Knowledge has the characteristic of a public good and generates externalities for the economy. Thus, even if a firm does not produce knowledge itself, it can benefit from the knowledge produced by other firms. Since production exhibits increasing returns to scale from using new technology, it follows that, other things being equal, the rate of economic growth depends on the rate of knowledge accumulation. The rate of investment in technology then becomes important.

International transactions are important for the acquisition of knowledge. Four channels (including trade) are identified through which knowledge externalities can be transmitted (Grossman and Helpman, 1991). Endogenous growth models show that trade will promote growth in developing economies through knowledge dissemination, except in the situation where knowledge flow is asymmetrical in favour of industrial economies. Thus, the insights into the export–growth linkages from the endogenous growth theories are essentially consistent with the argument for economic openness by neo-classical economists.

There is strong empirical evidence supporting the hypothesis that outward strategies tend to be associated with or lead to superior economic performance (Krueger, 1978; Michaely, 1977; Belassa and Associates, 1982; Feder, 1982; Dollar, 1990; World Bank, 1987, 1991; Edwards, 1993b). This conclusion holds whether the linkage is examined in the framework of neo-classical economics or endogenous growth theories.

One of the problems with empirical work is how to quantify different policy regimes, particularly outward-oriented versus inward-oriented strategies. The determination of a country's trade regime is often arbitrary. It is difficult to extract stylised facts characterising individual countries as outward- or inward-oriented. Clear boundaries for different policy regimes are not easy to define, given the complexities of national trade policies. Three approaches may be adopted to approximate policy orientations: subjective classifications according to certain criteria (World Bank, 1987; Krueger, 1978), export growth or growth of the share of exports in GDP (Feder, 1982; Belassa, 1985), the extent of trade distortions (e.g. real exchange rates) (Edwards, 1993a; Dollar, 1992).

None of these approaches is perfect, but the majority of studies based on cross-section data have shown that there is a positive relationship between export growth and output growth (Edwards, 1993b). Results based on time-series data are less clear. Time-series data have limited degrees of freedom, making it difficult to detect the effect of policy change, unless the change is large.

Whatever relationships are detected between exports and growth, there is an issue of causality between trade regimes and growth, or between exports and growth. For example, when a positive link between an outward-oriented strategy and growth is established, it does not automatically lead to a conclusion that the strategy causes growth. It could be the other way around, or causation could go both ways. The lack of a causality test is one of the major drawbacks in the earlier studies on the export–growth relationships (e.g. Michaely, 1977; Belassa, 1978, 1985; Tyler, 1981).

Causality tests have so far produced mixed results. While Chow (1987) found some evidence of two-way causality between exports and growth, Darrat (1986) and Hsiao (1987) rejected the causality relationships. Jung and Marshall (1985), Bahmani-Oskooee *et al.* (1991), and Dodora (1993) found inconclusive or weak evidence. Given that the positive relationship between export and growth is less frequently detected using time-series data, this is not surprising, as causality studies have to use time-series data. A more recent study by Bahmani-Oskooee and Alse (1993) seems to have identified some major defects in previous causality studies. Using the cointegration and error correction models to overcome the shortcomings in the previous studies, they show that there is a long-run positive relation between growth of real exports and output in developing economies.

Another issue in the literature is how different characteristics of individual countries affect the relationship between export and growth. Two questions are relevant. First, does the composition of a country's exports matter in the context of export–growth linkages? Manufactured exports which involve learning-by-doing tend to have a greater externality effect than primary exports (Eswaran and Kotwal, 1993; Sprout and Weaver, 1993). Second, does the stage of development influence the effectiveness of export-led growth? At early stages of development, countries may benefit more from exports because of the catching-up effect (Balassa, 1985; Edwards, 1992): it is difficult to generalise because it apparently contradicts the evidence that the exports of primary commodities generate fewer export externalities. Since low-income developing economies tend to concentrate on primary exports, these countries would be disadvantaged. Factors other than exports may also be responsible for 'catching-up'.

While there is strong evidence to support the proposition that export and output growth are reinforcing, derivation of benefits is not clear. Some of the empirical work cited above is based on rigorous theoretical framework (such as Feder, 1982), but other work is *ad hoc* in nature. Early studies tend to regress the growth of output against export growth or the growth of its share in GDP. Because primary factors are omitted from the models, it is unclear whether these models have actually captured the accounting relationship between exports and output or the efficiency gain associated with export expansion or externalities. More recent studies have explicitly incorporated primary factors in their models as well as the export variable. The results imply that are efficiency gains from exporting (Feder, 1982).

Incorporating export externalities in GTAP

In an endogenous growth framework, trade liberalisation has implications for growth as well as for resource allocation. It is difficult, however, to incorporate the endogenous theories in a comparative static model, not least because these theories are still evolving and are yet to be fully developed. In addition, empirical tests of these theories are limited. More needs to be done to examine the explanatory power of these models. An attempt will be made here to build export externalities into a comparative static model, using the results of empirical research on export–growth linkages (for details of how this was done, see Yang, 1995).

This represents an extension of the Global Trade Analysis Project (GTAP) model, as developed by Hertel and Tsigas (forthcoming). The key feature of the extended model is that technological change is endogenous, driven by export growth. There is no explicit specification of the mechanism through which export growth is translated into technological change, and the implicit assumption is that export-generated externalities have the effect of raising productivity.

There are both theoretical and practical issues in the incorporation of externalities in a neo-classical CGE model of perfect competition and constant returns to scale. How export externalities are to be built into a model depends on the externalities under consideration. Normally, if externalities are internal to firms, they are not compatible with standard perfect competition models, such as GTAP. Firms able to reap the benefits of externalities can become monopolies. In the framework of differentiated products, monopolistic competition is the likely outcome.

In a perfectly competitive model, positive pure profits arising from monopolistic competition are not allowed. To overcome this problem, it is assumed that export externalities are internal to the industry, instead of the firm. In this situation, the benefits of externalities can be regarded as technological change occurring in the industry. This treatment of export externalities therefore continues to allow a perfect competitive market in the model. In other words, only primary factors (labour, capital and land) receive explicit compensation, whereas export externalities determine the efficiency of their use, in the same manner as technology.

Export externalities are built into GTAP in line with the work by de Melo and Robinson (1990) and Gao (1993), although the issues addressed in their models are different. The strength of this extended GTAP model is that while its aggregate externalities are largely based on empirical evidence, at the sectoral level they take into account of the differing externality effects of various commodities. The presence of externalities in a multi-country model, in contrast with the single-country models of de Melo and Robinson and Gao, also provides opportunities for insights into the impact of externalities on the international competition.

In the context of trade liberalisation in the Uruguay Round, differences among various commodities in generating export externalities are important, because export composition varies among countries. Even a uniform tariff reduction is unlikely to lead to uniform *ad valorem* changes in exports. This gives variation in externalities among commodities an important role to play. In the extended version of the GTAP model, different elasticities governing the magnitude of externalities are calibrated from economy-wide estimates in the literature (Feder, 1982; Gao, 1993; Song and Chen, 1993; Sengupta, 1993; Belassa, 1985; Esfahani, 1991; Tyler, 1981).

The effect of externalities also varies with the openness of individual sectors. It is plausible that the more open a sector, as measured by a higher share of exports in output, the greater are the export externalities accruing to it. However, the effect of externalities does not occur linearly to the share, there are diminishing returns to openness. That is, at the margin each dollar of exports is likely to generate fewer export externalities for a more open sector than for a less open one, although the higher export share may mean that the overall impact of exports on the more open sector may still be larger than that on the less open sector. This is consistent with the empirical finding of diminishing effects of export growth on GDP growth (Kohli and Singh, 1989; Bacha, 1984; Ocampo, 1986).

The implicit assumption is that not all externalities generated by the exports of a particular sector are captured by that sector; some become economy-wide public goods. As a result, a less open sector which has a low starting level of 'knowledge' is able to benefit more from the pool of public goods. In other words, there is greater 'catching-up' for this sector, analogous to catching up for a less developed economy. Accordingly, curvature is built into the externality elasticities. Other things being equal, the higher the export share, the lower is the externality elasticity.

Implementing the Uruguay Round reform in the model

The modified GTAP model used to simulate the Uruguay Round agreements has ten countries (and country groups) and ten commodity groups. The ten countries are Australasia (Australia and New Zealand), United States, EU, Japan, the NIEs (Hong Kong, Republic of Korea and Taiwan), ASEAN (Indonesia, Malaysia, Philippines, Singapore and Thailand), China, South Asia, Latin America and the rest of the world.

The ten commodity categories in the model are intended to represent the commodities that are of major interest to the East Asian economies: agriculture, mining, processed food, textiles, clothing, iron and steel, machinery and equipment, transport equipment, other manufactures, and services (see the appendix for commodity details in each of the above

Table 7.1. *Production subsidies (negative entries are production taxes),* *percentage of domestic market prices*

	Austral-asia	North America	EU	Japan	NIEs	ASEAN	China	South Asia	Latin America	Rest of the world
Agriculture	1.4	8.9	21.1	13.8	14.4	0.3	−2.8	−2.0	1.6	4.7
Mining	−1.3	−6.5	−0.1	−2.7	−0.2	−1.3	−7.5	−8.0	−1.3	−3.9
Processed food	−1.3	−3.1	−0.5	−9.7	−11.8	−4.9	−10.0	−10.0	−2.3	−6.6
Textiles	−1.0	−0.9	−0.8	−2.0	−0.6	−1.5	−7.8	−7.8	−0.9	−2.2
Clothing	−1.1	−0.5	−0.8	−1.8	−0.9	−2.2	−7.4	−7.2	−2.7	−2.2
Iron and steel	−0.9	−2.9	−1.1	−3.6	−0.4	−1.3	−13.0	−13.0	−0.1	−3.1
Transport equipment	−0.8	−1.3	−0.9	−5.6	−3.2	−1.8	−9.1	−9.1	−0.7	−2.9
Machinery and equipment	−1.1	−1.1	−1.2	−2.6	−1.7	−0.8	−10.2	−10.2	−1.4	−2.5
Other manufactures	−0.8	−2.2	−1.1	−4.5	−1.5	−1.6	−10.7	−11.2	−1.5	−3.5
Services	−2.3	−5.6	−1.2	−3.2	−3.0	−2.0	−7.6	−7.8	−2.7	−3.3

Source: GTAP data base, version 2.

categories). It is also the intention of this commodity classification to iden-tify explicitly the commodities that are subject to significant non-tariff bar-riers (NTBs), such as the Multifibre Arrangement (MFA).

The effect of the Uruguay Round trade liberalisation depends on several factors, not least the estimated magnitude of the initial distortions. A summary of the magnitude of these distortions in the GTAP data base is presented in tables 7.1–7.4. All industrial economies (except Australasia) have production subsidies for agriculture; the EU has the highest support (table 7.1). North America and the EU also maintain supports for agricul-tural exports (table 7.3).

Tariffs or their equivalents on agricultural commodities are very high in the EU, Japan and the NIEs (table 7.2). They are also quite high in ASEAN and China. Among industrial goods, only processed food, textiles and clothing are subject to relatively high tariffs in industrial economies.

In GTAP, the MFA is modelled as export taxes imposed by exporting countries, as they normally take the form of voluntary export constraints (VERs). On average, restrictions on clothing are much higher than on tex-tiles (table 7.4). Across importing countries, restrictions on textiles are higher in the EU than in North America, while the opposite is true for restrictions on clothing. Among exporting countries, ASEAN, China and South Asia are the most severely restricted. They also tend to be low-cost efficient producers targeted by the MFA.

Table 7.2. *Nominal rates of border protection, percentage of c.i.f. border prices*

	Austral-asia	North America	EU	Japan	NIEs	ASEAN	China	South Asia	Latin America	Rest of the world
Agriculture	4.5	10.2	45.2	97.9	113.5	23.3	12.2	8.1	10.7	8.8
Mining	0.3	0.6	0.5	0.8	3.6	7.2	9.8	4.2	4.7	3.7
Processed food	8.4	11.8	25.0	36.3	14.7	13.6	37.9	11.4	16.0	11.6
Textiles	15.4	12.0	11.7	7.2	3.3	22.8	64.2	13.2	19.6	13.0
Clothing	21.0	21.0	13.2	14.0	1.2	8.6	94.7	13.9	19.4	12.1
Iron and steel	14.2	10.3	7.2	4.0	5.4	6.4	13.7	9.5	10.8	9.3
Transport equipment	20.9	4.8	8.1	3.0	9.1	18.6	37.5	12.7	15.9	12.2
Machinery and equipment	20.4	15.2	9.6	3.4	7.4	12.1	29.9	10.9	16.7	10.5
Other manufactures	16.6	7.4	7.6	4.7	5.1	12.2	27.0	9.0	14.5	11.0
Services	0.0	0.0	0.0	0.0	0.0	0.0	2.2	0.0	0.2	0.0

Source: GTAP data base, version 2.

Table 7.3. *Export subsidies (negative entries are export taxes), percentage of f.o.b. border prices*

	Austral-asia	North America	EU	Japan	NIEs	ASEAN	China	South Asia	Latin America	Rest of the world
Agriculture	−1.0	3.7	60.4	0.0	0.0	−3.3	0.0	0.0	0.1	−0.6
Mining	−1.3	0.0	−2.0	0.0	0.0	−3.0	−0.2	0.0	−0.7	−0.1
Processed food	0.5	1.5	14.5	0.0	0.0	−2.9	0.0	0.0	−1.8	−4.8
Textiles	−1.6	0.0	−0.2	0.0	−0.9	−4.0	−3.4	−8.6	−5.3	−3.9
Clothing	−0.9	0.0	−0.1	0.0	−11.0	−16.5	−8.6	−20.2	−14.3	−6.9
Iron and steel	0.0	0.0	0.0	0.0	0.0	−5.1	0.0	−0.2	−0.1	−0.7
Transport equipment	1.6	0.0	−3.1	−0.3	0.0	−0.4	0.0	-0.5	1.0	−1.1
Machinery and equipment	−0.1	0.0	−0.1	−2.0	−0.1	−0.8	0.0	0.0	0.0	0.0
Other manufactures	−1.1	0.0	−3.6	−0.4	−0.1	−1.5	−0.2	−0.3	−0.7	−1.3
Services	−0.4	0.0	0.5	0.0	0.0	−1.3	0.0	0.0	0.0	−0.1

Source: GTAP data base, version 2.

140   *Yongzheng Yang*

Table 7.4. *Export tax equivalents of MFA quotas, percentage of f.o.b. border prices*

	Textiles		Clothing	
	North America	EU	North America	EU
NIEs	8.1	9.3	15.9	14.0
ASEAN	10.7	13.8	26.7	27.6
China	15.9	21.5	28.8	26.5
South Asia	16.0	21.5	28.8	26.5
Latin America	8.7	12.4	16.8	15.0
ROW	4.4	5.8	8.0	8.0

Note:
The magnitudes presented in table 7.4 are smaller than those in the original GTAP data base. The modifications are made based on estimates by Saad (1993) and Yang (1992).
Source: Based on GTAP data base, version 2.

A second important factor determining the effect of trade liberalisation is the extent of such liberalisation. One of the problems with estimating the extent of trade liberalisation resulting from the Uruguay Round is that tariff undertakings by developing economies often take the form of tariff bindings; it is difficult to estimate the extent to which these tariff bindings constitute effective trade liberalisation. In addition, the absence of precise estimates of the increases in market access agreed under the Uruguay Round prevents any precise attempt to estimate effective tariff cuts at this stage. Following Brandão and Martin (1993), the implementation of the agreement is assumed to be as follows. Support for agricultural production is reduced by 20 per cent, while subsidies on agricultural exports are cut by 36 per cent. Note that tariff reductons on agriculture include both existing tariffs and tariffied non-tariff restrictions. Phasing out the MFA is represented by reducing export tax equivalents to zero. Tariff reductions are implemented as outlined in table 7.5. There are two exceptions in applying these reduction rates. For North America, the more recent GATT (1994d) estimates of tariff reductions of 15 and 10 per cent for textiles and clothing and transport equipment, respectively, are used instead of the developed country averages. For developing economies, it is assumed that their trade distortions are reduced by two-thirds of the developed country reductions, in line with their commitments to agricultural reforms in comparison with developed countries.

While the implementation of the Uruguay Round agreements will be carried out over a period of about ten years and its effects will probably go well beyond the transitory period, the model can capture only the

Table 7.5. *Tariff reductions in industrial economies agreed under the Uruguay Round, percentages*

	Rate of tariff reductions imported from:		
	All	Developing	Developed
Agricultural products	36.0	—	—
Mining products	34.4	35.0	33.7
Processed food	21.3	22.4	19.5
Textile and clothing	20.0	21.2	18.9
Iron and steels	62.2	66.7	60.6
Machinery and equipment	48.8	48.6	48.8
Transport equipment	21.6	18.4	21.8
Other manufactures	41.9	39.7	42.5

Source: Computed from GATT (1993a), Table 11.

comparative static effects. No time path of the trade liberalisation process is traced; such an exercise would require a dynamic model. The dynamic path of the liberalisation is important, not only because information on what occurs in the short run is useful for economic management, but also because even in a comparative static framework the sequence of reforms can influence the outcome. For example, if the phasing out of the MFA proceeds more slowly than tariff reductions, the cost of the MFA is likely to rise (Yang *et al.*, 1995).

An important determinant of the effect of the Uruguay Round agreement is the economic environment within which trade liberalisation is carried out – the model closure. The standard GTAP general equilibrium closure is used for neo-classical experiments. All prices and quantities are endogenous except the price for savings (the numeraire) and supplies of factors of production (land, labour and capital). Exogenous variables include all technical change and policy variables. The rate of return to investment is allowed to equalise across countries, so that savings demand can be met by investment in other countries, as well as by the country's own investment. The elasticity of the expected rate of return to investment with respect to end-of-period capital stocks is set at 10, making the supply of new capital goods quite insensitive to the expected rate of return. Export externality experiments use the same closure, except that output augmenting technology is now endogenous.

One limitation of these closures is its treatment of factor markets, especially with respect to capital and labour. As investment does not come on line in the next period of economic activity, potentially higher savings resulting from higher income following trade liberalisation in the previous period cannot be used to generate more income. Baldwin (1989, 1992) has shown that such effects can be important. This medium-term growth effect can be incorporated in a comparative static CGE framework.

In the present version of the GTAP model, labour supply is essentially demand-driven as there are no explicit labour supply equations. This essentially offers only two extreme scenarios of labour market closure. One is to assume that labour supply is fixed and wages are allowed to change. The other is to assume that wages, either nominal or real, are constant while labour supply is infinitely elastic. The former is adopted here, although it tends to lead to under-estimation of the effect of trade liberalisation, as labour supply does not respond to economic incentives.

With these considerations in mind, results in the following sections should be interpreted within the framework in which the Uruguay Round is implemented. The focus of this study is the medium- to long-term comparative static effects of the Uruguay Round Final Act. It is possible, and even likely, that in a period of ten years the comparative static effect dominate the overall impact of the trade reform. In the longer run, the dynamic effect is likely to be more important.

Liberalisation in the conventional neo-classical framework

In a neo-classical framework, welfare gains from trade liberalisation for the world as a whole derive solely from more efficient resource allocation. If the Uruguay Round Final Act is implemented as described, the global welfare gain is around US$69 billion (table 7.6). This estimate is substantially smaller than the results of some previous studies, which put the gain of the Uruguay Round in the order of US$90–270 billion (Nguyen *et al.* 1991; Goldin *et al.*, 1993; Brandão and Martin, 1993).

Several factors explain the difference. This estimate is based on the 1992 data base, whereas the earlier studies report a projected estimate for the year 2002, the year when the Uruguay Round reform was expected to be completed. Earlier studies used the Dunkel draft of the Uruguay Round Final Act (GATT, 1991), which proposed more trade liberalisation than was ultimately agreed at Marrakesh. In addition, some studies (Nguyen *et al.*, 1993) included estimates for trade liberalisation in the service sector and reductions in export taxes which were not included in the Uruguay Round outcome. Another factor relates to the Armington assumption (Armington, 1969a) applied in this model. Some of the earlier studies adopted the homogeneous product assumption for agriculture and the Armington assumption for manufacturing. Aggregation of sectors may

Table 7.6. *Welfare effects of Uruguay Round trade liberalisation (equivalent variation)*

	Agricultural reform		MFA reform		Tariff reductions		Total
	(US$ million)	% of total	(US$ million)	% of total	(US$ million)	% of total	(US$ million)
Australasia	955	108	112	13	−182	−21	885
North America	3 705	26	11 525	81	−956	−7	14 274
EU	10 884	49	8 827	40	2 556	11	22 267
Japan	10 122	43	−1 019	−4	14 360	61	23 463
NIEs	2 731	184	−2 981	−201	1 731	117	1 481
ASEAN	994	23	3 269	75	68	2	4 331
China	648	13	3 696	76	504	10	4 848
South Asia	46	3	1 624	105	−122	−8	1 549
Latin America	1 650	253	−1 064	−163	67	10	653
ROW	37	−1	−3 671	77	−1 128	24	−4 762
World	31 772	46	20 319	29	16 897	24	68 988

also affect the welfare estimates. These differences from earlier studies are also examined in the previous chapter.

One of the striking features of the Uruguay Round is to bring agriculture and the textile and clothing industries under GATT rules. Major gains from the Round are from these non-traditional reforms (table 7.6). Agricultural reform accounts for nearly half of the total gain in this model. The benefits from traditional tariff reductions (including those in textiles and clothing) are only 83 per cent of that from the phasing-out of the MFA alone.

Industrial economies are the major beneficiaries of the Uruguay Round liberalisation. Japan gains the most; Japan, like Australia, benefits mainly from agricultural reform and conventional tariff reductions for industrial goods. In fact, Japan loses from reform of trade in textiles and clothing because, as a net importer, its terms of trade deteriorate when world prices for textiles and clothing rise. Australasia gains from reform in textiles and clothing, because of increases in exports of raw materials to Asia, as that region expands textile and clothing exports.

As the second largest beneficiary of the Uruguay Round, the EU's gain is largely from agricultural reform (49 per cent). North America is the third largest beneficiary with over two-thirds of its welfare gain being derived from phasing-out the MFA. The gain from agriculture is surprisingly small for North America, as a percentage of its total gain, and is the smallest gain from agriculture among industrial economies.

Table 7.7. *Terms of trade effects of trade liberalisation, percentages*

	Agricultural reform	MFA reform	Tariff reductions	Uruguay Round
Australasia	1.0	0.1	−0.9	0.2
North America	0.4	0.8	−0.3	0.8
EU	−0.3	0.4	−0.1	−0.1
Japan	−0.3	−0.1	1.2	0.7
NIEs	−0.2	−0.9	0.2	−0.8
ASEAN	0.2	−0.5	−0.4	−0.7
China	0.4	−0.6	−1.0	−1.1
South Asia	0.4	−1.2	−0.3	−0.8
Latin America	0.6	−0.4	−0.5	−0.2
ROW	0.0	−0.4	−0.3	−0.6

Among developing economies, China turns out to be the largest beneficiary from the Uruguay Round. Its main gain derives from reform of textiles and clothing trade. This is also the case for ASEAN. South Asia gains
substantially from the phasing-out of the MFA, but only marginally from
agriculture. It loses considerably from traditional tariff reductions. Latin
America gains from agricultural reform and tariff reductions. The rest of
the world loses overall from the Uruguay Round, because of losses from
both the phase-out of the MFA and tariff reductions.

The NIEs, Latin America and the rest of the world lose from the phase-
out of the MFA because of increased competition from other clothing
exporters, such as ASEAN, China and South Asia. Exports of textiles and
clothing fall in all the three regions, leading to contraction of production.

In a comparative static model such as GTAP, there are two major potential sources of welfare changes from trade liberalisation for individual
economies. One is from more efficient resource allocation, and the other
from changes in terms of trade. While countries which liberalise tend to
improve the efficiency of their resource allocation, the terms of trade effect
may improve or deteriorate depending on the nature of liberalisation. The
terms of trade effect is particularly pronounced in models built under the
Armington product differentiation assumption. In certain circumstances,
such terms of trade effects can dominate the outcome of trade liberalisation.

With the current settings of elasticities in GTAP, agricultural reform is
likely to improve the terms of trade for countries other than the EU, Japan
and the NIEs, which have high initial protection and have to liberalise substantially according to the Uruguay Round (table 7.7). However, these
countries are able to benefit substantially from agricultural reform despite
the mild deterioration of their terms of trade (table 7.6).

Table 7.8. *Welfare effects of the Uruguay Round: sensitivity analysis,*
US$ million

	Central scenario	Halving elasticities	Doubling elasticities
Australasia	885	568	1 501
North America	14 274	9 524	22 317
EU	22 267	10 893	42 890
Japan	23 463	17 274	36 493
NIEs	1 481	−785	5 088
ASEAN	4 331	908	9 646
China	4 848	1 167	10 926
South Asia	1 549	815	2 826
Latin America	653	−8	2 309
ROW	−4 762	−6 103	−2 263
World	68 988	34 253	131 734

Phasing-out the MFA by 2005 will have major terms of trade effects. For North America and the EU, improved terms of trade are a major contributor to their overall gains, but at the expense of exporting countries, which suffer from adverse terms of trade effects. It is the combined adverse effect of terms of trade and increased competition resulting from the reform of trade in textiles and clothing that lead to welfare losses to the NIEs, Latin America, and the rest of the world.

Perhaps more striking are the terms of trade effects of tariff reductions. Several regions lose from tariff reductions (table 7.6). This tends to correlate with the deterioration of terms of trade as a result of tariff dismantling (table 7.7). The Armington assumption may have exaggerated the terms of trade effect of these regions' liberalisation. Under the Armington assumption, the terms of trade effect depends on the elasticities of substitution and market shares. The elasticities are determined by the nature of commodities, the market structure and the time period within which the economies are allowed to adjust. In the long run, the world economy would be expected to be much more responsive than in the short run. Trade liberalisation itself may increase the flexibility of the world economy and individual economies. In contrast, if an economy is unable to adjust sufficiently, it may not be able to benefit from trade liberalisation, or even loses due to changes in external conditions.

To capture the effect of possibly different adjustment capacities, two experiments on the Uruguay Round outcome are undertaken with different trade elasticities. To make the experiments manageable, all trade elasticities are doubled in the first experiment, but halved in the second experiment (table 7.8). The global welfare gain from the Uruguay Round

Table 7.9. *Welfare effects of the Uruguay Round reform with externalities*

	Welfare effect (US$ million)	Welfare increase due to externalities (%)[a]	Terms of trade (%)
Australasia	1 962	122	0.7
North America	26 881	88	1.2
EU	30 414	37	0.0
Japan	22 878	−2	0.4
NIEs	7 637	416	−0.7
ASEAN	14 595	237	−1.9
China	11 935	146	−2.1
South Asia	3 880	151	−2.4
Latin America	10 245	1 469	0.2
ROW	15 695	n.a.	−0.1
World	146 121	112	—

Notes:
[a]This is the increase over the numbers in the last column of table 7.6.
n.a.=Not available.

is almost linearly related to the changes in the trade elasticities. Halving the elasticities reduces the gain by 50 per cent, and doubling them increases the gain by a factor of 0.91. In addition, all regions except the rest of the world benefit from the Uruguay Round; even in the case of the rest of the world, the loss is reduced substantially. These two experiments highlight the importance of the flexibility of world markets in accommodating to changes resulting from the Uruguay Round.

Liberalisation with export externalities

With the externalities-driven endogenous technological change in the model, the impact of the Uruguay Round trade liberalisation becomes more profound. The global welfare gain from such export-driven technological change amounts to 112 per cent of the conventional comparative static gain (table 7.9). This gain represents only the effect of export externalities in the transitory period of trade reform and any benefits beyond the period are not captured. One striking feature of trade liberalisation with externalities is that all countries gain from the Uruguay Round. The reversal of the welfare position for the rest of the world is particularly significant, as it demonstrates that adverse terms of trade effects of trade liberalisation can be overcome by technological progress arising from it. This is even more significant when one takes into account that trade expansion, and hence the terms of trade effects, tend to become larger when technological change occurs during trade liberalisation.

Table 7.10. *Export share in gross output, percentages*

	Austral-asia	North America	EU	Japan	NIEs	ASEAN	China	South Asia	Latin America	Rest of the world
Agriculture	31	14	4	1	8	15	4	3	11	8
Mining	58	9	4	2	7	57	18	25	35	62
Processed food	24	6	5	0	4	18	7	3	8	5
Textiles	8	9	9	11	44	24	17	13	5	13
Clothing	6	6	15	1	64	59	72	42	14	26
Iron and steel	16	7	39	10	11	27	7	3	13	21
Transport equipment	10	26	17	40	40	29	50	6	18	20
Machinery and equipment	20	28	26	22	53	82	26	3	27	26
Other manufactures	13	10	8	6	25	42	24	6	10	18
Services	4	2	2	1	9	9	3	4	3	4
Average	10	6	5	5	20	26	13	5	8	12

Source: GTAP data base.

Industrial economies, except Japan, gain less than the average, ranging from 37 per cent for the EU to 122 per cent for Australasia. Australasia's above-average gain arises from its greater openness than the larger industrial economies in North America and Europe (table 7.10). Despite its export expansion, Japan is slightly worse off with endogenous technical change, because of a decline in its terms of trade. Overall, industrial economies gain 35 per cent when export externalities are incorporated.

Developing economies gain more from technological change than industrial economies. In fact, developing economies are nearly seven times better off than without allowance for technological change. In value terms, their total benefit from the Uruguay Round increases from US$8.1 billion in the neo-classical scenario to US$64 billion with endogenous technological change. This large gain results partly because the export externalities are greater for developing than for industrial economies. However, this has also to do with the greater openness and export composition of East Asian economies, as well as the nature of the Uruguay Round reforms. Most developing economies, especially Asian economies, export a larger portion of their output than industrial economies. This tends to generate greater externalities. In the case of textiles and clothing, when the MFA is phased-out, exports of these products expand substantially (table 7.12, p. 149). Coupled with the openness of these two sectors (see table 7.10), the MFA removal leads to large export expansion, which in turn leads to

Table 7.11. *Welfare effects of agricultural, MFA and tariff reduction reforms in the Uruguay Round, US$ million*

	Agricultural reform	MFA reform	Tariff reductions
Australasia	1 178	732	861
North America	4 947	17 303	4 520
EU	13 902	11 551	3 709
Japan	11 410	−2 689	12 092
NIEs	4 451	−1 080	7 426
ASEAN	1 920	15 770	4 623
China	1 475	14 948	4 584
South Asia	465	4 530	693
Latin America	3 361	583	11 391
ROW	1 927	1 848	14 941
World	45 037	63 496	64 841

technological progress. While export expansion also occurs in the neo-classical framework, the technological change generated by the export expansion leads to greater efficiency in textile and clothing production. This also makes more resources available to other sectors in these economies

Not all developing economies gain equally from endogenous technological change. The rest of the world gains the most, followed by Latin America. This results not only from export externalities but also from improvements in their terms of trade in comparison with the neo-classical scenario. Given that these two regions gain only slightly or even lose in the neo-classical scenario, the effects of externalities are particularly important for them.

Because of the considerable changes in terms of trade from the neo-classical scenario, it is difficult to evaluate the effect of economic openness on welfare gains from trade liberalisation. While the more open economies of the NIEs and ASEAN experience larger proportional welfare improvements than the less open economies of China and South Asia, such results may have been largely influenced by changes in terms of trade (table 7.9).

While the effect of economic openness on welfare gains is muted by changes in terms of trade, the varying externality effects of different commodities are unambiguous. In the neo-classical scenario, agricultural reform is the most important outcome of the Uruguay reform in terms of global welfare. When externalities are included, however, agricultural reform is the least significant, while phasing-out the MFA and tariff reductions become more important (table 7.11). Tariff reductions, the least important reform in the neo-classical scenario, become the most important,

Table 7.12. *Uruguay Round reform: changes in net exports as percentages of total exports, percentages*

	Austral-asia	North America	EU	Japan	NIEs	ASEAN	China	South Asia	Latin America	Rest of the world
Agriculture	9.0	30.1	−133.3	−651.3	−35.3	−21.7	6.4	−3.1	18.7	20.7
Mining	6.1	13.2	24.0	20.8	−43.7	−21.0	−13.7	−23.2	−6.0	0.1
Processed food	14.4	3.6	−8.9	−33.7	22.9	−13.3	−21.7	−14.5	3.4	16.2
Textiles	−26.7	−9.2	−10.5	10.9	33.3	−70.1	−20.2	15.1	−12.9	−7.8
Clothing	−212.1	−1043.2	−278.2	−675.2	20.2	492.6	62.3	206.5	−28.2	−54.9
Iron and steel	−15.3	−17.3	2.4	−7.8	−8.9	74.6	−58.3	−91.2	5.8	13.4
Transport equipment	−65.1	−6.9	−15.5	1.5	−11.6	−33.2	−19.4	−140.9	86.0	46.4
Machinery and equipment	−23.8	−0.5	4.9	−1.4	−7.2	−4.2	62.3	−115.2	−17.5	−7.4
Other manufactures	−13.3	2.5	7.4	8.1	5.4	−16.2	−18.9	−35.6	−13.6	−1.3
Services	0.8	5.9	9.0	2.4	−4.9	−15.4	−9.2	−24.9	−6.9	−2.2

simply because they generate more export externalities as commodities affected most by tariff cuts have above-average externality effects.

Despite the large demonstrated gains from export externalities, these estimates are likely to be conservative, because the technological change in this model is driven solely by export growth (table 7.12). Countries which do not experience export growth following trade liberalisation are therefore unable to benefit directly from externalities (table 7.13). This is a restrictive assumption. In the real world, it is possible – even likely – that a sector whose exports contract as a result of trade liberalisation may experience technological progress. After all, a contracting sector has to be more innovative to survive the more competitive environment, especially in the long run. The induced technological change from the contraction of exports would be assisted by expanded imports with embodied technology, as discussed above.

Gains from trade liberalisation

CGE research on the evaluation of trade liberalisation has focused on the gain from increased allocative efficiency. Given the evidence that more rapid export expansion leads to or is associated with more rapid output growth, it is likely that there are gains arising from trade liberalisation in addition to those from improvements in resource allocation. In light of this empirical finding, a simple general equilibrium model incorporating

Table 7.13. *Technological changes resulting from the Uruguay Round reform, percentages*

	Austral-asia	North America	EU	Japan	NIEs	ASEAN	China	South Asia	Latin America	Rest of the world
Agriculture	0.2	0.3	0.0	0.0	0.2	0.0	0.1	0.0	0.5	0.3
Mining	0.2	0.0	0.0	0.0	0.0	0.0	0.0	0.0	0.0	0.0
Processed food	0.6	0.1	0.0	0.0	0.3	0.0	0.0	0.0	0.2	0.2
Textiles	0.0	0.0	0.1	0.2	3.5	4.5	0.3	1.3	0.0	0.0
Clothing	0.0	0.0	0.0	0.0	2.4	35.3	7.4	17.9	0.2	0.0
Iron and steel	0.0	0.1	0.7	0.0	0.0	8.4	0.0	0.0	1.5	2.8
Transport equipment	1.2	0.2	0.0	0.3	0.0	0.0	0.0	0.0	8.9	5.8
Machinery and equipment	0.0	0.1	0.4	0.0	0.0	0.0	10.0	0.0	0.0	0.3
Other manufactures	0.1	0.2	0.2	0.2	0.9	0.0	0.0	0.0	0.0	0.4
Services	0.0	0.0	0.0	0.0	0.0	0.0	0.0	0.0	0.0	0.0

export externalities has been constructed. In this model, export expansion drives technological change. While the economy-wide aggregate effects of export externalities are based on empirical estimates in the literature, varying degrees of export externalities are allowed at the sectoral level. This is consistent with empirical evidence that externalities are generated at different rates by different commodities.

With export externalities, the global welfare gain arising from the Uruguay Round Final Act can be more than twice as large as in conventional neo-classical models. Trade liberalisation is more likely to be a Pareto improvement when externalities are taken into account. The potential losses resulting from the deterioration in the terms of trade can be easily over-offset by the much larger gains from export externalities.

With large variations in the current trade distortions among different sectors, both in industrial and developing economies, the sector-specific externalities can be important in determining the benefits of the Uruguay Round trade liberalisation. The export expansion for sophisticated manufactures generates larger externalities, but wider benefits arise, for economies which are already more open have the advantage of reaping externalities.

This model is not suitable for explaining the difference in growth performance among countries, but its results point to the possibility that the increasing openness of East Asian economies may have generated a continuous stream of externalities much larger than those for the more closed economies of, say, Latin America. Thus, even without taking into account the possible growth effect of greater openness, more open economies can significantly out-perform less open ones over a long period with on-going reform. Rapid export growth may depend on sound economic policy, but with export externalities, the difference between sound and less sound policies becomes even more important.

Appendix: The 10×10 version of the GTAP model

Table 7A1. *Commodity details*

Commodity	Commodity description
Agriculture	Paddy rice, wheat, grains, non-grain crops, wool, other livestock, forestry, fisheries, processed rice
Mining	Coal, oil, gas, other minerals, non-metallic minerals
Processed food	Meat products, milk products, other food products, beverages and tobacco
Textiles	Textiles
Clothing	Wearing apparels
Iron and steel	Primary ferrous metals
Machinery and equipment	Machinery and equipment
Transport equipment	Transport industries
Other manufactures	Leather, etc., lumber, pulp paper etc., petroleum and coal, chemicals rubbers and plastics, non-metallic minerals, non-ferrous metals, fabricated metal products, other manufacturing
Non-tradeable services	Construction, trade and transport, electricity water and gas, other services (private), other services (government), ownership of dwellings

Source: Author's compilation.

8

A review of Uruguay Round modelling

WILL MARTIN

F13   F43

D58   F47

Economic modelling played an important role in guiding negotiating positions in the Uruguay Round and in gaining acceptance for the completed
package. During the Round, model-based analyses by a number of
researchers, and particularly by Tyers and Anderson (1992), helped to
demonstrate the potential gains from agricultural liberalisation and hence
to build support for the inclusion of agriculture. Analyses of the overall
package by Nguyen *et al.*, (1993) and other researchers demonstrated the
potentially enormous gains from the overall liberalisation effort. Once the
shape of the final agreement had become clear, the publication of results
from the joint World Bank–OECD study (Goldin *et al.*, 1993) and the OECD
study (1993) helped provide the momentum needed to conclude the
Round.

Most of the analyses conducted during the Round were based on relatively stylised representations of the agreement. Now that the Final Act has
been signed, and the detailed results are available, a major challenge is to
go further and to analyse, as nearly as possible, the actual agreements
reached in the Round. New developments in modelling techniques also
make it possible to extend previous analyses by including model features
such as economies of scale, export externalities, technology changes and
the introduction of new products.

The two studies in this volume by Francois–McDonald–Nordström
(chapter 6) and Yang (chapter 7) are more sophisticated than the earlier
studies and include some 'dynamic' effects of trade liberalisation,
although the estimates are still based only on tariff reductions and non-
tariff barrier (NTB) liberalisation affecting manufacturing and agricultural
trade. The Francois–McDonald–Nordström results are the most sophisticated and disaggregated estimates released so far. They are also the largest
estimates for trade expansions (allocative and terms of trade effects) and
for net welfare gains in the year 2005, compared with what would have
happened without the Uruguay Round Final Act.

The Francois–McDonald–Nordström study is an extremely impressive and ambitious study which goes beyond the Harberger triangle measures of welfare gains, and introduces scale economies (external and internal to the firm), gains from increased product variety and some dynamic estimates of gains from trade liberalisation. An important feature of this study is that it is based on actual data from the Uruguay Round schedules for manufactures, rather than simply formula cuts based on statements of intent. Francois, McDonald and Nordström use their own model built on the GTAP data base of global production and trade. The public availability of this data base from Tom Hertel's GTAP modelling group at Purdue University has obviated the need for each modelling team to spend vast amounts of resources on constructing its basic data, and promises to increase greatly the use of formal models for global and regional trade policy analysis (Hertel and Tsigas, forthcoming).

The tariff rate reductions in the Francois–McDonald–Nordström study are calculated using a rule that a tariff is reduced only in cases where the final binding is below the initial applied rate. If tariffs do vary over time, this will ignore the liberalising effects of bindings above initial applied rates, and over-state the marginal impact of bindings below the initial applied rate. As a first cut, it is a reasonable and consistent approach to the problem, particularly if protection rates show little variation over time. Where data are available, a better general approach to the problem might be as set out in Martin and Francois (1994). Under this approach, the tariff is taken to be stochastic, depending upon a wide range of factors, relative prices, the trade position of the economy; the cost of collecting revenue; the structure of the particular industry and idiosyncratic factors (such as whether the Minister involved prefers Frederick List or Milton Friedman as his preferred academic scribbler!). A tariff binding at B in figure 8.1 maps all of the potential rates of protection above B onto point B. As a consequence, it lowers both the mean (from μ_0 to μ_1) and the variance of protection, potentially allowing the introduction of a binding to be mapped into an equivalent reduction in the tariff rate.

The Francois–McDonald–Nordström study contains an excellent summary of the multifibre arrangement (MFA) and of agricultural protection issues. The agricultural protection estimates are based on formula cuts applied to agricultural distortions data obtained from the major OECD and US Department of Agriculture analyses of global agricultural protection. This approach gives an excellent measure of changes in the trade barriers once these have been declared ('tariffied'), but over-states the amount of liberalisation achieved because of the extent to which tariff equivalents of protection were set above the average rate of protection previously applying because of the process of 'dirty tariffication' (Ingco, 1994).

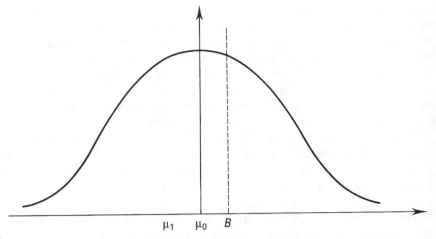

Figure 8.1 The distribution of tariffs and the effect of a tariff binding

This study provides some extremely useful decompositions of the results by source of reduction in protection, by model structure and by base year (tables 6.8–6.10, pp. 120–1, 123–5). These results give important insights into the reasons for the sometimes wide differences in estimated income gains from trade liberalisation. Unless these differences are dissected and understood, the art of modelling will not be regarded as credible by the policy makers for whom the model results are intended.

The pro-growth effects of trade liberalisation and export expansion have been a strong positive influence on the process of East Asian growth. Yang's chapter 7 focuses on this elaboration. These effects are now important far beyond East Asia, with rapid progress being made in trade liberalisation throughout the developing world, as other countries seek to emulate the performance of the East Asian economies. In fact, the lessons about the benefits from open trade strategies which East Asia has provided have been learned so well by other regions that East Asia is in danger of being left behind. The pace of trade liberalisation in Latin America since the mid-1980s has far outstripped that of East Asia (Dean *et al.*, 1994).

In chapter 7, Yang sets out a taxonomy of possible sources of welfare gains from trade liberalisation, including the Harberger triangles and revenue rectangles which measure improvements in allocative efficiency; greater exploitation of scale economies; enhanced rates of technical progress; greater availability of imported inputs; and the range of potential dynamic gains associated with higher rates of accumulation of knowledge.

While Yang would like to focus on the dynamic effects which are central in the endogenous growth literature, he is constrained both by his modelling framework, and by the available estimates of growth effects, to deal with comparative static effects. In his framework, income growth results from growth in exports, or higher income results from higher levels of exports. Thus, there is no mechanism of the kind sought in the endogenous growth literature, where changes in the level of a variable such as exports or human capital can lead to a permanent change in the growth rate.

Having carefully defined his objective, Yang adapts the available empirical evidence on economy-wide export externalities to allow its incorporation into his model. While these effects, and the literature on which it is based, refer to these effects as externalities, the actual measures encompass any effect of increased exports on the volume of measured output. Hence, they could include other sources of output increase, such as gains from exploitation of scale economies, or increases in the variety of intermediate inputs available to producers. A strength of this approach to extending the conventional measures of trade liberalisation is that it is based on real econometric estimates which capture these phenomena. Clever use is made of a logistic function to ensure that the gains are bounded.

The measures of actual trade liberalisation were the best available at the time of writing, but need to be further refined in future work. The decline in the agricultural production subsidy is estimated at the 20 per cent reduction agreed for the Aggregate Measure of Support (AMS) in the Uruguay Round Agreement. Unfortunately, there is considerable room for countries so inclined to dodge and weave extensively in the implementation of this reduction. Given the range of exemptions allowed, it seems reasonable to conclude that the AMS provision will exert very little discipline on domestic support. The 36 per cent reduction in agricultural export subsidies is much more tightly specified, and this reduction, or the 21 per cent reduction in the volume of subsidised exports, seems likely to bind much more tightly.

The model closure used by Yang provides for international capital mobility – allowing resources to move to take advantage of opportunities created by liberalisation. Labour supply is fixed, so that there are no 'free' gains from reducing unemployment. The Armington elasticities are taken from the SALTER model. Yang also reports some new estimates of the rents accruing under the MFA obtained from recent studies undertaken at the National Centre for Development Studies at the Australian University. This is a particularly important set of parameters that is likely to be widely used (see the Francois–McDonald–Nordström model in chapter 6).

The model simulation by Yang gives a small welfare gain of around US$60 billion. This does not match the Francois–McDonald–Nordström figure, or other recent studies on welfare estimates from the Uruguay Round. But Yang uses a different data base for the world economy (1992) and different specifications for the agricultural sector. Moreover, Yang's model uses different regional/country divisions from the Francois–McDonald–Nordström model, giving greater emphasis to developing countries, and especially East Asia. But the unique contribution of Yang's study is to introduce export externalities into the model using estimates obtained from the literature. He shows that by doing so the total welfare gains from liberalisation are almost doubled. And, more important, his results show a redistribution of benefits from developed economies to developing countries, because of technology transfers generated by higher levels of trade, and associated investments. These results have particular relevance to the East Asian economies.

In all of the modelling work on the Uruguay Round, and on other cases of trade liberalisation, the important thing is not the specific numbers which are generated. Rather, it is the insights that formal model-based analysis can provide into the implications of different policy measures, and the importance of different market structures and parameter values. The Yang and the Francois–McDonald–Nordström studies complement each other very well by illustrating the importance of differences in the assumptions made about issues such as whether markets are perfectly competitive, and whether markets are characterised by export externalities.

III

Trade issues for East Asia

9

What the Uruguay Round means for East Asia

GARY P. SAMPSON

F13   019

In recent decades, East Asian countries[1] have taken full advantage of the rules-based multilateral trading system by adopting domestic policies to promote growth through export expansion. Conducting trade according to rules based on non-discrimination (most-favoured-nation (Mfn) and national treatment) rather than regional preferences has served these countries well.[2] Consequently, one of the most important outcomes of the Uruguay Round for East Asian countries has been the strengthening of the rules of the multilateral trading system and the extension of multilateral rules to new areas of activity. Tightened disciplines on subsidies, safeguard measures, countervailing and anti-dumping duties, and diminution of 'grey-area' measures such as voluntary export restraints (VERs), where East Asian countries have frequently found themselves on the receiving end, will not only improve access to export markets but also increase predictability and reduce uncertainties for East Asian exporters. New areas in which East Asian countries stand to gain include GATS, TRIMs and TRIPs.

A well documented outcome of the Uruguay Round is that all small and medium-sized countries, such as the developing countries of East Asia, will benefit from the strengthening of the rules of the multilateral trading system. What is yet to be researched is the trade liberalisation commitments undertaken during the Uruguay Round by East Asian countries and the new market opportunities for products of export interest to them. What does the Uruguay Round mean for East Asian countries in terms of their improved market access for industrial and agricultural goods? What do the undertakings of the East Asian countries in the Uruguay Round mean for their economies? What policy conclusions can be drawn from these assessments?

Market access negotiations

In the Uruguay Round, the negotiations to liberalise trade in industrial products were primarily directed towards reducing border protection (tariff barriers). For agriculture, the objective was to reduce border protection (tariff barriers and tariffied non-tariff barriers (NTBs)), internal market support and export subsidisation.

The tariff is, in principle, the only instrument of protection allowed by the GATT. Not surprisingly, tariff negotiations have been the essence of the GATT. For nearly twenty years, GATT negotiations related almost exclusively to tariffs. Eight GATT negotiating rounds held since 1947 have reduced the average level of tariffs on industrial goods in industrial countries from more than 40 per cent to the post-Uruguay Round level of 3.9 per cent. GATT negotiating rounds have been far less successful in ensuring security of market access commitments through the binding of tariffs.

The concept of 'binding' a tariff is important in any discussion of trade liberalisation.[3] If a tariff reduction negotiated during a GATT round can be unilaterally raised, the tariff liberalisation may have little or no value to foreign exporters because the future treatment of the export is uncertain. Binding is particularly important in GATT negotiations; countries which agree to bind previously unbound tariffs are given negotiating credit even if the tariff is bound at a level above that currently applied (as is the case for East Asian developing countries). When a government agrees to bind a tariff on a tariff-line item, it commits itself not to increase the tariff above that level. Countries can permit imports at less than (but not more than) bound rates, provided this treatment is extended to all GATT contracting parties.

A number of issues remained open for negotiation in the area of tariffs prior to the Uruguay Round. In most industrialised countries, high tariffs (tariff peaks) still sheltered certain key or sensitive industries (such as footwear, textiles and clothing). The industrial countries also generally maintained a higher level of tariff protection for agricultural products than for manufactured goods, and tariff escalation was considered a problem for developing countries. Tariffs were much higher in developing countries than industrial countries, and the proportion of bound tariffs was in most cases very low or nil in developing countries. Further, duties below 5 per cent were considered 'nuisance' tariffs, since the revenue collected did not cover the costs incurred in customs processing. While these were all issues to be addressed, the priorities to be assigned to them, and the targets to be met, had to be negotiated.

The Ministerial Declaration in Punta del Este in September 1986 stated:

> Negotiations shall aim, by appropriate methods, to reduce or, as appropriate, eliminate tariffs including the reduction or elimination of high tariffs and tariff escalation. Emphasis shall be given to the expansion of the scope of tariff concessions among all participants.

The first meeting of the Negotiations Group on Tariffs was held on 10 February 1987. At the Mid-Term Review of the Uruguay Round by Ministers in Montreal in December 1988, several important issues relating to how tariffs were to be negotiated were settled. It was agreed that a target would be set that would be at least as ambitious as in the Tokyo Round; negotiators were to reduce tariffs by at least one-third. Second, the base rates which would provide the starting point for the negotiations would be the bound Mfn rates or, in the case of unbound rates, the tariff rates which were actually applied at the time of the launching of the Uruguay Round in September 1986. Third, it was agreed that the scope of tariff bindings would be substantially increased; therefore, negotiating credit was to be earned through both the reduction in tariffs and the increase in the bindings.

Technical considerations

The data presented here are drawn from the Integrated Data Base (IDB) maintained by the GATT Secretariat. The IDB contains data for forty-three countries (the twelve Member States of the EU counting as one). They include all industrial economies, a number of transitional economies and the major developing countries. Collectively these countries account for approximately 98 per cent of the merchandise trade of GATT contracting parties and approximately 90 per cent of total world merchandise trade. Of the ninety-three developing economy participants in the Uruguay Round, twenty-six are included in the IDB. Those twenty-six participants account for approximately 80 per cent of the merchandise exports (excluding petroleum) of the ninety-three developing economy participants. As far as data for trade flows are concerned, these relate to the most recent year for which countries provided tariff data to the GATT Secretariat. For the countries in the East Asia region, the years vary between 1988 and 1992.

Given that tariff schedules contain thousands of tariff-lines,[4] in any overview of the negotiations to reduce tariffs it is necessary to average the results; this brings with it a number of conceptual and practical problems. In the aftermath of the Kennedy Round, Jan Tumlir and Ladislav Till drew the conclusion that:

> There is no satisfactory method of averaging the rates of a customs tariff. For the most frequent purpose of such averaging – namely, the need to express in one figure or a simple set of figures the protective effect of a tariff – it is even difficult to indicate what the ideal method should be. (Tumlir and Till, 1971)

There have been no major breakthroughs in the period since Tumlir and Till's important work. In fact, there are not only the conceptual problems in tariff averaging that they identified, there are also practical problems such as selecting trade weights for averaging tariffs. For example, a large part of world trade is not the subject of multilateral negotiations. Trade flows within free-trade areas (for example NAFTA), customs unions (for example, the EU) and non-reciprocal preferential trading arrangements (for example the Lomé Convention) receive preferential treatment and do not face Mfn tariff rates; tariffs on these trade flows are therefore not the subject of negotiation. In what follows, only imports that face Mfn – referred to as 'imports from Mfn sources' – have been included in the trade weights. Similarly, in the trade flow data, a distinction is made between total imports from all sources and imports from Mfn sources.[5]

It is not obvious which tariffs should be averaged. Many GATT contracting parties have both bound and unbound Mfn rates in their tariff schedules. The Mfn tariffs may be ceiling bindings, but rarely, if ever, applied in practice. Ceiling bindings may apply to individual products or there may be an 'across-the-board' binding of all tariff-line items at a certain rate. The margin between the rate which is actually applied (the applied rate) and the bound ceiling rate represents the extent to which the country may increase its tariff in a manner which is legally consistent with GATT obligations. There are at least two options with respect to the 'average' tariff. It could be argued that only bound rates, including ceiling bindings, should be used as these are the only 'legally certain' rates. As noted above, the base rates for the tariff negotiations in the Uruguay Round were the bound rates; if rates were not bound, the rates actually applied at the start of negotiations were to be used. While this may describe the legal situation with respect to tariffs, it could be argued that it would not necessarily give an accurate picture of the level of protection in terms of the tariff rates actually applied. A better measure for the purpose of assessing market access possibilities would be to average the tariff rates actually applied, irrespective of whether they were bound or not.

Two sets of tariff averages have been calculated here. First, the base rates notified by governments for the purposes of negotiations (which include the bound Mfn rates (including ceiling bindings) and the unbound rates as of September 1986). The post-Uruguay Round rates are the bound rates (including ceiling bindings) and the rates which remain unbound after the Uruguay Round. (The base rates offered for negotiations could in reality be above those actually applied, as a base rate above the applied rate was in some cases tabled for negotiating purposes.) These are referred to as base rates. Second, the applied rates have also been calculated. In this case, these rates are those that were actually applied, both bound and unbound before and after the Uruguay Round. Thus, while these applied rates include bound Mfn rates, they exclude ceiling bindings if the ceiling bindings were not applied. The base and applied rates can be different for two reasons. Ceiling bindings may not be applied or governments may not have notified, as base rates, the tariffs that were actually applied in September 1986. If rates were not bound in September 1986, governments may have notified a base rate that was higher than their applied rate. This would permit such countries to negotiate from a higher starting point. This distinction is particularly important for East Asian developing countries, all of which have bound ceiling rates which in many instances are relatively high. Further, not all East Asian countries notified their applied rate in 1986 as their base rate. This is not the case for the major industrial countries.

An important technical consideration for negotiating purposes is the decision that both the reduction in tariffs and the increase in bindings were to be taken into account for negotiating purposes. There is no objective means available, however, to compare the value of tariff reductions with increases in the scope of bindings. While negotiators attempted to formalise an approach where a matrix of combinations of tariff reductions and increased bindings would assign 'values' to the different combinations of tariff cuts and bindings, this approach was never adopted. Thus, the relative value of bindings and tariff reductions remained subjective and the object of trade-offs in negotiations.

A final technical problem relates to the difficulties in evaluating bindings by calculating the trade coverage. Finding a measure of coverage means confronting many of the weighting problems that arise in calculating tariff averages. One option is to calculate the share of tariff-lines which are bound. Following this approach means that a high share of tariff-lines bound could result even if some important tariff-lines (in trade terms) were left unbound. An alternative would be to calculate the share of trade in bound tariff-lines. A large share of trade in bound tariff items could still mean that a large number of tariff-lines remain unbound. Therefore, in most instances below, the simple average of tariff-lines which are bound, as well as the share of trade in bound tariff-lines, have been calculated.

Industrial products

For the industrial economies, the target established by Ministers in Montreal of matching the outcome of the Tokyo Round (a one-third reduction in tariffs) was met (table 9.1). These economies, which currently

Table 9.1. *Tariff reductions on industrial products (excluding petroleum), by industrial countries from selected groups of countries, US$ billion and percentages*

Importing country group	Import value (US$ billion)	Weighted average		
		Pre-UR %	Post-UR %	Percentage reduction
All industrial products (excluding petroleum)				
Industrial economies	736.9	6.3	3.9	38
Developing economies (other than least developed economies)	167.6	6.8	4.3	37
LDCs	3.9	6.8	5.1	25
Excluding textiles and clothing, fish and fish products				
Industrial countries	652.1	5.4	3.0	44
Developing economies (other than LDCs)	125.2	4.9	2.4	51
LDCs	2.1	1.7	0.7	59

Note:
UR=Uruguay Round.
LDCs=Least developed countries.
Source: Data drawn from the GATT IDB.

account for about two-thirds of world imports of industrial products other than petroleum, reduced tariffs by 38 per cent for industrial products.[6] The average trade-weighted tariff will be reduced from the pre-Uruguay Round level of 6.3 per cent to 3.9 per cent.[7] These tariff reductions involve smaller percentage tariff cuts and higher average post-Uruguay Round tariffs for the mix of products currently imported from developing countries and from least-developed countries (LDCs). These results are reversed, however, if 'textiles and clothing' and 'fish and fish products' are excluded from the calculations. Both product groups are important in exports of developing economies, and especially LDCs (almost one-half of their exports to industrial economies), but are product categories for which tariff reductions were below the average for industrial products as a whole, and for which post-Uruguay Round tariffs are above the average.

The Uruguay Round objective of increasing the scope of bound tariffs was also met. The percentage of tariff lines which are bound for industrial products has risen from 78 to 99 per cent for industrial economies, from 22 to 72 per cent for developing economies and from 73 to 98 per cent for transitional economies (Czech Republic, Slovak Republic, Hungary and

Table 9.2. *Pre- and post-Uruguay Round scope of bindings for industrial products (excluding petroleum), number of lines, US$ billion and percentages*

Importing country group or region	Number of lines	Import value (US$ billion)	Percentage of tariff lines bound		Percentage of imports under bound rates	
			Pre-UR	Post-UR	Pre-UR	Post-UR
By major country group						
Industrial economies	86,968	737.2	78	99	94	99
Developing economies	157,805	306.2	22	72	14	59
Transitional economies	18,962	34.7	73	98	74	96
By selected region						
North America	14,138	325.7	99	100	99	100
Latin America	64,136	40.4	38	100	57	100
Western Europe	57,851	239.9	79	82	98	98
Central Europe	23,565	38.1	63	98	68	97
Asia	82,545	415.4	17	67	36	70

Note:
UR=Uruguay Round.
Source: Data drawn from the GATT IDB.

Poland) (table 9.2). While the level of bindings is lower in developing economies than in industrial or transitional economies, the increase in bindings was the most substantial for this group. In terms of imports of industrial products of each country group, virtually all imports facing Mfn tariffs of the industrial economies (US$737.2 billion) and of the transitional economies (US$34.7 billion) will enter under bound tariffs after the Uruguay Round, as well as more than half the imports of developing economies (59 per cent). A major result of the Uruguay Round, therefore, is an improvement in the security of market access for industrial products through bindings.

The value of imports of industrial products into the East Asian countries and increases in tariff bindings as a result of the Uruguay Round are shown in table 9.3. Column (1) identifies the importing country, column (2) the value of imports which receive Mfn treatment and column (3) total imports from all sources. There is very little difference in the value of imports from Mfn sources and world sources (US$291 billion compared to US$308 billion),[8] which follows because East Asian countries do not discriminate between sources of supply through preferential trading arrangements.

The share of tariff lines subject to bindings in East Asian economies has increased sharply as a result of the Uruguay Round (from 6 to 56 per cent)

Table 9.3. *Imports of industrial products, value of trade and tariff bindings*

Importer (1)	MFN imports (US$ million) (2)	Total imports (US$ million) (3)	Number of tariff lines (4)	Share of tariff lines bound (%)	
				Pre-UR (5)	Post-UR (6)
China	50.0	72.1	5,399	0	77
Hong Kong	115.5	115.5	5,111	1	23
Indonesia	12.6	13.6	7,717	30	92
Korea	40.6	42.3	8,883	24	89
Malaysia	11.3	13.7	10,461	2	79
Philippines	9.2	9.9	5,384	9	67
Singapore	36.9	38.8	4,953	0	73
Thailand	14.6	16.0	5,140	12	70
Total	290.7	307.5	53,048	6	56
Japan	132.9	133.4	7,338	89	96

Note:
UR=Uruguay Round.
Source: Data drawn from the GATT IDB.

(table 9.3, columns (5) and (6)). The regional share of bindings is reduced by the low level of bindings in Hong Kong (23 per cent), although most of that country's applied rates are set at zero. Hong Kong accounts for 40 per cent of the industrial imports in the region. In the case of Japan, 89 per cent of trade was in bound tariff lines prior to the Uruguay Round, and this will increase to 96 per cent.

The trade-weighted averages of tariff rates for the East Asian developing countries before and after the implementation of the Uruguay Round results show reductions in average base duties of 25 per cent, and a reduction of 22 per cent in applied rates (table 9.4). The levels of tariffs and tariff reductions are influenced by the inclusion or exclusion of ceiling bindings. The Uruguay Round reduced average base duties by 11 per cent from 12.8 per cent to 11.3 per cent. For applied rates, the average tariffs will be reduced from 10.2 per cent to 8.0 per cent: a 22 per cent reduction.

The average level of tariffs in each of the East Asian countries, as well as their percentage reduction, varies greatly across countries. In some instances, the results vary greatly depending on whether base rates or applied rates are used. With a zero level of bindings prior to the Uruguay Round (table 9.3), Singapore chose to notify base rates for the purposes of negotiations which were higher than the applied rates. Thus, the pre-Uruguay Round base rate for negotiating purposes was 12.4 per cent compared with an applied rate of 0.4 per cent. Starting from a high base rate

Table 9.4. *Imports of industrial products, trade-weighted tariff reductions*

	Weighted average tariff rates					
	Base duties including ceiling bindings			Applied duties excluding ceiling bindings		
Importer	Pre-UR	Post-UR	(%)	Pre-UR	Post-UR	(%)
China	29.0	33.1	. . .	27.0	24.0	10
Hong Kong	0.0	0.0	0	0.0	0.0	0
Indonesia	20.4	36.9	. . .	12.4	11.9	4
Korea	18.0	8.3	54	15.3	7.9	48
Malaysia	10.2	9.1	11	9.4	6.9	27
Philippines	23.9	22.2	7	22.6	20.6	9
Singapore	12.4	5.1	59	0.4	0.3	25
Thailand	37.3	28.0	25	37.0	27.0	27
Total	12.8	11.3	11	10.2	8.0	22
Japan	3.9	1.7	56	2.9	1.7	41

Notes:
UR=Uruguay Round.
. . .=Negligible.
Source: Data drawn from the GATT IDB.

meant that Singapore recorded a significant absolute tariff reduction (7.3 percentage points) and a 59 per cent cut in the base rates. In the case of Hong Kong, even though only 1 per cent of its tariff lines were bound, it offered its applied rates of zero for negotiation purposes. There was, by definition, a zero percentage reduction (that is, from zero to zero) in tariff rates for Hong Kong. For Indonesia, the pre-Uruguay Round trade weighted average of the applied rates was 12.4 per cent and the post-Uruguay Round average of base rates, after the negotiations, was 36.9 per cent. This is a reflection of the fact that the Indonesian tariff offer consisted of an across-the-board ceiling binding of 40 per cent (with some exceptions); the result was an increase in bindings from 30 to 92 per cent of trade (table 9.3) accompanied by a very significant increase in bound rates compared to the Uruguay Round applied rates. This provides an example of the trade-off of higher tariffs as compared to higher bindings that some countries are prepared to accept.[9]

The significance of industrial countries' imports of manufactures from the East Asian countries is shown in table 9.5. For all industrial products, the average applied duties will be reduced from 7.6 per cent to 5.4 per cent (a 29 per cent reduction), as a result of the Uruguay Round.[10] Because of the composition of East Asian exports, this is less than the average reduction of 38 per cent for all developing countries (table 9.1). The reduction in

Table 9.5. *Imports by industrial economies from East Asian developing countries, tariff reduction by industrial product group, US$ million and percentages*

Product category	Imports from world (US$ million)	Imports from East Asia[a] (US$ million)	Simple and trade-weighted average tariff (%)					
			Pre-Uruguay weighted average		Post-Uruguay weighted average		Percentage reduction weighted average	
			Applied duties excluding ceiling bindings	Base duties including ceiling bindings	Applied duties excluding ceiling bindings	Base duties including ceiling bindings	Applied duties excluding ceiling bindings	Base duties including ceiling bindings
All industrial products (excluding petroleum)	1,146,617	180,745	7.6	8.2	5.4	5.5	29	33
Textiles and clothing	93,361	40,388	15.8	16.2	13.2	13.2	16	19
Metals	116,083	12,148	4.0	4.5	1.8	1.9	55	58
Mineral products, precious stones and metals	110,500	11,949	2.7	4.1	1.7	1.7	37	59
Electric machinery	115,938	28,824	5.0	6.3	3.0	3.0	40	52
Leather, rubber, footwear and travel goods	41,154	17,147	9.3	9.4	8.1	8.1	13	14
Wood, pulp, paper and furniture	91,996	10,150	4.3	4.9	1.8	1.8	58	63
Fish and fish products	24,951	7,160	6.2	6.7	4.8	4.8	23	28
Non-electric machinery	177,302	19,837	3.4	4.3	1.1	1.2	68	72
Chemicals and photography supplies	104,886	6,855	5.9	6.5	3.9	4.1	34	37
Transport equipment	172,126	4,876	4.5	4.8	3.8	3.8	16	21
Other manufactured articles	98,320	21,411	6.0	6.4	2.8	2.8	53	56

Note:
[a] Excluding imports under tariff lines where duties are not available in percentage terms.
Source: Data drawn from the GATT IDB

base rates, however, meets the Uruguay Round objective of a one-third reduction in tariffs.

Because of the limited use of ceiling bindings in industrial countries there are only small disparities in the base and applied rates for each product. The absolute level of average tariffs, however, differs considerably across the various product categories. For the East Asian developing countries, trade in textiles and clothing is important. For these products, the tariff reduction was less than the industrial average; in fact both base and applied average tariffs are two-and-one half times the industrial average. From the perspective of improved market access, however, the Uruguay Round Agreement to phase-out restraints applied under the multifibre arrangement (MFA) is of particular importance. For those products where the MFA quota is the binding restraint, the tariff equivalent of the quota exceeds the ordinary tariff. The tariff-equivalent of MFA quotas has been calculated to be considerably higher than the Mfn tariff in a number of cases (GATT, 1994d). The other product category where both the base and the applied rates remain above the industrial average is leather, rubber, footwear and travel goods (8.1 per cent compared with the industrial average of 5.5 per cent) is also of importance for exports of East Asian countries. In both textiles, clothing and footwear, and in travel goods, the percentage reduction in base tariffs (19 and 14 per cent respectively) was also considerably less than the industrial average (33 per cent). One tariff-related result of the Uruguay Round that has been criticised by a number of East Asian developing countries is that the reduction in Mfn tariffs has led to an erosion of their tariff preferences in the industrial countries markets under the Generalised System of Preferences (GSP). While there has been an erosion of GSP preference margins, tariff preferences remain potentially significant for a number of product categories.

Agricultural products

In earlier rounds of GATT negotiations, agricultural products were largely excluded from tariff reductions and use of tariff bindings has remained low compared with industrial products. In addition, there remain numerous exceptions to the GATT prohibition on quantitative restrictions (QRs) and no effective binding provisions on export subsidies. The Agreement on Agriculture negotiated in the Uruguay Round embodies a comprehensive package of measures to initiate a process of reform over a six-year implementation period (1995–2000). The main provisions of this Agreement cover specific binding and reduction commitments in all areas which affect competition in agricultural trade, namely: market access; domestic support and export competition.[11] Specific provisions granting more favourable treatment to developing countries (lower reduction commitments and longer implementation periods in particular) are included in the Agreement.

The Uruguay Round negotiations relating to domestic support resulted in a commitment to reduce the level of support, expressed in terms of an Aggregate Measure of Support (AMS), by 20 per cent relative to the base period (1986–8). The Agreement provides for the exception of certain policies under the so-called 'green and blue boxes'. Exceptions under the green box are those that have been accepted as having no, or at most minimal, trade distortion effects or effects on production. Exceptions under the blue box meet other conditions concerning, in particular, production limitations. Domestic support policies that do not exceed 5 per cent of the total value of production are not subject to reduction commitments (the *de minimis* provision). As the provisions relating to developing countries will apply to East Asian developing countries, the domestic support policies of these countries which are classified as development policies, including investment subsidies and support to encourage diversification from the growing of illicit narcotics, are exempted from reduction commitments. The *de minimis* provision for East Asian developing countries is set at 10 per cent.

The section of the Agricultural Agreement on export competition clarifies the definition of export subsidies and subjects them to reduction commitments. Export subsidies are subject to budgetary and quantity reduction commitments, respectively 36 and 21 per cent from the 1986–90 average, by the end of the implementation period. The base period of 1991–2 or the average between 1986–90 and 1991–2 may be used as the starting point for reductions under some circumstances. However, volume and budgetary commitments to be reached by the end of the implementation period are based on the reference period of 1986–90. East Asian developing countries (EADCs) have the same flexibility as other developing countries and will be subject to budgetary and quantity reduction commitments, 24 and 14 per cent, respectively. Subsidies are bound in the sense that countries are not to provide export subsidies other than in conformity with the Agreement and the commitments specified in the national Schedule.

Market access negotiations required the conversion of non-tariff border measures into tariff equivalents (tariffication of non-tariff measures). All customs duties, including those resulting from tariffication, are required to be bound from 1995, and reduced on average by 36 per cent, with a minimum reduction of 15 per cent for each tariff line, over a six-year period from 1995 to the year 2000. East Asian developing countries are required to reduce tariffs and other tariffied measures by two-thirds of the reduction applying to industrial countries (24 per cent), and to implement tariff cuts over a ten-year period from 1995 to 2004. The tariffication requirement also includes the maintenance of import opportunities representing at least the quantity of imports in the 1986–8 base period, and minimum access provisions where current access quantities represent less than 5 per cent of domestic consumption of the same product in the base period. These minimum access opportunities are implemented on the basis of tariff quotas, provided on a Mfn basis, at low or minimal tariff rates. The initial quantity of the tariff quota generally represents 3 per cent of domestic consumption, rising to 5 per cent by the end of the implementation period.

For both Korea and Japan, the treatment of agricultural products (in particular rice) was a dominant concern in the market access negotiations in the Uruguay Round. One outcome of importance for these two countries is that if certain conditions are met, they will not have to tariffy the border protection of rice. In such circumstances, minimum access opportunities for Japan are set at 4 per cent of domestic consumption, rising to 8 per cent at the end of the implementation period (six years). For a primary agricultural product that is a predominant staple in the traditional diet of a developing country – such as rice in Korea – the minimum access opportunity is initially set at 1 per cent of domestic consumption to be raised in steps to 4 per cent at the end of the implementation period (ten years).

The average percentage reductions in tariffs and tariffied non-tariff measures in agriculture varied widely among East Asian countries (table 9.6.)[12] The tariff reduction for Hong Kong, for example, is zero as tariffs and other charges were zero at the outset. For Singapore, the percentage tariff reductions are substantial (61 per cent), with the next largest reduction being Indonesia (33 per cent). The overall average reduction for the region is 21 per cent, a figure which is heavily influenced by the Hong Kong result. In fact, no country other than Hong Kong registered an average tariff reduction below the average for the East Asian developing countries as a group.

In the past only a very small proportion of agricultural tariffs have been bound. The share of tariff lines that were bound before and after the implementation of the Uruguay Round results has risen sharply (table 9.6): the figures point to the low level of bindings of agricultural trade prior to the Uruguay Round and the fact that all tariffs will be bound as a result of the Round.[13]

Table 9.6. *Imports of agricultural products, tariff reductions, bindings and share of trade duty free*

Importer	Total imports (US$ million)	EADC imports (US$ million)	Simple average tariff reductions (%)	Share of tariff lines bound	
				Pre-UR (%)	Post-UR (%)
China	4,234	492	26	0	100
Hong Kong	8,419	3,547	0	3	100
Indonesia	1,313	291	33	69	100
Korea	4,598	446	28	24	100
Malaysia	932	268	28	4	100
Philippines	1,079	90	30	29	100
Singapore	2,103	500	61	1	100
Thailand	1,048	223	25	18	100
Total	23,726	5,857	21	48	100
Japan	25,970	5,665	36	60	100

Note:
UR=Uruguay Round.
Source: Data drawn from the GATT IDB.

Table 9.7 shows the value of agricultural imports from East Asian developing countries including the sub-category of tropical products. Imports from all sources are shown as well as imports from the East Asian countries. The percentage reduction in tariffs and tariffied non-tariff barriers as a result of the Uruguay Round are also shown. Among the first twelve agricultural product categories in table 9.7, tariff reductions by industrial economies range from a low of 25 per cent for dairy products to a high of 49 per cent for flowers, plants and vegetable materials. The average tariff reduction for agricultural products as a whole is 37 per cent. The three most important categories for the exports of East Asian countries are fruit and vegetables, oilseeds fats and oils and other agricultural products, all of which face tariff cuts that are greater (or equal to) the average for all agricultural goods. The category of tropical agricultural products – of export interest to many developing economies in the East Asian region – has an above-average reduction in tariffs (44 per cent).

Policy conclusions

The emergence of the East Asian economies as major players means that the world is increasingly regarded as tri-polar. North America, Europe and a region centred on Japan (Snape *et al.*, 1993). Two of the three zones are

Table 9.7. *Imports of agricultural products from East Asian developing countries, tariff reductions by agricultural product group, US$ million and percentages*

Product category	Total imports (US$ million)	Imports from East Asia (US$ million)	Percentage reduction in tariffs in industrial countries
All agricultural products	115,939	12,923	37
Coffee, tea and cocoa	14,198	892	36
Sugar	3,709	327	29
Spices and cereal preparations	4,929	824	35
Fruit and vegetables	22,042	4,124	37
Oilseeds fats and oils	14,373	2,216	40
Other agricultural products	19,629	2,296	49
Animals and products	12,594	963	32
Beverages and spirits	9,199	223	38
Flowers, plants and vegetable materials	3,235	510	49
Tobacco	3,955	221	36
Grains	5,947	326	38
Dairy products	2,131	1	25
Tropical products	34,121	6,372	44
Tropical beverages	12,963	854	48
Tropical nuts and fruits	6,656	1,218	37
Certain oilseeds, oils	4,379	1,843	41
Roots, rice and tobacco	5,663	1,484	39
Spices, flowers and plants	4,460	973	54

Source: Data drawn from the GATT IDB.

actively increasing the geographic scope and the economic depth of their economic integration through the creation of formal institutional mechanisms. The maintenance and strengthening of the multilateral trading system following the successful conclusion to the Uruguay Round will be an important factor in determining the future of regional trading arrangements in East Asia and elsewhere.

The scenario of three competitive trading blocs envisaged inward-oriented policies being adopted if the Uruguay Round failed, as an alternative to the non-discriminatory multilateral system. For East Asia, the Uruguay Round means strengthened rules, improved market access and the binding of domestic liberalisation commitments. This positive result will greatly reduce the likelihood that inward-oriented preferential arrangements will be formed in the region out of frustration with the multilateral trading system. As far as the future of regional trading arrangements for other countries is concerned, it has been argued that the results of the Uruguay Round will provide parties to such arrangements with the option of pursuing an open approach to trade. Viewed in this perspective, a viable multilateral trading system is not a complement to an outward-looking regional trading arrangement – it is a precondition (Sutherland, 1994). This is a positive result for those countries that are not members of preferential trading arrangements.

The results here show that considerable potential benefits should accrue to East Asian countries as a result of new market access opportunities. While average tariffs on industrial goods imported into industrial countries from East Asian countries remain higher than for industrial imports from all sources, there have been substantial reductions in the order of 30 per cent on average. While in some individual sectors the tariffs remain high (textiles and clothing and leather goods), there have nevertheless been important tariff reductions in what are very sensitive product categories in industrial countries. In the case of textiles and clothing, the results of the tariff negotiations should be assessed along with the phasing-out of the MFA. Similarly, the very substantial reduction of tariff escalation, a long-standing objective of all developing countries, is a positive outcome for East Asian developing countries (GATT, 1994d).

While it is true that GSP preferences will be eroded for East Asian developing countries due to the tariff reductions for industrial goods, this is to be measured against reduced or zero bound tariffs on products of export interest to them. Further, even though the loss of these preferences may well have implications for East Asian developing countries – as these countries have been the principal beneficiaries of GSP preferences – it should come as no surprise. The objective of GSP preferences is not to divert trade from other exporters, but rather to permit preference-receiving countries to compete on an equal footing with producers in the importing market. Past experience has shown that this objective is more effectively met through the elimination and binding of tariffs in multilateral trade negotiations than through preference schemes. GSP schemes frequently place *a priori* restrictions and criteria on the granting of preferences. This is not the case with negotiated reductions of tariffs that are bound in national schedules. Further, in many instances, tariff preferences are temporary and non-contractual. In contrast, tariff commitments made in the GATT are legally binding commitments. It is only by providing compensation to suppliers that bound rates can be increased. Finally, GSP treatment may be viewed as the advanced implementation of Mfn tariff reductions offered to East Asian developing countries. The subsequent elimination of tariffs for non-GSP countries can be viewed as the extension of zero tariffs to non-GSP beneficiaries. In short, the binding of tariff reductions implemented in the context of GATT negotiations provides security of market access for East Asian countries, fosters trade expansion, and consequently industrialisation and economic growth.

Irrespective of how they are measured, average bound tariffs for some East Asian countries remain high, particularly when compared to the average levels in the industrial countries as well as other countries in the region (Hong Kong and Singapore). In some instances, the high ceiling bindings are coupled with applied rates that are well below the bound rate (Indonesia, China), suggesting that the high bound rates are being maintained to gain future negotiating credit. The high applied rates in some countries (China, Indonesia, Philippines, Thailand) shows there is scope for further domestic liberalisation. The significant differences in average tariffs between countries make it hard to imagine that a customs union between them is a realistic possibility. If there is to be a serious free trade area among these countries, the disparity in tariff levels means that a very effective set of rules of origin will have to be developed.

The different results that follow from measuring the level and reduction in tariffs when both base and applied rates are calculated, points to the complexities of any quantitative evaluation of the market access negotiations, not only for the East Asian countries, but for all countries that do not apply bound rates. This should be taken into careful consideration in drawing policy conclusions from any quantitative study using tariff averages. In fact, the method of tariff averaging is important not only for evaluating the results of market access negotiations, it is also important for the calculation of effective rates of protection, tariff escalation and partial and general equilibrium models measuring trade creation, trade diversion and income gains through tariff liberalisation. The results also point to the difficulties in assessing the results of the negotiations when both tariff cuts and increased bindings are to be taken into account. The lack of an objective measure of the value of bindings *vis à vis* tariff reductions leaves much open to interpretation by individual participants in the negotiations. The trade-off available to negotiators also encourages countries to bind at a level above the applied rate of duty in order to gain future negotiating credit.

NOTES

Director of the Development Division, General Agreement on Tariffs and Trade, Geneva, Switzerland. The author wishes to thank members of the Statistics and Information Systems Division of the GATT Secretariat, in particular, Philip Obez, for assistance in the preparation of the quantitative material. The views expressed in this chapter are those of the author and not the organisation for which he works.

1. East Asia is taken to include all East Asian developing countries that are con-
    tracting parties to GATT – Korea, Hong Kong, Indonesia, Malaysia,
    Philippines, Thailand and Singapore – and Japan. China is also included as a
    developing country. Although not a contracting party, China has been in the
    process of accession to GATT since 1986, was an active participant in the
    Uruguay Round (particularly in the services negotiations) and is of major eco-
    nomic importance in the region. Japan is treated separately from the East Asian
    developing countries.
2. In accordance with GATT procedures, almost sixty free-trade areas and
    customs unions between GATT contracting parties have been notified
    since 1947. Japan, Hong Kong and Korea are the only GATT contracting parties
    that are not members of customs unions or free-trade areas. While the ASEAN
    Free-Trade Area was signed in 1987, the preferences and coverage have been
    limited and the period for implementation is very long-term. Its predecessor –
    the ASEAN Preferential Trade Area – did little to promote intra-trade.
3. Bindings are also of value for domestic producers using the product as an
    input. Where investment decisions are taken on the basis of the price of the
    imported good inclusive of the reduced tariff, bindings provide a means to
    consolidate domestic reform programmes. The tariff-line is the most dis-
    aggregated product classification and is used for the purpose of levying tariffs
    on imports. While it is possible to increase a bound tariff, this can be done only
    through the renegotiation of the concession with affected trading partners; the
    country raising the tariff faces the possibility of having to pay compensation to
    those foreign exporters adversely affected by the increase in the bound tariff.
4. There are, for example, over 60,000 tariff-lines in East Asian countries (see table
    9.3).
5. Trade under GSP has, however, been included as imports from Mfn sources.
    GSP rates are not bound, are applied selectively to less than all industrial prod-
    ucts and, in many instances, there are quantitative limits on imports receiving
    GSP treatment.
6. This is the trade-weighted average reduction in base rates (as described above),
    inclusive of ceiling bindings. In fact, for developed countries, the inclusion of
    ceiling bindings does not greatly change the results as they apply to a relatively
    insignificant part of total trade. This is not the case for East Asian developing
    countries.
7. In calculating the trade-weighted tariff averages, the results are not sensitive
    to the inclusion of ceiling bindings due to their relative unimportance in devel-
    oped countries.
8. This was justified in terms of the (unadopted) Chairman's Guidelines on credit
    for tariff bindings. According to the Chairman's proposal: 'Developing coun-
    tries which bind 100 per cent of their tariff lines . . . below 40 per cent, . . .
    achieve the Montreal target of tariff reductions', (MTN.GNG/MA/W/131,
    19 December 1991).
9. Note that the reduction is less than the average for imports of industrial goods
    from all Mfn sources as shown in table 9.1. Also average tariffs remain higher
    on imports from developing countries.

10. As with industrial goods, the focus of this chapter is improved market access through reductions in border protection. The results of the negotiations in the areas of domestic support and export competition are, however, summarised below in general terms for the sake of completeness.

11. Under the modalities for the establishment of specific binding commitments, the coverage of border measures to be tariffied – other than customs duties – included: quantitative import restrictions, variable import levies, minimum import prices, discretionary import licensing, non-tariff measures maintained through state enterprises, VERs and any other schemes similar to those listed above, whether or not the measures are maintained under country-specific derogations from the provisions of the GATT 1947. The calculation of the tariff equivalents, whether expressed as *ad valorem* or specific rates, were to be made using the actual difference in internal and external prices for the years 1986–88.

12. The *ad valorem* equivalent of the pre- and post-Uruguay Round tariffs have not been calculated due to the high incidence of specific customs duties and other measures. Unlike *ad valorem* tariffs – which are assessed as a percentage of the value of imports of the particular product – specific tariffs are charges based on volumes of imports (for example, US$100 per ton of wheat) and cannot be easily converted to *ad valorem* tariffs. The simple average of the percentage reduction in *ad valorem* tariffs and specific duties charged on imports has, however, been calculated.

13. Punta del Este Declaration, Part I.B(vii).

10

What the Uruguay Round means: the case of Australia

GRAEME THOMSON

Establishing what the Uruguay Round outcome means for any one country (or group of countries) is no simple task. Trade reforms promote economic efficiency in the use of productive resources and when these reforms are implemented multilaterally the gains are enhanced by extending specialisation in production and consumption ('the division of labour . . . must always be limited . . . by the extent of the market', Adam Smith, *Wealth of Nations*). In addition to these traditional gains from trade liberalisation, the Uruguay Round offers benefits from the strengthening of GATT disciplines to reduce evasions of commitments, and from the inclusion within World Trade Organisation (WTO) disciplines of investment and other measures that have effects similar to border barriers to trade. The GATT rules are also extended by the Uruguay Round agreements to cover new areas of trade, including services, intellectual property and agriculture. All this liberalisation, strengthening of rules and expansion of coverage should serve to reduce uncertainties associated with production and consumption in Australia and in other countries.

Australian negotiators played an active role in the Uruguay Round. The results in terms of average reductions in tariffs on Australia's exports to major overseas markets were above the average reductions by industrial countries (see table 10.1). In addition, significant concessions were achieved in access to agricultural and primary commodity markets (coal) for the first time. These improvements in access to overseas markets were matched by unilateral liberalisation of the Australian import regime and the binding of 95 per cent of Australia's tariff lines, compared with 25 per cent after the Tokyo Round. These bindings are still at much higher levels than other OECD countries, but the applied rates are on the whole, well below the bound rates. The Uruguay Round negotiations helped to sustain reform and change in the Australian economy and made producers and consumers aware of the need to globalise their economic activities. Ultimately, the extent to which a country benefits from multilateral trade liberalisation and strengthening of the rules and disciplines depends on its

Table 10.1. *Bound tariff reductions on industrial products*

	Trade-weighted tariff averages	
	Pre-UR	Post-UR
Developing countries	6.3	3.8
United States	5.4	3.5
EU	5.7	3.6
Japan	3.9	1.7
Australia	19.3	10.9

Note:
UR=Uruguay Round.
Source: GATT/Department of Foreign Affairs and Trade.

domestic policies and the structural flexibility of its industries. Australia's adoption of structural reform while the Uruguay Round was in progress has enhanced competitiveness and created a good position from which to exploit the trade opportunities arising from the Round.

The Australian experience in the Uruguay Round demonstrates how small and medium-sized economies can secure new trade opportunities from multilateral negotiations. For the first time Australia went into a round of multilateral trade negotiations determined not only to be a 'wheeler' but also a 'dealer', with a vision based on important principles: in particular, to restore and improve the multilateral 'rules-based' trading system and to extend the scope of that system to include agriculture and other sectors neglected in earlier GATT Rounds. As a key participant in virtually all negotiating committees with its commitment to make the domestic adjustments, Australia achieved a place as an influential stakeholder in the Round. Australia established the Cairns Group of 'fair trading' agricultural countries, and was active in several important committees (for example, services and market access). This experience showed that medium-sized countries can play a role in trade negotiations, especially when the major players become deadlocked or attempt to force through their own solutions.

Like other small and medium-sized economies, Australia stands to gain from the re-securing of the GATT rules and the continuing operation of the free and open multilateral trading system under new WTO institutions. In recent years the GATT system has been in decline as contracting parties have by-passed the rules or sought solutions to trade difficulties that fall outside them. The maintenance of order and stability in the trading system is particularly important for the Western Pacific economies which have relied on expanding exports to underpin strong economic performance.

The expansion of effective participation in the Uruguay Round negotiations to a much larger number of countries as concerned and active players was of fundamental importance. Previous GATT Rounds involved less than twenty active countries. This time forty or more countries were significant participants. Importantly, East Asian economies were brought into the core group of participating countries. This helped to achieve a better balance between the traditional, dominant influence of North America and Western Europe, and the dynamic growth economies of East Asia and Latin America. This has also created some active new stakeholders in the WTO, with interests in securing the implementation of the Uruguay Round agreements and sustaining the long-term health of the liberal, multilateral trading system.

Developing countries will receive broadly equal treatment with other members in their rights and obligations under the new WTO rules and agreements. While longer transition times and lower levels of commitments are still provided, there is no wholesale 'special and differential' treatment accorded developing countries. This should promote economic development and strengthen demands for equal treatment in trade liberalisation and under the trade rules of the new institution. The Uruguay Round Agreement establishing the WTO is a single undertaking which precludes exemptions or reservations on specific agreements. (This does not apply to the Plurilateral Trade Agreements on civil aviation, government procurement, bovine meat, and dairy products.)

Finally, negotiations are continuing under some agreements (for example, the General Agreement on Trade in Services, or GATS) and will recommence with reviews of progress with the implementation of some other agreements in 1999 (for example, agriculture and TRIPs). These commitments will make the liberalisation of trade a continuing process and the widening of WTO membership will spread the benefits of economic integration. At the same time, the Uruguay Round took major steps to strengthen GATT dispute settlement procedures for resolving trade disputes. This may be one of the most significant outcomes of the Round.

All these changes will increase the predictability of trade and investment throughout the globe. The magnitude of the benefits for the international economy are examined above (part II), and some of the hazards of estimating trade and income changes are reviewed. Estimating the effects of the Uruguay Round changes on the Australian economy is an attempt to show what individual countries may expect to achieve.

Estimating Uruguay Round effects

The Round is estimated to add about US$3.3 billion (A$4.4 billion) per year to Australian incomes when fully implemented (Industry Commission, 1994); US$1 billion in additional exports will accrue to agriculture (Andrews *et al.*, 1994). The overall increase in annual exports is estimated to be US$4 billion (8 per cent higher than they would have been without the Uruguay Round liberalisation). These are static gains arising from tariff reductions and the Agricultural Agreement. Liberalisation from the GATS and other agreements and strengthening of GATT trade rules are not included in the model. No dynamic effects are allowed for (see chapters 6 and 7).

In the industrial sector, the average tariff reduction on Australia's exports to her main trading partners is calculated at 53.5 per cent (trade-weighted basis). Within this, the average cut by Japan is 75 per cent, United States 57 per cent, Republic of Korea 68 per cent, EU 49 per cent, India 27 per cent and Thailand 33 per cent. With manufactured exports comprising an increasing component in Australia's exports, these improvements in access and returns are important. Exports from the non-agricultural sectors are expected to increase by US$1.5 billion a year by the end of the implementation period, with most of the benefits occurring in the first five years (Industry Commission, 1994).

Particular benefits will flow to the coal industry, non-ferrous metals, pharmaceuticals, medical and scientific equipment, construction equipment, beer and steel. The coal industry will derive significant benefits, with exports estimated to rise by US$750 million a year by 2002 as a result of the agreement negotiated with the EU. The EU has agreed to a standstill on subsidies for coal production, followed by an annual reduction of subsidies.

The agricultural package negotiated in the Round contains important and lasting benefits for the Australian farm sector. These benefits will result from improvements in market access and reductions in domestic price support and export subsidies. Estimates indicate that by 1999, the implementation date for the Agricultural Agreement, Australia's beef exports should increase by US$250 million, dairy products by US$160 million, grain exports by US$280 million, rice exports by US$25 million and sugar exports by US$7 million. Other farm sectors should also benefit.

In terms of market access, there is reason for some disappointment with the Uruguay Round outcomes. The United States and the EU focused their attention on achieving a bilateral package, with only occasional reference to major outsiders such as Japan. In consequence, the scope of agreements was scaled down where these two major players had mutual interests. This twice eroded the Agreement on agriculture in the final stages of the round (the Blair House Accord), and this, in turn, opened the way for US negotiators to reduce the US contribution to market access liberalisation. This triggered spiralling but selective reduction by both EU and US negotiators in areas of particular sensitivity, including textiles and clothing, electronics, scientific equipment, and ultimately non-ferrous metals (especially aluminium). The GATS was also constrained by US–EU bilateral tensions. Each of these had significant interest for Western Pacific countries and affected their benefits adversely. In the process of pulling key elements of the market access package apart, an opportunity was provided for many other participants to pull back from earlier offers, or to refrain from making expected improvements as part of final efforts to obtain overall balance in the commitments. Efforts in the final days of the negotiations were directed at halting the backsliding rather than extending or enlarging the scope of the Final Act. Faced with diminishing contributions, Australia also cut-back some of its offers.

Another disappointment for Australia was the failure to conclude an agreement on trade in steel and steel products. Strictly speaking, the steel negotiations were not part of the Uruguay Round. However, talks on steel ran in parallel with the Uruguay Round negotiations, and failure to reach agreement left a major area for future trade disputes.

Agriculture

While the GATT was intended to cover agricultural trade as much as other trade, many of the rules and disciplines were ineffective because of the exceptions and waivers granted. The major industrial countries see agriculture as a special case, with the livelihood of farmers regarded as a social or cultural rather than an economic issue.

When the Uruguay Round negotiations began in 1986, the EU and the United States were engaged in an agricultural trade war using a heavy-handed combination of price supports, export subsidies, and market access controls to protect domestic agricultural production. Total transfers from taxpayers and consumers to agricultural sectors were estimated to be US$335 billion in 1993, with 88 per cent of the distortions occurring in the United States, the EU and Japan (OECD, 1994b).

The Australian government had a clear view of what it wanted to achieve from the early stages of the Uruguay Round: to bring agricultural trade within the purview of GATT rules. This required removing discrimination in trade by adopting most-favoured-nation (Mfn) tariffs as the only acceptable form of protection, greater acceptance of market forces in price determination as a way to improve competition and to stabilise world prices for agricultural products. Agricultural trade has been an area of major trade disputes, often involving the major countries, so strengthening GATT dispute settlement procedures was crucial.

Despite its slowly diminishing significance in Australia's total exports, the agricultural sector still accounted for half Australia's export earnings when the Uruguay Round negotiations began. Agricultural trade featured high among Australia's interests. In forming the Cairns Group of 'fair trading' agricultural countries (August 1986),[1] the intention was to provide a third force to confront the EU and the United States in the agricultural negotiations.

The Cairns Group accounts for 20 per cent of world agricultural exports. The members have a combined population equal to that of the EU and the United States together. The Group met resolutely both at ministerial and at ambassadorial level in Geneva during the Uruguay Round negotiations. At an early stage in the negotiations, the Cairns Group decided to address the basic problems in agricultural trade. The Group insisted on specific formula-based reductions in three areas:

- domestic supports (e.g. price supports)
- market access (e.g. import quotas, variable levies, tariffs)
- export competition (subsidies).

This represented a major change in the approach to agricultural negotiations in the GATT. Previously, efforts had been confined to border measures and had not focused on domestic policies. This was a major challenge. The agricultural settlement in the Uruguay Round addresses the cycle of over-production/price support/rising trade barriers/ export disposal problems, entrenched in most of the OECD countries. But this was not achieved without some obstinacy on the part of Cairns Group members, both at the Mid-Term Review (Montreal, December 1988) and at the GATT Ministerial Meeting (Brussels, December 1990). The Cairns Group adopted the position that the Uruguay Round could not conclude successfully without substantial results on agriculture and held tenaciously to this position (Cairns Group Ministerial Communiqués: Bariloche, 23–26 February 1988; Waitangi, 17–19 March 1989; Chang Mai, 21–23 November 1989). Without these efforts the Agricultural Agreement would have been much less far-reaching. The Cairns Group members decided in Marrakesh that they should continue to meet, to ensure that the agreement is implemented properly and to keep agricultural trade reform prominently on the WTO agenda.

The Agreement on Agriculture is in three parts.

Market access
This is guaranteed by the 'tariffication' of all existing measures of protection. Quantitative restrictions on imports, embargoes, variable import levies, minimum import schemes, etc. must be converted to tariff equivalents. These tariff equivalents must then be reduced by 36 per cent over the six-year implementation period, and bound. Within that average cut, the minimum reduction on any tariff must be 15 per cent. Any tariff that exceeds the bound rates must be renegotiated with trade partners, who may demand compensation. Developing countries are required to undertake the same procedures, but tariffication and reductions (minimum 10 per cent) can be phased in over ten years.

Domestic support
Measures that distort agricultural trade must be reduced by 20 per cent overall. This places a cap on over-production which has severely distorted world agriculture markets. However, genuine relief to farmers by way of so-called 'green box' measures can continue, for disaster relief, research, disease control, infrastructure assistance, environment protection, and food security. A major disappointment for the Cairns Group was the watering down of this commitment by allowing it to be applied on an aggregate basis rather than commodity by commodity as proposed in the Dunkel Draft Final Act (1991) and the generous extension of green box measures to include CAP payments and US deficiency payments.

Export subsidies
These are reduced according to both value and quantity, and applied commodity by commodity rather than on an aggregate basis, as is the case with market access and domestic supports.

This 'triple discipline' was fought for by the Cairns Group. The EU wished only to undertake commitments on money expenditure. If agreed, this would have allowed governments subsidising exports to switch expenditure between commodities and markets, and would have reduced the discipline. Countries are required to reduce the value of direct export subsidies to a level 36 per cent below the 1986–90 average, and to reduce the quantity of subsidised exports by 21 per cent. In consequence, there will be 50 million tonnes less of subsidised wheat and flour on world markets over the period 1995–2000. World markets for other products will also be improved: 1 million tonnes less of subsidised beef, 1 million tonnes less of subsidised rice, and over 400,000 tonnes less of subsidised cheese than if export subsidy levels had simply continued at 1994 levels. These cuts in export subsidies will relieve downward pressures on international prices. Without the Uruguay Round, subsidies might have increased.

Australian commitments to reduce assistance to agriculture will be small because domestic protection is already low: reduced support for tobacco, removal of sales tax concessions on fruit and vegetable juices (Industry Commission, 1994); a few products will experience marginal reductions in tariff protection.

The complexity of the individual market sectors makes it difficult to summarise the outcomes, although some are obviously very significant. The market for meat will be significantly liberalised with the elimination of widespread quotas, and renewed assurances given that the EU will not ship subsidised beef into Australia's key Asian markets. Significant advances have been made on the grains market, particularly with Japan and South Korea agreeing to begin opening their rice markets. Measurable improvements have been gained in access to the ASEAN and US dairy markets and the United States has undertaken to reduce sales of subsidised skim milk powder. Other modest advances were made in sugar, fish and horticulture. The phasing-out of the Multifibre Arrangement (MFA) over ten years should have positive effects for wool and cotton prices.

The Uruguay Round outcomes provide opportunities for Australian agriculture. World agricultural trade will be fairer and freer, though markets will remain fiercely competitive, particularly in terms of quality control, product development, marketing, distribution and financing. Australia's primary producers will have to adapt to remain competitive. The temptation by some governments to backslide will require vigilance during the implementation period. The major achievement has been to bring agricultural trade within the multilateral trading rules and the binding of agricultural protection levels. Continuation of the liberalisation process depends on the achievements during the implementation period and the attitudes adopted in the resumed negotiations in 1999. The WTO Committee on Agriculture, established as part of the settlement, will monitor implementation of the Agriculture Agreement.

The Agreement on the application of sanitary and phytosanitary (SPS) measures also has direct relevance to agricultural trade. It builds on existing GATT rules to prevent the use of quarantine measures for trade protection. The agreement maintains the sovereign right of any government to provide the health protection it deems appropriate, but takes steps to prevent misuse of SPS measures to create barriers to international trade.

Table 10.2. *Countries that Australia negotiated with in the Uruguay Round*

Argentina	Austria	Brazil	Canada	EU
Finland	Hong Kong	India	Indonesia	Japan
Korea	Malaysia	Mexico	Norway	Pakistan
Philippines	Poland	Romania	South Africa	Singapore
Sri Lanka	Sweden	Switzerland	Thailand	United States

The transparency of SPS measures is improved. Members have to establish that measures are taken after an appropriate assessment of the actual risks and, if requested, must make known the basis of such assessments, including the level of risk regarded as acceptable. The agreement clarifies that measures to ensure food safety and to protect animal and plant health should be based on objective and accurate scientific data. A committee of the WTO Council – the SPS Committee – will review compliance with the Agreement, discuss potential trade impacts, and cooperate with appropriate technical organisations. In a trade dispute arising from the application of SPS measures, the WTO dispute settlement procedures will be used and advice from scientific experts may be sought.

Non-agricultural trade

Australian industries have much-improved access to foreign markets as a result of the Uruguay Round. Nearly 80 per cent of processed and manufactured exports have improved and there is more predictable market access through bound tariff commitments by major trading partners, including developing countries. The average bound tariff facing Australian exports of non-agricultural products will be less than 2 per cent. Some high tariffs and other barriers remain in some markets, but a major improvement was achieved in the Uruguay Round. Nearly 50 per cent of all Australia's exports will enjoy duty-free access to significant markets; less than 6 per cent of Australia's exports of industrial products will face tariffs higher than 15 per cent following the negotiations.

Australia negotiated bilaterally with twenty-five trading partners, according to the traditional GATT 'offer and request' procedures (see table 10.2). (Various across-the-board formulae for tariff reductions were rejected in favour of parallel bilateral negotiations on an offer and request basis on market access.)

Major trading countries will eliminate tariffs over ten years on pharmaceuticals, construction equipment, furniture, medical equipment, beer, distilled spirits and paper. Most OECD countries will harmonise tariffs on chemicals at low levels. The EU's commitment to reduce subsidies for coal production for the first time is a major outcome for Australia: subsidised coal production in Germany and other EU countries will be largely phased out by 2002. Some other countries have also improved market access for coal imports. Overall coal exports from Australia are expected to rise by US$1 billion a year.

Australian exports of non-agricultural products will be US$3.3 billion a year higher when the Uruguay Round liberalisation is fully implemented (Industry Commission, 1994). Australia's commitments to liberalise import barriers in the Round can be met largely within the current programme of unilateral tariff cuts announced in 1988 and 1991. On light beer and some medical equipment the tariff cuts need to continue beyond 1996 levels, to become zero in 1999. If the continuing steel negotiations reach an agreement, Australia may be required to eliminate some steel tariffs over ten years.

Australia's commitments in the Round amount to a 44 per cent reduction in the bound tariff average, giving an average bound trade-weighted tariff of 10.9 per cent after full implementation. Tariffs on 97 per cent of merchandise imports and 95 per cent of tariff lines will be bound. Most of Australia's commitments will be ceiling bindings, and applied tariff rates will generally be lower. By July 2000, the government's current tariff-cutting programme will be completed and the average applied tariff will be less than 2.9 per cent. The higher applied tariffs will be 25 per cent for apparel and 15 per cent for passenger motor vehicles; all other tariffs will be at or below 5 per cent.

According to the Industry Commission's estimates, total merchandise exports will be 8 per cent higher when the Round's agreements are fully implemented, while imports will be 7 per cent higher. These figures indicate greater specialisation in production and consumption as a result of Uruguay Round liberalisation. Adjustment in Australia's industrial structure, already under way with the unilateral trade liberalisation programme, creates an environment that will facilitate adoption of changes to take advantage of the new trade opportunities. These arise not only from improved access to overseas markets, but also from the faster growth generated throughout the world economy (see chapter 6).

Trade in services

The GATS provides a comprehensive framework of general rules for trade in services. An initial package of standstill and liberalisation measures applies only to services where a specific commitment has been made. This 'positive' list approach (as opposed to a 'negative' list approach where only exceptions are notified) has watered down the effectiveness of the GATS. It means also that negotiations are continuing to establish conditions that will allow more extensive commitments in some important service sectors (including maritime services, financial services and telecommunications). Negotiations have also begun on the role of qualifications and standards in trade in professional services. Nevertheless, a first step has been taken to include a significant traded sector in the WTO. The GATS requires negotiations to re-open in 1999.

International trade in services requires different rules from those applying to merchandise trade. Trade in services often requires establishment in the market itself. Local regulations governing such operations, and other factors such as movement of personnel to deliver the services, means that the GATS has a complex structure. It consists of (a) a Framework Agreement, (b) sectoral Annexes dealing with issues affecting specific services (financial services, personnel movements, telecommunications and aviation services) and (c) country-specific schedules of commitments on market access and national treatment. The Framework Agreement incorporates the GATT principles, such as Mfn treatment, national treatment, market access, transparency, the free flow of payments and transfers, and dispute settlement procedures.

International trade in services is growing at around 12 per cent a year, much faster than merchandise trade (GATT, 1989). The role of services has increased strongly in the Australian economy, accounting for 73 per cent of GDP in 1994. Services are valued at around 22 per cent of Australia's merchandise exports and income from services grew at more than 10 per cent a year in real terms during 1993–4 (DFAT, 1995). More than half this foreign income was from tourism, which is higher than for some high-profile sectors, such as coal, wool, iron ore and wheat. The United States and Japan are traditional markets for Australian service exports and the fast-growing markets in Asia offer new opportunities.

The adoption of a global agreement on the liberalisation of trade in services was an important outcome of the Uruguay Round for Australia. The GATS establishes rules to give transparency and non-discrimination in this rapidly expanding sector of international trade. It has also extended GATT rules into new areas such as foreign investment rules, which means that future negotiations will have wider scope. The GATS opens new areas of policy for economic liberalisation, and importantly, requires members to enter into a new round of services negotiations within five years.

Strengthening GATT rules

The Uruguay Round Final Act included the Agreement establishing the WTO as well as twenty ministerial Decisions, three ministerial Declarations and one Understanding (Annex 10.1). Most of the agreements are concerned with clarifying and elaborating GATT rules to reduce uncertainties in the multilateral trading system.

Two of the agreements represent a significant extension of GATT powers. The Agreement on trade-related aspects of intellectual property rights (TRIPs), addresses the problems of piracy and counterfeiting. It draws on existing treaties: the Paris Convention for the Protection of Industrial Property (1967), the Berne Convention for the Protection of Literary and Artistic Works (1971), the International Convention for the Protection of Performers, Producers of Phonograms and Broadcasting Organisations (Rome, 1961), and the Treaty on Intellectual Property in Respect of Integrated Circuits (Washington, 1989). Members are obliged to implement laws which provide protection as set down in these previous conventions. In addition, the Agreement recognises GATT principles: national treatment, Mfn treatment for all contracting parties, transparency of procedures, and now, dispute settlement processes as agreed in the Uruguay Round. Making the protection of intellectual property an integral part of the WTO establishes common standards for all contracting parties (the previous treaties had limited memberships – for example, the Rome Convention had only fifty-seven signatories).

Every year, export income is lost to Australia because of piracy and counterfeiting of patents, copyrights and trademarks in telecommunications, chemicals and pharmaceuticals. Creative material produced by artists, musicians, designers, etc. is similarly lost. Improved protection of intellectual property will help to protect these incomes. TRIPs will also facilitate technology-related investment and the transfer of technology to Australia and other countries. In the long run, this will increase economic growth prospects. Expansion of patent and trade mark applications lodged by Australians, both domestically and overseas, is among the fastest growing in the OECD: external patent applications filed by Australians between 1981 and 1991 increased by 17.5 per cent a year. Industries expected to benefit from TRIPs include wine-making, medical equipment and copyright materials (music, books, films, etc.).

The Agreement on trade-related investment measures (TRIMs) prohibits contracting parties from using investment measures that are inconsistent with GATT Articles III and XI. By attempting to reduce instruments that distort international trade flows and investment, this Agreement should also improve resource allocations and increase prospects for economic growth. The TRIMs Agreement reaffirms commitments to existing GATT disciplines, and identifies two measures as inconsistent with Articles III and XI: local content requirements (equivalent to import-content limits) and trade balancing requirements. Other TRIMs, such as export requirements, domestic sales targets and foreign exchange balancing restrictions, are not tackled. Inconsistent TRIMs have to be notified to the WTO within ninety days and are required to be phased out by industrial countries in two years, by developing countries in five years and by LDCs in seven years. By condoning the continuation of TRIMs that violate GATT obligations, this Agreement may be regarded as retrograde. The commitment to the TRIMs Agreement, however, does establish a framework for dealing with trade and investment issues. This Agreement also requires a future review of its operation, including an assessment of the need for provisions on investment policy and competition policy. The agenda of the WTO has been widened, even if the initial step is little more than a standstill on existing derogations from GATT rules.

The remaining agreements annexed to the WTO Agreement are concerned with strengthening GATT rules to restrict abuses and evasions. Contingency protection, which has become a serious issue since the end of the Tokyo Round (Robertson, 1992), comes under new scrutiny with new agreements on safeguards (Article XIX), subsidies and countervailing measures (Articles VI and XVI), anti-dumping (Article VI) and the Agreement on textiles and clothing. How effective these new agreements prove to be will depend on their implementation, but a serious effort was made in the Uruguay Round to close many gaps in the original GATT exceptions clauses. The anti-dumping provisions remain open for general use and the effectiveness of the Round's attack on 'grey-area' measures will depend on this weak link.

Many of the other agreements make incomplete attempts to deal with perceived weaknesses in GATT Articles: rules of origin, Article XXIV, customs procedures (Article VII, preshipment inspection, etc.), Articles XVII, XVIII and XXVIII, etc.

Australia has a strong interest in increasing predictability in trade and in strengthening trade rules to reduce opportunities for countries to evade commitments. In this context, the attempts made to close gaps in the rules are welcome. Uncertainty will also be reduced for small and medium-sized economies by the improved dispute settlement procedures.

Dispute settlement

International disputes are inevitable in the complex, competitive atmosphere of international economic relations. Settlements depend on sovereign nations being willing to submit to a dispute settlement procedure that may require changes to existing policies. GATT, and now the WTO, represents an institution that has an agreed set of processes for dealing with non-compliance by a Member. These processes have evolved based on case-law experience, the challenge is to maintain flexibility while retaining remedies against non-compliance.

The Uruguay Round negotiations reviewed dispute settlement because of widespread concerns that had evolved about delays and uncertainties. The understanding in the Final Act provides a unified dispute settlement procedure for all the agreements, and for the WTO. Many of the agreements have special or additional rules, procedures or dispute settlement provisions, and the separate negotiations during the Round did not allow the texts to be made fully consistent. In consequence it was agreed that the Dispute Settlement Understanding should apply to all of the other agreements, except where there are special or additional rules.

The Uruguay Round Agreement on dispute settlement takes GATT Articles XXII and XXIII, along with the procedural rules that had developed, and introduces a stricter and more legalistic regime. It provides for automatic progression from one step to the next, unless there is specific agreement by the parties not to proceed. In addition, the Dispute Settlement Body is established to supervise the new, consolidated process. This still seeks resolution outside the formal processes, where possible. The preliminary stage of consultations continues before any formal action is taken, but a strict time limit is introduced. Under the new procedures a panel is formed automatically; the panel stipulates deadlines for submissions and may seek expert technical advice and information from any source.

Introducing an Appellate Body is a major new provision. Seven experts in trade law are appointed; only three would be required for any appeal. No consensus is required for a panel's report to be adopted. Previously a 'defiant defendant' could prevent the adoption of the panel report by the GATT Council (or Tokyo Round Code Committees). Adoption is now automatic unless a member gives notice that it intends to appeal to the Appellate Body. The WTO Dispute Settlement Body may decide by consensus not to adopt a report. The Appellate Body may uphold, reverse or modify the decision of the panel. The deliberations however, are 'limited to issues of law covered in the panel report and legal interpretations developed by the panel' (Dispute Settlement Understanding, Article 17.6).

Within thirty days of the adoption of the Panel's report, a defendant must indicate how it intends to implement the decision. Where not implemented within a reasonable period of time, a complainant may seek compensation. If this fails, the complainant may request the Dispute Settlement Body to approve retaliation, using suspension of concessions or other obligations under the relevant Agreement. As in the past, the Agreement offers special procedures for developing countries and LDCs.

These new procedures provide a system of rules for the settlement of disputes. It is the most comprehensive procedure employed so far in international law and sets a new course towards a more 'legalistic' approach.

Australia's trade policy

During the past decade Australian attitudes to trade policy have undergone a revolutionary change with the adoption of unilateral dismantling of protection and industrial supports. The Uruguay Round negotiations, with their far-reaching objectives, could not have come at a better time in terms of Australia's capacity to adapt to the new trade opportunities the Round provided. The strengthening of GATT rules and the new dispute settlement procedures also increase Australian confidence in the WTO and the new open multilateral trading system it supports. Some worries remain about the spread of regionalism, anti-dumping legislation and bilateralism, but the Uruguay Round Final Act has dealt with much of the recent backsliding.

In some respects the Uruguay Round outcomes fell short of Australia's original hopes after the Punte del Este Declaration, especially in agriculture, processed minerals and certain industrial products and services. Estimating the benefits from the Uruguay Round outcomes, however, probably under-states the actual gains that will occur by the end of the implementation stage. Estimates using various economic models have tended to focus on traditional trade liberalisation of tariffs and other easily quantifiable changes; this time, agriculture and textiles and clothing were included for the first time. Nevertheless, the benefits to Australia in terms of increased real incomes and net gains in the trade balance are valuable, even measured using static analysis, and are much higher than from any earlier GATT Round.

Even so, the main benefits for Australia, like other participants, are likely to arise from dismantling of trade barriers and strengthening of rules that are difficult to estimate, either because of uncertainties about the real content of the complex agreements or because of insufficient technical background to measure the effects (for example, trade in services, TRIPs, etc.). The main achievement in some agreements may only be a standstill against new protectionism. But these agreements also contain machinery for review and extension that provide a firm foundation for future liberalisation across a broad front and for strengthening of disciplines under the WTO. GATS, TRIPs, TRIMs and agriculture will all begin reviews in 1999.

Making the WTO Agreement a single undertaking (with the exception of the four plurilateral agreements which may be acceded to separately) has given new strength to the WTO. Both in terms of active signatories and the scope of the agreements, this provides a strong foundation for future liberalisation. Apart from the largest players, all members depend on a rules-based trading system for their well-being in international economic relations.

NOTE

1. The Cairns Group met at Australian invitation in Cairns in August 1986. Its members are Argentina, Australia, Brazil, Canada, Chile, Colombia, Fiji, Hungary, Indonesia, Malaysia, Philippines, New Zealand, Thailand and Uruguay.

11

Competition policies as irritants to East Asian trade

J. DAVID RICHARDSON

Even before the Uruguay Round negotiations were concluded, a new agenda of trade issues was being compiled, and in some cases used to belittle the Uruguay Round achievements as the answer to yesterday's problems (Feketekuty, 1992; OECD, 1992). Prominent on the new trade agenda are divergences in domestic competition policies; the other major issues are the environment and trade, policies on foreign investment and labour standards. All these issues involve domestic economic policies and intrude on domestic policies in ways previously not accepted in trade negotiations. The Uruguay Round agenda encouraged negotiations on trade in services and trade-related investment measures (TRIMs) which necessarily resulted in incursions into domestic regulations (for example, financial sectors). These negotiations led on to discussions of many domestic policies previously regarded as outside the GATT sphere of interest.

One of the most contentious new agenda items is competition policies. The debate concerns two main aspects: substantive differences between countries' competition policies (anti-trust, price restraints, etc.), and differences in the application of these policies as between domestic and foreign enterprises. This leads to three main questions.

- Are competition policies significant irritants to global trade and investment?
- Do they cause significant inefficiencies to global trade and investment?
- If so, what could, and should, be done to reduce/eliminate these distortions?

Competition policies have become a significant source of international friction between several East Asian economies and the EU and US authorities. Intense competition from East Asian industries, in the form of exports and foreign investment flows, has aroused concerns about domestic market structures as well as market access. The objections to competition policies and their implementation are receiving attention in bilateral negotiations as well as in multilateral fora, and they will be a major issue on the WTO agenda. The specific issues still have to be defined precisely, but it is evident that discussions and negotiations will proceed at global, regional and bilateral levels in the coming years.

Basic issues

Two problems motivate concerns about competitive distortions. First, private business practices can act as barriers to market access that impede international trade and investment. This makes them contrary to the spirit (if not always the letter) of the GATT and other international agreements. Traditionally, most such private practices fall within the domain of anti-trust laws and policies, a sub-set of competition policies. The standards of nations, however, in the application of these laws and policies are not uniform.[1] Indeed, many nations have not formally implemented any competition laws or policies. Competition-policy conventions at an international level are thought by some to be one means to reduce such barriers to global market competition.

Second, in some areas the impacts of international commercial policy and competition policy overlap, but actual practices differ.[2] In these cases, it would be desirable to make the two sets of policies consistent so that they do not act against each other[3] and, if possible, to move them toward 'best practice'.

To address these concerns wisely requires more detailed research. First it is necessary to identify domains of competition policy that are relevant to international trade. Second, the extent of international divergence and of internal inconsistency in commercial and competition policies has to be established and measured, with special emphasis on substantive differences among national policies that create economic inefficiency and/or international tension.[4] Third, the extent of average divergence from some definition of 'best practice' has to be determined (Graham and Richardson, forthcoming).

Substantive international competition-policy issues

Priority global issues in international competition policies have been identified and grouped in tables 11.1 and 11.2.

Column (1) in table 11.1 and 11.2 classifies issues according to market structure, firm conduct, exemptions, trade policy, or other. These categories are not always mutually exclusive – for example, predation (classified under firm conduct) is very similar to anti-dumping (classified under

Table 11.1. *Criteria for a global competition-policy agenda: detail*

			State of convergence	
Category (1)	Economic clarity (2)	Toward best practice (3)	Toward each other (4)
---	---	---	---
I *Issues pertaining to market structure*			
Cartelisation	Clear	Low	High
Unwarranted horizontal restraints	Clear	Moderate	Moderate
Vertical arrangements			
• resale price arrangements	Murky	. . .	Low
• foreclosure	Murky	. . .	Low
Strategic alliances	Murky	. . .	Low
Mergers and acquisitions regulation	Clear minus	Moderate	Moderate
II *Issues pertaining to firm conduct*			
Predation	Clear minus	. . .	Moderate
Price-fixing	Clear	High	High
Price discrimination	Clear minus	. . .	Moderate
Abuse of market power	Murky	. . .	Low
III *Exemptions*			
Functional (e.g. for research and development)	Murky	. . .	Moderate
Sectoral (e.g. for telecommunications)	Murky	. . .	Moderate
Temporal (e.g. for recession cartels)	Murky	. . .	Low
'Efficiency defence'	Murky	. . .	Low
IV *Trade policy measures raising competition concerns*			
VERs, OMAs, etc.	Clear	Low	Low
VIEs	clear minus	Moderate	Low
Anti-dumping	Clear	Low	Low but becoming higher
National treatment issues			
• for imports	Clear	High	High
• for foreign direct investors	Clear	Moderate	Moderate but becoming lower
V *Other related issues*			
Intellectual property protection	Murky	. . .	Moderate but becoming higher
State aids to industry/subsidies			
research and development	Murky	. . .	Low
production	Clear minus	Moderate	Low

Note:
. . . Indicates that best practice is not clearly delineated and/or controversial.

Table 11.1 *cont.*

Category (1)	Feasibility of further convergence[a] (5)	Gains from further convergence[a]	
		Efficiency gains (6)	Conflict reduction (7)
I *Issues pertaining to market structure*			
Cartelisation	Moderate	High	Moderate/High
Unwarranted horizontal restraints	Moderate	High	Low/Moderate
Vertical arrangements			
• resale price arrangements	Moderate	Low	Low
• foreclosure	Moderate	Low	High
Strategic alliances	?	Moderate	?
Mergers and acquisitions regulation	Moderate/High	Moderate	Moderate
II *Issues pertaining to firm conduct*			
Predation	Low	High	High[a]
Price-fixing	High	High	Low
Price discrimination	Low/Moderate	Low	High
Abuse of market power	Low	Indeterminate	Low
III *Exemptions*			
Functional (e.g. for research and development)	Moderate	Low/ Moderate	High
Sectoral (e.g. for telecommunications)	Low but improving	Moderate	High
Temporal (e.g. for recession cartels)	Moderate	Moderate	Moderate
'Efficiency defence'	Low	Indeterminate	Moderate
IV *Trade policy measures raising competition concerns*			
VERs, OMAs, etc.	High[b]	High	Moderate
VIEs	?	High	High
Anti-dumping	Low	High	High
National treatment issues			
• for imports	(in place)	Low	Low
• for foreign direct investors	Moderate	Moderate/ High	Moderate but growing
V. *Other related issues*			
Intellectual property protection	Moderate/High[b]	Moderate	High
State aids to industry/subsidies			
research and development	Moderate[b]	Moderate	Moderate/High
production	Moderate[b]	Moderate	Moderate/High

Notes:
[a]Toward each other and/or towards best practice.
[b]Based on successes and failures in GATT negotiations during the Uruguay Round.
? indeterminate.

Table 11.2. *Criteria for a global competition-policy agenda: summary*

Category (1)	Economic clarity (2)	State of convergence		Feasibility of further convergence[b] (5)	Gains from further convergence[a]	
		Toward best practice (3)	Toward each other (4)		Efficiency gains (6)	Conflict reduction (7)
I Issues pertaining to market structure	Clear minus	Moderate	Moderate	Moderate	Moderate	Moderate
II Issues pertaining to firm conduct	Clear minus	...	Moderate	Low	Moderate	Moderate
III Exemptions	Murky	...	Low	Moderate	Moderate	High
IV Trade policy measures raising competition concerns	Clear	Low	Moderate	Moderate	High	High
V Other related issues	Murky	...	Moderate	Moderate	Moderate	High

Notes:

... Indicates that best practice is not clearly delineated and/or controversial.

[a]Toward each other and/or towards best practice.

[b]Based on successes and failures in GATT negotiations during the Uruguay Round.

trade policy). These categories allow substantively similar issues to be placed in separate categories if the regulatory process treats them separately.

Column (2) in table 11.1 and 11.2 is an attempt to categorise these issues by the criterion of economic clarity – whether there is strong consensus among economists as to what is best practice towards the issue. If there is such a consensus, the issue is labelled as 'Clear', whereas if there is no such consensus, the issue is described as 'Murky'. On some issues where a majority consensus exists but also a minority of specialists who disagree, the category 'Clear minus' is used. No attempt is made to explain the consensus position.

If there is to be any sort of international convergence on the issues listed, the best practice with respect to the issue should be clear or, at least, clear minus (columns (3)–(4)).[5] If there is no intellectual consensus on what is the best practice, international convergence would serve no function. Indeed, it could be counterproductive. What would be the point of converging on a bad practice?

Columns (3)–(7) in tables 11.1 and 11.2 describe aspects of convergence with respect to each practice. Columns (3)–(4) describe the status quo; columns (5)–(7) describe the feasibility and desirability of changing the status quo, with respect to reducing both inefficiency and international conflict.

Column (5) indicates feasibility of further convergence. That is political feasibility, whether there is any consensus among policy officials and legislatures about what would be normatively better practice. Low feasibility refers to (a) substantial difference among officials of different nations on desirable practice; or (b) a substantial difference between branches of a single government as to desirable practice.[6] If an issue is not characterised by a high or at least a moderate level of feasibility in this sense, there is probably little hope of any convergence.

Column (6) represents an effort to judge gains in terms of economic efficiency from moving to a regime where there is some sort of convergence upon best practice. In areas where the substantively best practice is murky, a judgement is made about the efficiency implications of continuing practices that economists agree lead to inefficiencies.[7] One way of looking at this judgement is: if economists agree on what is substantively best practice, and this agreement has economic merit, what would be gained? (Column (7) represents a similar effort to judge gains from conflict reduction.)

The areas where a triad of at least moderate clarity, feasibility, and efficiency is present are:

- cartelisation;
- other horizontal restraints;
- mergers and acquisitions;
- price-fixing;
- VERs, OMAs, etc.;
- national treatment for foreign direct investors and services.[8]

Several important areas of conflict do not make this list although they have high efficiency and conflict-reduction implications. These include anti-dumping (implying predatory pricing) and voluntary import expansions (VIEs). Efficiency gains would be substantial here if the political will existed to implement reforms (Itoh and Nagaoka, Lipstein and Krugman, in Graham and Richardson, forthcoming). Intellectual property and related issues remain unclear because the debate over welfare trade-offs between strong intellectual property protection (which can foster monopoly or single-firm dominance but also foster technological advancement) and greater rivalry will never be fully resolved. State aids to industry also remain controversial. (Is there such a thing as a good subsidy?) Among these issues, the last three do not make the list because the underlying economics of each issue remains murky. Hence what is normatively best practice is difficult to determine. The first does not make the list because it is politically infeasible at the present time.

Column (7) in tables 11.1 and 11.2 indicates issues where failure to reach any sort of convergence will lead to high or growing international tension. Remarkable and disturbing is the observation that many of the issues rated are quite dissimilar from items where there is both some hope for and some gain to be had from convergence.

There is no obvious elixir to the malady posed by this disjointedness. It is clear that most of the global competition issues on which it is important to achieve substantive convergence (judging by the criteria in tables 11.1 and 11.2) are ones on which it will be difficult to reach any sort of consensus (judging by the criteria of columns (3)–(4) of the tables).

Substantive issues in an Asia Pacific context

How would the classifications (tables 11.1 and 11.2) look if the information were restricted to the Asia Pacific theatre? What would be the priority issues in competition policies?

They would be different. Any answer would begin with: 'because of variant conceptions of firms, markets, competition, conglomerates, alliances, and correspondingly variant philosophies of competition policy' (Matsushita and Rosenthal, in Graham and Richardson, forthcoming).

Asian firms are sometimes historical extensions of families, or socially construct themselves that way. External capital markets play less of a role in monitoring and directing Asian firms; internal discussion and decision-making are more important. (Hence Japan has been characterised as a market economy, but not a capitalist one.) Incumbency is usually honoured; attempted entry is often seen as an affront. Maximisation of market share may be explicitly pursued;[9] its consequence may be foreclosure or exit (due, arguably, to predation). The largest Asian firms are usually diversified conglomerates, much more so than elsewhere in the world.[10] Conglomeration does not automatically imply either horizontal or vertical concentration. Hence concentration is not itself a focus of competition policy except in so far as it affects market power and its abuse. Yet conglomerates raise unique issues: Are there institutional barriers to external takeovers of one or another narrow product line? So certain product lines protect others from competition via cross-subsidisation? Is conglomeration in general a deterrent to entry and, if so, does the deterrence discriminate against foreign firms?

In terms of specific entries in an Asia Pacific version of tables 11.1 and 11.2, there are likely to be wider gaps and larger gains from increasing convergence on vertical arrangements, especially foreclosure (both efficiency gains and conflict reduction), strategic alliances, exemptions, and national treatment for investors. On exemptions and national treatment, the gaps are sometimes quite large. Formal competition policies are at early stages in some countries, each sector is treated uniquely as an exemption, and formal acceptance of national treatment for investors is a long way off. An important type of exemption to normal competition policies in East Asia is the degree of reliance on export processing zones with special or uniquely advantageous competition-policy rules. This is an example of a geographical exemption from normal competition policy.

Investment disparities may be eased as more East Asian economies apply to join the OECD (Korea is intending to join the OECD formally in 1997; negotiations to do so have prominently concerned investment and national treatment), and a reduction in exemptions from competition-policy requirements may take place as part of the process of negotiations described below. In addition, as East Asian markets in financial services liberalise and deregulate, and become subject to normal competition-policy strictures, there will be a natural tendency for information markets to work more swiftly and predictably, especially for information about corporate plans and performance, supplied by accountants, brokers, and industry specialists, bond and credit-rating agencies. Better markets for information, in turn, make other markets work more competitively, one of the most common goals of competition policy.

Alternatives for an international competition-policy process

There are three generic alternative means by which competition policies can be carried into international markets, to reach situations that fall outside or spill over any particular nation's borders: (i) via non-cooperative unilateral actions; (ii) via cooperative unilateral actions; or (iii) via variants of supranational mechanisms.

The status quo default option includes all unilateral actions or efforts undertaken by one nation to reach objectionable practices in some other nation.[11] The shortcomings of non-cooperative unilateralism are immediately apparent. There is no consensus among national authorities as to what action, if any, is warranted. If the differences in the objectives of nations are substantial, as seems the case in the Asia Pacific region, the actions of one could generate severe frictions. A target country might respond with blocking statutes or other measures designed to frustrate the nation initially taking action. Indeed, column (7) of tables 11.1 and 11.2 could be seen as a judgement of how much friction is, or could be, generated by unilateral actions on issues of competition policy.[12]

Supranational mechanisms have been implemented within the EU. The European supranational authority has worked quite well overall (Vernon and Nicolaïdis, in Graham and Richardson, forthcoming). Only a few cases decided by the EU Competition Directorate (DGIV) have caused significant internal frictions within the EU (for example, the de Havilland case). The European experience, however, is probably not repeatable at the international level. Early on, the member states of what is now the European Union were willing to allow the European Court of Justice to act as final arbiter on competition-policy cases, and this court generally has sided with DGIV and enhanced the powers of the agency. This willingness has allowed competition issues within Europe to transcend national sovereignty. It is very unlikely that sovereign states not presently members of the EU or seeking to become members would be willing to cede sovereignty to a supranational agency to a similar extent.

The Australia/New Zealand experience (Thomson, in Graham and Richardson, forthcoming), by contrast, suggests some substitutes for supranationality that could be adopted more generally. These are largely consistent with cooperative unilateralism (alternative (ii) above). This approach has much promise. The following might be achievable.

Positive comity

Under positive comity, a national government which held a grievance that pertained to another nation's competition policy (for example, private practices that created barriers to imports or direct investments) would appeal to the authorities of that nation to investigate and, if appropriate, to take action under their own competition laws to address the grievance. In responding to the complaint, these authorities would take into account the interests of the complaining nation. Both the NAFTA Agreement and the September 1991 Agreement Regarding Application of Their Competition Laws between the United States and the EC Commission provide guidelines for positive comity.[13]

One extension of positive comity might be enlargement of the rights of firms (including foreign firms) to bring private cases before competition-policy authorities (or the courts) of the relevant country where there was an alleged violation of its competition laws. These rights might be made contingent on a demonstration of material injury (even if this injury was of the nature of lost opportunity) to the firm (Jackson, 1990). Another extension might be to increase the scope for cooperative investigation and regulation of conduct that crossed national boundaries (for example, where mergers or alliances were transborder in nature).

Extension of WTO (or other international) consultation and dispute settlement procedures into the domain of competition policy

Consultation provisions are a natural and necessary companion of positive comity. Extending WTO dispute settlement, however, to encompass competition policy would require the creation of a body of international competition law and/or experience,[14] something that seems unlikely in the near future given the considerations outlined above. Thus, any extension of international dispute settlement mechanisms will be dependent upon implementation of law and policy at the national level.

An oversight mechanism

What might be envisaged is a procedure for situations where one government is aggrieved by private practices occurring within the jurisdiction of another government, and it is not satisfied with the results of consultation with the relevant authorities and an appeal to positive comity. If it believes that the impasse is the result of improper application of the second country's law, the first country could then appeal to an impartial expert body whose function would be to investigate and report on the alleged improper application. This body would have to be accorded full access to the record of the proceedings of the authorities of the country it was investigating. A promising model for this regard is the procedure established under the Canada–US Trade Agreement (CUSTA) for reviews of anti-dumping and subsidies cases. National law still prevails but an international tribunal can, under certain circumstances, investigate and report on whether proper procedure has been followed under national law.

One question that arises is: what could happen if the expert body were to rule that, indeed, the application of the law had been improper? One possibility would be to allow the complaining country to impose sanctions by withdrawing concessions under the GATT. The sanctions would have to be commensurate with the losses suffered by aggrieved parties. Who would determine what would be the magnitude of these? Under current procedures, the complaining country makes this calculation. A more acceptable approach might be to allow the expert body to recommend on this and also give it the power to determine whether any sanctions actually carried out were consistent with its recommendations. (There is little logic to this, of course, because sanctions tend to aggravate the losses of the complaining country and cannot mitigate the losses of the complaining industry.)

These proposals would give the impartial body more power than present GATT panels. However, for there to be any meaningful international application of competition policy, these proposals represent something like a minimal set. Anything less seems too weak to be meaningful. At the same time, these proposals would not be subject to a standard argument against any effort to bring competition policy into the GATT, notably that to do so would weaken existing national or regional law and policy. Implementation of these proposals certainly would not have this effect.

Process in the Asia Pacific region

Which of these elements of international process for competition policy might have relevance in the Asia Pacific region? Competition-policy issues will remain a significant friction and source of inefficiency in Asia Pacific trade relations (tables 11.1 and 11.2). Moreover, these issues will grow in intensity.

Neither positive comity nor consultation rights and obligations need be threatening, and both are naturally implemented on a bilateral basis. But recent attempts at bilateral discussions of grievances, especially by the United States in the Structural Impediments Initiative (SII) and 'framework' talks with Japan and Korea, have achieved only moderate success; they may have increased grievances rather than resolving them. This is no doubt why the APEC Eminent Persons Group (EPG) has recommended 'multilateralising' the grievance-resolution process (EPG, 1994). With respect to competition-policy questions, for example, a commitment to five annual reports on the state of and trends in barriers to competition within the Asia Pacific domain, prepared by an APEC multinational team, would increase information on these issues. More ambitious ideas for future implementation might be gleaned from provisions of the Havana Charter chapters on restrictive business practices, prescient for their time (see the appendix below).

An Asia Pacific process on 'Trade-Related Competition-Policy Measures' would not have to begin with the full range of substantive issues, either. Investment issues and national treatment might be an important yet tractable place to start (EPG, 1994). Joint report drafting, as practised in the SII, might be a fruitful way to begin exploring thornier substance, such as anti- and pro-competitive aspects of vertical arrangements and the value of private access and judicial oversight. Among other things, such joint studies might allow the time for apolitical reflection on both competition and competition policies.

There is scope for both cooperative unilateral process and multilateral reporting on the international conflicts and inefficiencies that spring from the overlap and interplay of competition policies and trade policies. Some initiatives along these lines could be carried out in an Asia Pacific or wider context. In either case, work could begin with only a sub-set of the full range of issues. For the Asia Pacific region, that sub-set might profitably include exemptions, foreclosure, or treatment of investors.

Appendix: The Havana Charter and competition policy

A remarkable documentary artifact concerning some of these issues is the chapter on restrictive business practices from the Havana Charter of the stillborn International Trade Organisation (ITO), a portion of which formed the framework for the GATT. Elements of its chapter on restrictive business practices include forty-four-year-old anticipations of modern issues. But are the anticipations really adequate? And even if so, is there any value in returning to this document for precedent? Whatever the answer to the first question, we believe the answer to the second question to be 'yes.'

The chapter included measures that preserved sovereign authority, while promoting classification, elaboration, and transparency, yet all in a nuanced manner. Specifically it included:

- obligations on members to prevent private 'business practices affecting international trade which restrain competition, limit access to markets [words that would seem most familiar today from trade parlance], or foster monopolistic control'; but reporting and suasion were the instruments most frequently mentioned, not sanctions;

- explicit identification of such practices as 'fixing prices . . . , excluding enterprises . . . , allocating territorial market . . . , fixing sales quotas or purchase quotas . . . or . . . production quotas . . . , discriminating against particular enterprises . . . , preventing by agreement the development or application of technology or invention whether patented or unpatented'; but freedom to contract – presumably with suppliers and distributors – was explicitly guaranteed as long as it was not used to support the practices sanctioned (see point above);

- procedural rules for modifying official identification of anti-competitive practices, for example, by further identifying 'any similar practices which the Organisation may declare, by a majority of two-thirds of the Members present and voting, to be restrictive business practices'; by implication, this provision might also be taken to allow de-certification, for example, of an identified restrictive business practice that in certain instances facilitated dynamic efficiency (innovation and productivity enhancement);

- authorisation for the Organisation 'to conduct studies . . . relating to . . . general aspects of restrictive business practices affecting international trade . . .', or relating to specific aspects such as 'incorporation, company registration . . . , fair trade practices, trade marks, copyrights, patents and the exchange and development of technology';

- recognition of 'special procedures with respect to services . . . such as transportation, telecommunications, insurance and the commercial services of banks'; and

- the clear application of such rules to state-owned as well as privately-owned enterprises.

Certain aspects of these provisions could serve as a beginning for initiatives, especially in an Asia Pacific context, that would aim at rationalising competition and trade policies. Specifically, the identification and study provisions offer promise of immediate results, especially if carried out by a multinational and inter-agency groups (that is, groups that would include trade officials and competition-policy officials, and preferably officials responsible for foreign investment regulation as well).

NOTES

1. Nor are the underlying philosophies always the same. Wide differences exist between the economic objectives of competition policy (broadly defined to include investment and trade policy). Is the policy intended to maintain some effective level of competition within specified sectors? Is it to maximise the static efficiency of production within these sectors (including consideration of natural scale economies)? Is it to maximise the dynamic efficiency of production (e.g. to optimise the rate of technological innovation and diffusion)? To what extent does competition policy strive to balance short-term interests of consumers (e.g. lower prices) with longer-term considerations (e.g. innovation and growth)? Should foreign consumers 'count' and, if so, how? Should competition policies allow for any explicit trade-off of consumer interests in favour of producer gains in international markets, gains that could be so large that national welfare improves? To what extent do competition policies strive to balance interests of initiating firms (e.g. two firms contemplating a merger) with interests of passive firms (who, for example, might be injured by the merger)? Should it matter that any of these firms has significant foreign ownership and, if so, why? Is avoidance of competition sometimes a goal, and if so why? Do nations wish to encourage the development of 'national champion' firms? Is 'bigness' encouraged as a means of achieving economies of scale or scope? Or is bigness seen *per se* as bad because of its alleged power over weaker agents?

2. For example, in the control of predatory behaviour in competition policy and anti-dumping in trade policy.

3. For example, where certain trade arrangements, such as voluntary export restraints (VERs), have anti-competitive effects, or where certain anti-trust exemptions, such as for export cartels, have anti-trade effects. The scope for rationalisation can only grow over time, as more and more countries adopt trade-remedies-as-harassment policies against foreign rivals. Most Asia Pacific countries, for example, have adopted some form of anti-dumping regime. As these begin to constrain European and US exports in Asia Pacific markets, anti-anti-dumping pressures will increase among the traditionally heavy initiators of such petitions.

4. One example is failure to control a private business practice in one nation that results in barriers to another nation's exports or investment, illustrated by Japanese tolerance of implicit collusion among its big producers of flat glass, used in vehicles and construction. Imports have been long stuck around 3 per cent of Japanese use (roughly US$6 billion per year), despite high-profile US complaints and negotiations and exhortation/intervention by both the Japan Fair Trade Commission and the Ministry of Trade and Industry. A second example is where one nation's GATT-legal trade policies have an anti-competitive effect that adversely affects another nation's interests, illustrated by the US Big Three automakers' use of the anti-dumping mechanisms to harass Japanese rivals.

5. In what follows, 'convergence' pertains both to convergence among the laws and policies of nations (necessary if any sort of international accord is to be

reached) and convergence between trade-policy and competition-policy positions on issue areas where there is substantial overlap (e.g. predation and anti-dumping). Presumably what is desired is convergence (in both contexts) towards best practice rather than convergence for its own sake!

6. For example, trade-policy officials may defend existing anti-dumping statutes, but competition-policy officials may see these as irrational when evaluated by standards for predation or price discrimination.

7. This latter, would have to be considered a soft judgement; an honest assessment might for all such cases be that the efficiency implications are indeterminate.

8. Though for the moment there is some backsliding on investment (Beltz, 1994; Warner and Rugman, 1994). The OECD has initiated negotiations for a broad multilateral investment agreement concerned with national treatment and is considering whether to involve non-OECD members. It is considering also the overlap between investment issues and competition-policy issues such as intellectual-property protection (*Inside US Trade*, May 13, 1994, p. 8).

9. Examples of declarations to that effect by Japanese firms are numerous, especially during Japan's catch-up growth; for a Korean counterpart, see, for example Soon (1994, chapter 4).

10. See *The Economist*, (July 17, 1993, pp. 61–2).

11. For example, efforts to enforce domestic law or policy on the non-domestic activities of firms via some concept of 'effects' doctrine, without working with or through the relevant authorities in the nation where the practices actually take place. Both the United States and the EC (but especially the former) have periodically attempted such an approach.

12. During the Spring of 1994 several US Congressmen, for example, introduced a bill, originally proposed by the Labor Industry Coalition for International Trade (LICIT), for a 'Section 311' of US trade law on foreign private anti-competitive practices. The bill would allow industries to petition relevant parts of the US government to bring suit against uncompetitive practices by foreign entities and foreign investors in the United States, who could consequently be subject to both civil penalties and trade sanctions. (*Inside US Trade*, May 20, 1994, pp. 21–2 and April 8, 1994, p. 3). We view this kind of proposal as having dubious efficacy (to say nothing of propriety) in light of what we say in the text.

13. Joelson (1993) in the NAFTA context; Vernon and Nicolaïdis (1994) in the EC–US context. In early June 1994, the United States proposed legislation that would allow the US Department of Justice and the Federal Trade Commission to negotiate mutual legal assistance agreements with foreign anti-trust authorities (*Wall Street Journal*, June 4, 1994, p. B8).

14. See Finger (1994) for a discussion of why agreement and precedent are necessary pre-requisites for formal dispute settlement mechanisms.

12

Japan's trade and investment in East Asia

MASAHIRO KAWAI

F21 F14 F13 O19

Rapid economic growth in East Asia has been made possible by deepening regional integration and increasing interdependence with the global economy. East Asian economies have pursued outward-oriented strategies by liberalising international trade and by deregulating capital flows. This has built strong trade and investment ties with the rest of the world. The expansion of trade and foreign direct investment (FDI) has been a vital source of growth in the region. The important interactions between trade and investment flows have promoted structural changes and economic growth.

Expansion of Japan's trade and investment in the region has played a pivotal role in promoting growth and economic interdependence. Although Japan has been investing in East Asia for many years, the volume of FDI did not increase substantially until the mid-1980s. Many Japanese firms undertook FDI as part of globalisation strategies, as production costs increased at home after 1985, with the sharp appreciation of the yen against other major currencies. By that time, several East Asian countries had firmly established outward-looking strategies, thereby attracting foreign enterprises and investment inflows. These parallel policy developments resulted in a sharp increase in Japanese and other countries' investments in East Asian economies.

Traditionally, Japanese investments overseas had aimed at securing supplies of minerals and raw materials for domestic industries. While some investments in primary industries continued, the appreciation of the yen provided reasons for investments overseas to reduce production costs. In order to retain competitiveness in labour-intensive production, Japanese firms shifted some production processes off-shore. In general, however, most overseas plants produced for exports to third countries as well as back to Japan. This type of Japanese FDI was described by Kojima (1968) as trade-creating rather than trade-reducing. Japan's FDI also stimulated her exports to East Asia to meet increased demand for high technology-intensive and human capital-intensive capital goods, parts and components. Trade expansion in turn encouraged FDI, leading to a virtuous circle of positive interaction. Because Japan was regarded as the role model and catalyst for East Asia's rapid economic development, an analysis of Japan's trade and investment links with the region has particular value.

Trends in Japan's FDI

Japan's postwar FDI abroad started in the first half of the 1950s and began to accelerate during the second half of the 1960s, reaching its first peak in 1973 when the yen appreciated. Until the 1960s, Japan's FDI went into the exploitation of natural resources in developing countries for export back to Japan's manufacturing industries, for example, oil drilling in Indonesia and copper mining in Malaysia. Early in the 1970s, Japan's FDI began to shift away from securing resource supplies to manufacturing and commerce. At this stage an increasing proportion of Japanese FDI went to labour-intensive manufacturing in East Asia, including clothing and textiles.

The 1973 oil-price shock slowed the growth rate of the Japanese economy and the subsequent structural adjustment diverted investment to domestic restructuring. For the remainder of the 1970s, Japan's FDI showed little growth, partly because Japanese firms were performing less profitably and partly because the world economy was growing slowly and inflationary uncertainties had increased. When capital transactions were gradually deregulated early in the 1980s, Japan's FDI outflows rose markedly to both developed and developing economies. (For a history of Japanese FDI, see Hamada, 1972; Kojima, 1985; Komiya, 1990; Komiya and Wakasugi, 1991; and Urata, 1993a, 1993b.) Healey (1991) presents detailed data of Japan's FDI in Asia Pacific economies.

From 1986 onwards Japan's FDI increased rapidly and underwent major changes in its direction and industrial pattern. The expansion of FDI outflows in the four year period 1986–9 was spectacular (table 12.1). FDI as a proportion of Japan's GDP rose to 2.4 per cent in 1989, from only 0.4 per cent in 1980. This surge in foreign investment coincided with a series of structural adjustments not only in Japan but also in other parts of East Asia.

Almost as dramatic was the reduction in Japan's FDI outflows in 1990, a trend which continued into 1993.

Japanese FDI falls almost equally into three broad sectors: resource development (agriculture, forestry, fisheries and mining), manufacturing, and services (construction, commerce, finance and insurance, transportation, real estate, etc.) (table 12.2). This stock of investments is concentrated in Asia, North America and Latin America. By 1985 the share of resource

Table 12.1. *Japan's FDI, US$ millions, 1970–93*

Fiscal year	North America	Latin America	Asia	Middle East	Europe	Africa	Oceania	World total	(% of GDP)
1970	192	46	167	28	335	14	123	904	0.44
1971	230	140	237	36	84	21	110	858	0.37
1972	406	282	402	236	935	34	42	2338	0.77
1973	913	822	998	110	337	106	208	3494	0.84
1974	550	699	731	64	189	55	108	2395	0.52
1975	905	371	1101	196	333	192	182	3280	0.66
1976	749	420	1245	278	337	272	162	3462	0.62
1977	735	456	865	225	220	140	165	2806	0.41
1978	1364	616	1340	492	323	225	239	4598	0.47
1979	1438	1207	976	130	495	168	582	4995	0.49
1980	1596	588	1186	158	578	139	448	4693	0.44
1981	2522	1181	3338	96	798	573	424	8931	0.76
1982	2905	1503	1384	124	876	489	421	7703	0.71
1983	2701	1878	1847	175	990	364	191	8145	0.69
1984	3544	2290	1628	273	1937	326	157	10155	0.80
1985	5495	2616	1435	45	1930	172	525	12217	0.91
1986	10441	4737	2327	44	3469	309	992	22320	1.12
1987	15357	4816	4868	62	6576	272	1413	33364	1.39
1988	22328	6428	5569	259	9116	653	2669	47022	1.62
1989	33902	5238	8238	66	14808	671	4618	67540	2.35
1990	27192	3628	7054	27	14294	551	4166	56911	1.94
1991	18823	3337	5936	90	9371	748	3278	41584	1.24
1992	14572	2726	6425	709	7061	238	2406	34138	0.93
1993	15287	3370	6637	217	7940	539	2035	36025	0.85

Source: Ministry of Finance, *Zaisei Kin-yu Tokei Geppo* (Monthly Statistics on Government Finance and Banking), various issues.

development in Japan's FDI declined sharply, the manufacturing share declined somewhat, while the share going into services rose markedly. After 1985 investments were directed increasingly to services and manufacturing in North America and Europe. In the period 1985–93, these two regions together absorbed two-thirds of Japan's FDI outflows. This contrasted sharply with earlier periods when most of Japan's outflows went to resource development in developing countries. Although the share of Japanese FDI directed to East Asia declined in the 1980s, investments in manufacturing in East Asia remained strong.

There were several reasons for the changes in the direction and the pattern of Japanese FDI after 1986.

First, the globalisation of Japanese business activities in line with other major players in the international economy, caused by improvements in Japanese firms' managerial and technological capabilities, resulted in a surge of Japan's FDI. The rapid and steep appreciation of the yen exchange rate against the major international currencies reduced the yen price of

Table 12.2. *Cumulative values of Japan's FDI, by area and industry activity,*
US$ million, 1970–93

Fiscal Year		North America	Latin America	Asia	Middle East	Europe	Africa	Oceania	World
1970	Resource development[a]	186	110	315	0	6	59	208	886
	Manufacturing	217	275	320	4	37	25	51	928
	Services[b]	468	177	98	2	590	7	22	1,362
	Total	912	567	751	334	639	93	281	3,577
1975	Resource development	428	653	1,478	24	853	308	456	4,209
	Manufacturing	815	1,536	1,932	125	252	60	317	5,037
	Services	2,433	678	757	61	1,340	131	152	5,542
	Total	3,916	2,882	4,218	976	2,517	501	931	15,942
1980	Resource development	832	1,385	3,309	42	861	529	1,023	7,981
	Manufacturing	2,428	2,781	4,571	1,064	844	96	789	12,573
	Services	5,978	1,953	1,828	124	2,639	817	699	14,039
	Total	9,798	6,168	9,830	2,259	4,471	1,445	2,525	36,497
1985	Resource development	1,508	1,693	6,546	194	866	654	1,504	12,977
	Manufacturing	7,706	4,560	7,517	1,260	2,088	215	1,055	24,400
	Services	16,917	9,318	5,141	244	7,589	2,487	1,666	43,359
	Total	26,965	15,636	19,463	2,972	11,002	3,369	4,242	83,650
1990	Resource development	2,723	1,980	7,882	404	1,594	691	3,360	18,634
	Manufacturing	40,322	6,281	18,659	1,277	12,540	231	2,302	81,613
	Services	91,568	32,452	20,192	302	43,094	4,900	12,293	204,502
	Total	136,185	40,483	47,519	3,431	59,265	5,826	18,098	310,808
1993	Resource development	3,256	2,359	8,945	801	2,142	724	4,333	22,561
	Manufacturing	54,513	7,277	28,349	1,656	19,371	258	3,687	115,112
	Services	125,381	40,203	28,030	396	59,717	6,365	17,640	277,732
	Total	184,868	49,917	66,517	4,447	83,637	7,351	25,817	422,555

Notes:
[a]Resource development includes agriculture, forestry, fisheries and mining.
[b]Services includes construction, commerce, finance and insurance, transportation, real estate and others.
Source: Ministry of Finance, *Zaisei Kin-yu Tokei Geppo* (Monthly Statistics on Government Finance and Banking), various issues.

foreign assets. At the same time, Japanese exports became less competitive on world markets. Both effects promoted FDI outflows from Japan.

The yen appreciated by 37 per cent between 1985 and 1988 on a real, effective basis (IMF index of relative normalised unit labour costs), significantly reducing Japan's international price competitiveness. To cope with the new international price structure, Japanese firms in the tradeables sector had three choices:

- they could reallocate their productive resources (capital, labour, research and development resources and managerial resources) away from tradeables towards non-tradeables sectors;
- they could upgrade technology and productivity to increase the proportion of high value-added products;
- they could shift production plants to foreign countries where production costs were lower.

All three courses were followed in Japan's industrial structural adjustment in the 1980s. This process has continued in the 1990s as the appreciation of the yen resumed.

Yen appreciation has a 'liquidity' or 'wealth' effect, which encourages capital outflows. In the 1980s, yen appreciation gave Japanese firms a bigger command over foreign resources and assets for a given yen value. This enabled them to finance a given stock of outward investments for fewer yen than previously, and improved their financial position. Liquidity was also injected into the economy by the Bank of Japan after 1986, pushing up the yen prices of Japanese shares and stocks and land. This asset-price inflation encouraged firms to seek cheaper assets overseas, which also increased FDI outflows (Kawai, 1994). The prices of Japanese shares and stocks (Nikkei Stock Index) rose by 80 per cent between 1987 and 1989. However, when the stock market index declined sharply (it fell almost 40 per cent between 1989 and 1990), Japan's FDI outflows were sharply curtailed.

Second, trade frictions with and protectionism by other industrial countries stimulated investments behind trade barriers. Trade frictions between Japan and the United States go back to the 1960s and spread from exports of clothing and textiles and electrical appliances, to iron and steel, automobiles and high-technology products such as machine tools and semiconductors in the 1980s. Some Japanese industries that encountered trade threats in the United States, such as textiles, colour TV, and iron and steel industries, were persuaded to adopt voluntary export restraints (VERs). Eventually other firms also started to invest in assembly or production plants in the United States, for example, the electrical appliance industry and the automobile industry. Some Japanese firms shifted their production plants to East Asia to avoid discriminatory, bilateral trade measures imposed by the US authorities. But in most instances such investment shunting was quickly countered by new restrictions against suppliers to the US market.

Third, as the scope of FDI by Japanese firms spread, new opportunities arose for financial and other supporting services to follow Japanese businesses overseas. The strong yen was an advantage for Japanese banks and

214 Masahiro Kawai

other financial institutions expanding their operations overseas, and for any Japanese firm or investor interested in real estate purchases.

Japan's FDI in East Asia

Since 1986, Japan's FDI in East Asia has gone primarily into manufacturing and service industries. The emphasis on manufacturing distinguishes Japanese investments in East Asia from those in other regions (table 12.2). The region's robust economic growth and stability, low unit labour costs, and a climate of trade liberalisation and investment deregulation have made the East Asian economies attractive locations for off-shore manufacturing.

The first wave of Japanese FDI in East Asia occurred early in the 1970s. As labour shortages developed, stricter environmental regulations were imposed, and yen appreciation reduced Japan's international competitiveness. Several East Asian economies with low-cost labour became attractive targets for investment. The transition from import-substitution to export-orientation in several Asian newly industrialising economies (NIEs) also reduced uncertainties; gradually some even adopted policies to promote inward foreign investment. Japan thus started to expand her investment in East Asia's labour-intensive and low-technology manufacturing, particularly in textiles and electrical machinery.

In the 1980s the second wave of Japanese FDI took place in Korea, Taiwan, and later in Thailand and Malaysia, as these economies shifted to outward-oriented economic development strategies. The trade, industrialisation, and foreign investment policies of these East Asian economies were formulated with an eye to export promotion, especially with the increased absorption of imports by the United States as domestic demand recovered and the dollar appreciated in the early 1980s. Robust economic growth, high labour productivity, and low nominal wages were important factors in attracting FDI from developed countries including Japan in this period.

The third wave was induced by yen appreciation after 1986. The four NIEs (Singapore, Hong Kong, Taiwan and Korea) and the ASEAN countries (Malaysia, Thailand, Indonesia and Philippines) attracted major FDI during this period. Policies in Korea, Taiwan and Singapore promoted inward foreign investment in pursuit of high-tech industrialisation; their strong economic growth came from simultaneous expansion of foreign trade and direct investment inflows. However, the growth of Japan's FDI in the four NIEs slowed late in the 1980s, just as total Japanese investment outflows peaked. The slowdown was attributable to the diminished cost advantages of some of these countries as wages increased and their currencies appreciated. Moreover, some graduated from the US Generalised System of Preferences (GSP) in 1989, which reduced their attractiveness as export platforms. Firms in Japan and other advanced economies turned to the ASEAN countries as alternative locations for new production sites. Some manufacturing firms shifted labour-intensive processes to ASEAN and other Asian countries.

Until the 1980s, Japanese direct investment in ASEAN had been mainly in the primary sector or in resource-intensive manufacturing, in keeping with the abundance of natural resources in the region. However, new investment from Japan in the 1980s went into manufacturing. The appreciation of the yen and other Asian currencies provided new opportunities in the ASEAN countries for export development. The ASEAN countries' shift from inward-oriented to outward-oriented strategies during the 1980s was prompted by the earlier success of the four NIEs' outward-oriented policies. Unilateral liberalisation of trade and direct investment regimes strengthened regional interdependence.

The record, however, was not uniform across the region (table 12.3). Political and social unrest in the Philippines, and its external debt problem, reduced its attractiveness to foreign investors. Thailand attracted Japanese manufacturing investment in large amounts, but those flows declined rapidly after peaking in 1989–90. The lack of industrial infrastructure and the shortage of local managers in Thailand have proved bottlenecks to further expansion. Japan's annual FDI in Malaysia, on the other hand, has not declined noticeably in the 1990s. Investment inflows into Indonesia remained strong, and in consequence, aggregate Japanese FDI in ASEAN remains strong.

Since 1992, China has become one of the largest recipients of Japanese FDI in Asia. China's gradual but persistent economic reforms, open-door liberalisation policy, and increasing acceptance of its political and social stability have brought in strong investment inflows since 1988. The coastal area of China has attracted capital from Japan, Hong Kong and Taiwan, and from ASEAN countries with large Chinese communities. This has contributed to China recording the highest economic growth in East Asia. Capital inflows are the vehicle of economic transformation in China, its changing trade patterns and its industrial adjustment. The strong interaction between FDI inflows and trade is the key to this transformation.

Table 12.4 shows that sources of FDI in East Asia have changed over time. Note that table 12.4 summarises FDI flows using recipient countries' data not comparable between countries, but indicating compositional changes in investment inflows from major investing countries and groups. Cross-hauling of investment flows within East Asia has increased greatly

Table 12.4 *cont*.

Investor Recipient		Japan		United States		Europe	
		Million US$	Share of world total	Million US$	Share of world total	Million US$	Share of world total
Thailand	1985	. . .	. . .	. . .	. . .	. . .	. . .
	1986	555	(58.2)	164	(17.2)	197	(20.7)
	1987	947	(48.7)	172	(8.9)	268	(13.8)
	1988	3045	(48.7)	673	(10.8)	1051	(16.8)
	1989	3524	(44.1)	549	(6.9)	1604	(20.1)
	1990	2706	(33.7)	1091	(13.6)	1450	(18.1)
	1991	1760	(35.3)	1131	(22.7)	1381	(27.7)
	1992	1967	(19.6)	1233	(12.3)	3281	(32.7)
	1993	2705	(63.0)	431	(10.0)	760	(17.7)
Indonesia	1985	127	(14.8)	141	(16.5)	195	(22.7)
	1986	329	(39.8)	154	(18.6)	124	(15.1)
	1987	532	(36.5)	73	(5.0)	607	(41.7)
	1988	247	(5.6)	672	(15.1)	1433	(32.3)
	1989	779	(16.5)	348	(7.4)	605	(12.8)
	1990	2241	(25.6)	154	(1.8)	1339	(15.3)
	1991	929	(10.6)	276	(3.1)	1187	(13.5)
	1992	1511	(14.6)	923	(8.9)	1365	(13.2)
	1993	836	(10.3)	445	(5.5)	930	(11.4)
Philippines	1985	26	(19.8)	58	(44.4)	32	(24.5)
	1986	22	(28.5)	22	(28.7)	17	(21.2)
	1987	29	(17.2)	36	(21.6)	26	(15.9)
	1988	96	(20.2)	153	(32.3)	36	(7.6)
	1989	158	(19.6)	131	(16.3)	73	(9.1)
	1990	306	(31.8)	59	(6.2)	45	(4.7)
	1991	210	(27.0)	83	(10.7)	330	(42.4)
	1992	72	(25.5)	62	(21.7)	48	(16.9)
	1993	112	(21.1)	88	(16.6)	126	(23.7)
China	1985	315	(16.1)	357	(18.3)	165	(8.5)
	1986	263	(11.7)	326	(14.5)	170	(7.6)
	1987	220	(9.5)	263	(11.4)	75	(3.3)
	1988	515	(16.1)	236	(7.4)	195	(6.1)
	1989	356	(10.5)	284	(8.4)	213	(6.3)
	1990	503	(14.4)	456	(13.1)	144	(4.1)
	1991	533	(12.2)	323	(7.4)	263	(6.0)
	1992	710	(6.4)	511	(4.6)	294	(2.7)
	1993	1324	(4.8)	2063	(7.5)	701	(2.5)

Table 12.4 *cont.*

Recipient		Four NIEs		World total	
	Investor	Million US$	Share of world total	Million US$	
Korea	1985	14	(2.7)	532	(100.0)
	1986	16	(4.5)	354	(100.0)
	1987	70	(6.6)	1060	(100.0)
	1988	15	(1.2)	1283	(100.0)
	1989	49	(4.5)	1090	(100.0)
	1990	21	(2.6)	803	(100.0)
	1991	21	(1.5)	1396	(100.0)
	1992	10	(1.1)	894	(100.0)
	1993	75	(7.2)	1044	(100.0)
Taiwan	1985	. . .	. . .	. . .	. . .
	1986	64	(8.3)	770	(100.0)
	1987	80	(5.7)	1419	(100.0)
	1988	115	(9.7)	1183	(100.0)
	1989	247	(10.2)	2418	(100.0)
	1990	248	(10.8)	2302	(100.0)
	1991	101	(8.6)	1179	(100.0)
	1992	162	(11.1)	1461	(100.0)
	1993	144	(11.8)	1214	(100.0)
Singapore	1985	. . .	. . .	444	(100.0)
	1986	. . .	. . .	546	(100.0)
	1987	. . .	. . .	688	(100.0)
	1988	. . .	. . .	824	(100.0)
	1989	. . .	. . .	833	(100.0)
	1990	. . .	. . .	1223	(100.0)
	1991	. . .	. . .	1425	(100.0)
	1992	. . .	. . .	1678	(100.0)
	1993	. . .	. . .	1966	(100.0)
Malaysia	1985	31	(23.4)	131	(100.0)
	1986	46	(22.7)	203	(100.0)
	1987	113	(37.8)	298	(100.0)
	1988	271	(35.3)	768	(100.0)
	1989	544	(43.3)	1256	(100.0)
	1990	1100	(47.8)	2302	(100.0)
	1991	1015	(45.0)	2255	(100.0)
	1992	325	(14.1)	2298	(100.0)
	1993	229	(24.1)	949	(100.0)

Table 12.4 *cont.*

Investor / Recipient		Four NIEs		World total	
		Million US$	Share of world total	Million US$	
Thailand	1985	. . .	. . .	. . .	. . .
	1986	263	(27.6)	953	(100.0)
	1987	498	(25.6)	1946	(100.0)
	1988	1684	(26.9)	6249	(100.0)
	1989	2011	(25.2)	7995	(100.0)
	1990	2696	(33.6)	8031	(100.0)
	1991	1584	(31.7)	4988	(100.0)
	1992	941	(9.4)	10022	(100.0)
	1993	600	(14.0)	4295	(100.0)
Indonesia	1985	53	(6.2)	859	(100.0)
	1986	141	(17.1)	826	(100.0)
	1987	172	(11.8)	1457	(100.0)
	1988	1591	(35.9)	4435	(100.0)
	1989	1181	(25.0)	4714	(100.0)
	1990	2600	(29.7)	8750	(100.0)
	1991	1983	(22.6)	8778	(100.0)
	1992	2668	(25.8)	10323	(100.0)
	1993	2637	(32.4)	8144	(100.0)
Philippines	1985	6	(4.7)	132	(100.0)
	1986	8	(10.2)	78	(100.0)
	1987	38	(23.0)	167	(100.0)
	1988	141	(29.8)	473	(100.0)
	1989	323	(40.1)	804	(100.0)
	1990	384	(39.9)	961	(100.0)
	1991	68	(8.8)	778	(100.0)
	1992	69	(24.2)	284	(100.0)
	1993	93	(17.6)	532	(100.0)
China	1985	966	(49.4)	1956	(100.0)
	1986	1342	(59.8)	2244	(100.0)
	1987	1610	(69.6)	2314	(100.0)
	1988	2118	(66.3)	3194	(100.0)
	1989	2280	(67.2)	3393	(100.0)
	1990	2166	(67.1)	3487	(100.0)
	1991	2969	(68.0)	4366	(100.0)
	1992	8799	(79.9)	11008	(100.0)
	1993	21277	(77.3)	27515	(100.0)

Notes:
For Korea, Taiwan, Thailand and Philippines approval data for all industries. For Singapore commitment data for manufacturing. For Malaysia approval data for manufacturing. For Indonesia approval data on new investment and expansion for industries other than finance and oil and gas. For China, execution data for all industries.
Sources: Japan External Trade Organisation, *JETRO White Paper on Foreign Direct Investment*, Tokyo, various issues; national sources.

since 1986. Although Japan is still a large direct investor in East Asia, the four NIEs have become the largest group of investors in ASEAN and China. Their FDI in ASEAN and China has similar causes to the earlier wave of Japanese investment in the NIEs: increasing wages and currency appreciation at home, and trade frictions with the United States and Western Europe.

Japanese FDI and trade

Japan's intra-industry trade

To examine interactions between trade and direct investment, it is necessary to look at the influence of Japan's recent investment outflows on her patterns of trade, particularly in East Asia. An essential link is to be found in intra-industry trade (IIT).

Traditionally, Japan has engaged in IIT, importing fuels, raw materials and products intensive in natural resources, and exporting labour-intensive products which gradually became skill- and capital-intensive. Most recently, Japan's exports have become more intensive in high technology and human capital. These patterns of trade are consistent with Japan's changing relative factor endowments and explained by the standard Hecksher–Ohlin–Samuelson trade model.

The sharp appreciation of the yen in 1985–8 brought major changes in the patterns of Japan's trade. The share of manufactures in total imports rose rapidly from 31 per cent in 1985 to 52 per cent in 1993. The increase in real incomes caused by the yen appreciation turned Japan into an attractive market for manufactured products from abroad. In addition, buoyant economic activity in Japan in the latter half of the 1980s and the import promotion policies pursued by the Japanese government helped to stimulate imports of manufactures. Machinery imports, for example, increased rapidly. These changes in Japan's imports and increasing outflows of investment in manufacturing in East Asia were important in the expansion of Japan's IIT.

Japanese firms attempt to site production facilities overseas to minimise costs in the world market. Such a global strategy naturally leads to an efficient cross-border, intra-firm division of production. The production of machinery requires a large number of manufactured parts and components, the production of which may be divided into several different processes. These processes do not have to be located in one country. Indeed, since different parts and components may require different technologies and factor proportions, factories engaged in different processes may be located in countries where the required technologies and factors of production are relatively abundant. In practice, parts and components that require high technology and human capital tend to be produced in Japan, and those that require standardised technology and skilled labour tend to be produced in Korea, Taiwan, Singapore, and more recently in Thailand and Malaysia. Components that require low technology and unskilled labour tend to be produced in Indonesia, the Philippines, and China. This type of 'vertical' intra-firm, inter-process division of production is expected to expand with the growth of international business activities by Japanese firms in the manufacturing sector (Dobson, 1993; Urata, 1994).

The sources of purchases and imports, and the destinations of sales and exports, by Japanese manufacturing firms' affiliates located abroad are summarised in table 12.5 (a) and table 12.5 (b). The data indicate that Japan's FDI in manufacturing depends on trade between overseas affiliates and firms in Japan (parent firms, in particular) or in third countries, accounting for a growing proportion of the affiliates' total sales. This tendency is pronounced in the sales activities of overseas affiliates: the share of exports to Japan in the total sales of affiliates located in Asia rose from 10 per cent in 1980 to 16 per cent in 1986 and 1989, which was the highest among all regions except in the Middle East, where the affiliates produce petroleum products to be shipped back to Japan. In addition, the share of exports from Asia to third countries was also high, in the 20–30 per cent range. Asian countries have become increasingly integrated into Japanese firms' global production networks. This integration is one of the driving forces behind the recent rapid expansion of international trade between Japan and the developing Asian economies. Furthermore, high export-orientation is a key feature of Japanese firms' manufacturing investments.

The trade–investment nexus in East Asian economies

The 'trade–investment nexus' has different significance for developing East Asian economies than it has for Japan (Petri, 1994). The nexus works as follows:

- Outward-oriented trade policies and open foreign investment regimes help to stimulate trade and attract capital inflows.
- FDI inflows create additional trade, and this in turn may give rise to more investment inflows.
- Vigorous trade and investment growth encourage governments to adopt policies favourable to international linkages.

Table 12.5. *Sources of purchases and imports and destinations of sales and exports, by Japanese manufacturing firms' affiliates located abroad, US$ million, 1980–9, percentages*

(a) Sources of purchases and imports

Fiscal year	North America	Latin America	Asia	Middle East	Europe	Africa	Oceania	World
1980								
Local purchases	39.9	66.7	42.2	19.1	39.3	27.0	19.5	42.5
Imports from Japan	49.1	24.5	41.5	25.7	44.5	43.6	60.9	42.8
Imports from third countries	11.0	8.8	16.3	55.2	16.1	29.4	19.6	14.7
Total purchases and imports	100.0	100.0	100.0	100.0	100.0	100.0	100.0	100.0
(US$ million)	(4,688)	(1,729)	(7,265)	(140)	(596)	(370)	(702)	(15,491)
1983								
Local purchases	28.5	67.3	44.8	78.4	39.4	23.5	33.0	39.7
Imports from Japan	68.7	30.2	38.4	6.2	44.3	58.1	65.3	50.4
Imports from third countries	2.8	2.5	16.9	15.4	16.3	18.4	1.7	9.9
Total purchases and imports	100.0	100.0	100.0	100.0	100.0	100.0	100.0	100.0
(US$ million)	(5,116)	(705)	(5,802)	(333)	(782)	(207)	(958)	(13,903)
1986								
Local purchases	32.3	60.5	42.2	93.9	33.1	34.6	31.4	36.9
Imports from Japan	62.3	26.5	45.3	3.5	51.2	45.0	65.5	53.0
Imports from third countries	5.4	13.0	12.6	2.6	15.6	20.4	3.1	10.2
Total purchases and imports	100.0	100.0	100.0	100.0	100.0	100.0	100.0	100.0
(US$ million)	(11,780)	(1,136)	(6,281)	(180)	(4,431)	(158)	(704)	(24,669)
1989								
Local Purchases	47.1	66.7	49.8	53.8	35.1	32.9	32.6	45.6
Imports from Japan	49.2	13.4	38.9	32.5	41.9	40.3	65.6	45.7
Imports from third countries	3.7	19.9	11.4	13.7	23.0	26.8	1.8	8.7
Total purchases and Imports	100.0	100.0	100.0	100.0	100.0	100.0	100.0	100.0
(US$ million)	(27,485)	(775)	(14,334)	(30)	(7,400)	(131)	(2,787)	(52,941)

Note:
The exchange rates used for conversion are 209.35, 224.00, 146.85 and 158.00 yen/dollar for 1980, 1983, 1986 and 1989, respectively.
Source: Ministry of International Trade and Industry, *Basic Survey on Japanese Business Activity Abroad*, no.1 (1983), no.2 (1986), no.3 (1989), and no.4 (1991), Government of Japan, Tokyo.

224 *Masahiro Kawai*

Table 12.5 *cont.*

(b) Destinations of sales and exports

Fiscal year	North America	Latin America	Asia	Middle East	Europe	Africa	Oceania	World
1980								
Local sales	84.9	82.6	63.9	13.9	74.6	97.0	80.6	72.9
Exports to Japan	7.8	9.4	9.8	72.3	0.3	0.0	13.8	10.9
Exports to third countries	7.3	8.0	26.4	13.8	25.1	3.0	5.6	16.2
Total sales and exports	100.0	100.0	100.0	100.0	100.0	100.0	100.0	100.0
(US$ million)	(8,009)	(4,926)	(11,981)	(1,106)	(1,704)	(681)	(1,430)	(29,835)
1983								
Local sales	87.3	72.1	66.9	10.9	68.9	91.8	81.6	73.2
Exports to Japan	7.7	12.2	10.8	73.0	3.3	0.0	16.1	11.6
Exports to third countries	5.0	15.8	22.3	16.2	27.8	8.2	2.2	15.2
Total sales and exports	100.0	100.0	100.0	100.0	100.0	100.0	100.0	100.0
(US$ million)	(9,337)	(2,294)	(12,396)	(875)	(2,305)	(480)	(2,207)	(29,896)
1986								
Local sales	92.8	80.5	54.7	17.2	70.3	92.2	83.5	77.1
Exports to Japan	3.3	4.1	15.8	79.1	1.2	0.0	14.7	7.8
Exports to third countries	3.9	15.4	29.5	3.7	28.5	7.8	1.8	15.1
Total sales and exports	100.0	100.0	100.0	100.0	100.0	100.0	100.0	100.0
(US$ million)	(29,342)	(3,953)	(21,810)	(1,173)	(11,268)	(678)	(3,195)	(71,419)
1989								
Local sales	93.1	69.9	63.9	29.5	66.5	72.1	90.3	79.6
Exports to Japan	4.5	10.9	15.8	66.0	1.7	0.0	7.4	7.9
Exports to third countries	2.5	19.2	20.3	4.5	31.8	27.9	2.4	12.4
Total sales and exports	100.0	100.0	100.0	100.0	100.0	100.0	100.0	100.0
(US$ million)	(43,959)	(2,691)	(25,794)	(495)	(13,291)	(223)	(3,983)	(90,436)

Note:
The exchange rates used for conversion are 209.35, 224.00, 146.85 and 158.00 yen/dollar for 1980, 1983, 1986 and 1989, respectively.
Source: Ministry of International Trade and Industry, *Basic Survey on Japanese Business Activity Abroad,* no.1 (1983), no.2 (1986), no.3 (1989), and no.4 (1991), Government of Japan, Tokyo.

This type of 'trade–investment nexus' has been an effective component of the East Asian 'miracle'. Petri presents some econometric evidence supporting the nexus hypothesis using data from twenty-seven low- and middle-income economies. He concludes that

> East Asian economies have consistently pursued less distortionary policies than other low and middle-income countries and have built stronger trade and investment relationships.

Japan's trade and FDI links

A *gravity model* can be used to analyse the extent of interactions between Japan's bilateral trade and FDI flows (Drysdale and Garnaut, 1982; Deardorff, 1984). A standard gravity model of international trade relates bilateral trade flows to the levels of economic activity in exporting and importing countries and to the geographical distance between them and other explanatory variables (e.g. regional trade arrangements). Recently, gravity models have been applied to direct investment flows where trade is treated as an explanatory variable (Eaton and Ho, 1993; Eaton and Tamura 1994).

In this section, two types of regression equations are run separately applying the gravity model to both trade (exports, imports, and total separately) and investment flows. To determine linkages, investment (FDI stock) is used as one of the explanatory variables in the trade equation. Other variables include GNP, *per capita* income, an APEC dummy variable, and an oil-exporter dummy variable. Similarly, trade is included as one of the explanatory variables in the investment equation. The other variables are the same as those in the trade equation:

Trade equation
$$\log(TRADE_{ij}) = \alpha_0 + \alpha_1(\log(GNP_i) + \log(GNP_j)) + \alpha_2(\log(GNP_i/POP_i)$$
$$+ \log(GNP_j/POP_j)) + \alpha_3 \log(DISTANCE_{ij}) + \alpha_4 APEC_i + \alpha_5 OILEXP_i$$
$$+ \alpha_6 \log(FDISTOCK_{ij}(-1)) + u_{ij}.$$

Direct investment equation
$$\log(FDIFLOW_{ij}) = \beta_0 + \beta_1(\log(GNP_i) + \log(GNP_j)) + \beta_2(\log(GNP_i/POP_i)$$
$$+ \log(GNP_j/POP_j)) + \beta_3 \log(DISTANCE_{ij}) + \beta_4 APEC_i + \beta_5 OILEXP_i$$
$$+ \beta_6 \log(TRADE_{ij}(-1)) + v_{ij}.$$

In these equations, subscript *j* refers to Japan and *i* refers to an individual trading partner ($i = 1, 2, \ldots, 75$ or 76).

The ordinary least-squares (OLS) regression results for the *trade equation* confirm earlier findings that the estimated coefficient of GNP is statistically

significant and positive; that *per capita* income is also positive and significant; and that distance has a negative impact on trade flows (Detailed
model description and results are available from the National Centre for
Development Studies, Australian National University, on request). The
trading arrangement dummy (*APEC*) has a positive coefficient which is
not always statistically significant. The oil-exporter dummy has a positive
coefficient which is in many cases statistically significant in the import and
export-plus-import equations. The new finding is that the coefficient of
FDI (*FDISTOCK*(−1)) is always positive and statistically significant.

When investment flow is used instead of stock in the trade equation, its
estimated coefficient in the import equation becomes small and statistically insignificant in the second half of the 1980s. This implies that Japan's
annual imports were not correlated with annual investment outflows, but
were strongly correlated with the cumulative value of investment outflows. It turns out that FDI stock explains trade better than does FDI flows:
Japan tends to trade more with countries where it has a large stock of direct
investment.

The regression results for the *direct investment equation* show that the size
variable (*GNP*) tends to have a negative coefficient, and it is statistically
insignificant in many cases. *Per capita* income has the expected positive
coefficient and is statistically significant. The coefficient of distance is
always positive, and significantly so in the first half of the 1980s.The coefficient of the APEC dummy is always positive but not always significant.
The oil exporter dummy almost always has a significantly negative coefficient; *ceteris paribus*, Japan tends to invest less in oil-exporting countries.

The most important coefficient is *TRADE*(−1), which captures the effect
of trade on direct investment outflows; the coefficient is always significantly positive where *TRADE* is the sum of exports and imports. The effect
of trade on direct investment flows is much more pronounced if *TRADE* is
represented by exports, while the effect is weaker if *TRADE* is represented
by imports. A large bilateral trade flow, defined as the sum of exports and
imports, induces greater FDI outflow from Japan.

The empirical evidence shows that Japan's bilateral trade and FDI are
positively related and causally interdependent. Thus Petri's (1994) hypothesis on the trade–investment nexus is supported by an analysis of data for
Japan's trade and investment with the world, and with East Asia in particular.

13

China: export growth and enterprise reform

FRANCES PERKINS

The completion of the Uruguay Round negotiations and the establishment of the World Trade Organisation (WTO) mean that the most important outstanding global trade issue is the re-admission of China to the GATT. Although China signed the Final Act in Marrakesh in April 1994, its 1986 application for re-entry to the GATT has to be agreed before China can be accepted as a member of the WTO and enjoy GATT privileges, such as most-favoured-nation (Mfn) treatment and reciprocal rights under all the WTO agreements. Several aspects of the Protocol of Accession, which sets out China's obligations as a contracting party, remain to be defined. Some contracting parties are suspicious about China's foreign trade policies, its tax system and its capacity to offer national treatment to foreign investors. A major concern arises about subsidised exports from state-owned enterprises.

Full Mfn access to industrial countries' markets would help to sustain China's recent strong export growth, as well as providing security of access to those markets. Under present observer status in the GATT, China's Mfn treatment is subject to annual review, which is used as a weapon by various social and commercial lobby groups, especially in the United States. Automatic Mfn treatment for China may be denied under Article XXXV, which allows existing contracting parties to deny GATT tariff schedules to a new member if no previous tariff negotiations have taken place between the two countries. At the same time, China's status as a developing country provides access to various exemptions in GATT, which could restrict other contracting parties' access to China's markets. After re-admission, China would become eligible for access to industrial countries' markets according to their systems of generalised preferences. Resort could also be made to exemptions under Article XVIII to allow increases in protection (tariffs and import quotas) to promote development of 'infant' industries or to help to correct balance of payments difficulties. China is now the world's eleventh biggest exporter, so it is natural that WTO members are cautious about conditions for China's re-entry.

On the other hand, economic reform in China has progressed rapidly and changes that have occurred have assuaged many of these concerns. In 1992, China declared its determination to establish a 'socialist market economy'. In 1991, the Chinese authorities took important steps to unify the tax system. It removed differences in income taxes levied on different types of enterprise (foreign-owned enterprises, joint ventures), and at the end of 1993, income tax laws relating to domestic enterprises (state-owned, collectives, and private enterprises) were unified at the same rate as enterprises with foreign investment. This unified income tax system is regarded as essential for competition in a market economy. At the same time, a complex system of turnover taxes were being combined into a system of value-added taxes, consumption taxes and business taxes. Unification of the tax system is an important step towards compliance with GATT national treatment requirements and regarded as evidence of the establishment of a competitive market economy (Wang, 1994).

The major obstacles to China's full admission to the WTO relate to the perception by trading partners that exports from state-owned enterprises are subsidised and that imports by some industries are still subject to licensing or planning restrictions. This chapter attempts to evaluate these perceptions. After reviewing the extent of China's trade reform programme and its demonstrated effect on trade flows, the results of a survey of trade performance by different enterprises in coastal regions subject to different regulatory regimes will be examined to see if subsidies and other trade interventions still influence China's trade patterns.

China's trade reform programme

China claims, with some justification, that it has reformed its trade regime, enterprise management and markets for goods and factors in preparation for entry to the WTO. However, trading partners still claim that reforms have not gone far enough. These reforms were designed to improve the efficiency and export-orientation of the industrial sector, including the dominant but largely moribund state-owned sector.

China's open-door policy for foreign investment and trade was initiated late in the 1970s. Previously trade was merely an adjunct to the national production Plan. The expectation was that liberalisation would provide access to modern technology and management to improve industrial efficiency and infrastructure, create employment opportunities and expand export industries. This partial liberalisation contributed to China's strong economic growth, but the central government has continued to affect performance through its planning and subsidisation of exports. Between 1978 and 1988 the number of mandatory imports in the foreign trade plan were reduced from 3000 categories to only seventeen, while only twenty export categories remained subject to mandatory controls in 1988. The value of planned trade was reduced further early in the 1990s; by 1992 only 15 per cent of exports by value and 18.5 per cent of imports were in categories still subject to mandatory planning. Moreover, the concentration of China's exports, which is both an indicator of government interference and economic under-development, declined sharply. The Hirschman commodity concentration index for China's exports dropped from 0.39 in 1972 to 0.12 in 1988 (World Bank, 1994e). The four NIEs had recorded a similar experience of rapid diversification of exports. China's import concentration, however, remained high throughout the 1980s at around 0.43. Import penetration was limited, occurring only in machinery and equipment, chemicals, textiles and raw materials. Nevertheless, a growing proportion of unclassified imports cover intermediate products imported by joint ventures and foreign-owned firms (World Bank, 1994e).

One of the earliest trade reforms was the establishment of special economic zones and open cities in several of the coastal provinces. It was intended that by providing superior infrastructure and more liberal trade, foreign investment, taxation and foreign exchange regulations,[1] these zones would attract export-orientated foreign firms (Lin, 1991; Wall, 1990). The Chinese authorities expected that such advantages would increase productivity and raise export growth. In the special economic zones, new industrial estates were established with subsidised factory space, specialised infrastructure including international telecommunication facilities and accommodation for workers. Improvements were made to port, airport, road and rail infrastructure serving these zones. These facilities were provided at a high cost to the Chinese economy (Lin, 1991). While attempts were made to improve dealings with the Chinese bureaucracy by enterprises in the zone, administrative regulations often remained confused and arbitrary. Whether the zones actually provide a significantly more attractive investment environment for foreign firms is uncertain (Wall, 1990).

To facilitate export expansion, the twelve foreign trade corporations owned by the central government were replaced with over 3600 dispersed trading companies. These new foreign trade corporations were allowed to act as agencies and to provide export services for client enterprises and to acquire goods for export outside the Plan. For commodities not subject to planning control, these reforms established for the first time links between domestic and international prices (Lardy, 1992). By 1987, Guangdong alone had 900 trading corporations. Large exporters had permission to export on their own account; by 1992, half of China's 10,000 state-owned enterprises were exporters. Firms trading on their own account have freedom to find international customers and to respond to their needs. Enterprises trading through foreign trade corporations had no direct link with their customers.

Although the foreign trade corporations continued to subsidise planned imports, efforts were made to reduce subsidies by raising domestic prices to international levels for imported commodities, such as iron and steel, non-ferrous metals and grains. Foreign trade corporations have exclusive rights to import 'key' commodities according to import licensing. These reforms and the abolition of export subsidies reduced losses through the Plan. In 1989 these losses were equivalent to 2.1 per cent of GDP and 85 per cent of the central government's deficit; by 1991, these losses had fallen to 0.9 per cent of GDP and 25 per cent of the government's deficit (World Bank, 1994e). In 1991 the Chinese government announced that export subsidies would be abolished and foreign trade corporations were made responsible for their own profits and losses. This reform also increased incentives for foreign trade corporations to export commodities offering the highest profit margins.

China's tariff and non-tariff barriers (NTBs) remain high. In 1992, the average tariff (unweighted) on China's imports was 43 per cent and the average tariff (trade-weighted) was 32 per cent, both higher than in 1987. A World Bank study (World Bank, 1994e) showed that China's average tariffs (both trade-weighted and unweighted) were higher than in other large developing countries, (Brazil, Argentina, Colombia, Egypt, Hungary, Kenya, Philippines). Only India and Pakistan had higher levels of protection. NTBs apply to 51 per cent of imports (by value), enforced through the mandatory import Plan.

An extensive regime of duty drawbacks for exporting enterprises means that import duties contribute little to government revenue: only 5.6 per cent of the value of imports compared to 51 per cent for India. The complex system of high tariffs and NTBs with many dispensations make effective rates of protection difficult to assess. This makes it difficult to assess whether exposure of industries to international competition will actually increase their competitiveness and their capacity to export.

Foreign trade performance has been one of the major successes of China's reform programme. The creation of special economic zones, the granting of permission for enterprises to manage their own exports and the curtailing of export subsidy schemes have promoted export growth. On the other hand, imports are still subject to licensing arrangements, and tariff and non-tariff protection remains high. Even so, between 1978 and

Table 13.1. *Selected provincial growth rates and exports, billion yuan, 1981–90*

	Output		Exports	
	Value 1990	Average real annual growth (1981–90, %)	Value 1989	Share of China's total exports (%)
Guangdong	169.1	16.9	42.6	20.1
Shanghai	110.0	6.0	26.3	12.4
Liaoning	121.6	9.1	23.1	10.9
Shandong	184.2	13.6	15.9	7.5
Jiangsu	216.2	13.0	12.7	6.0
Zhejiang	114.4	13.8	9.7	4.6
Tianjin	47.5	8.7	8.8	4.1
Hebei	95.7	11.8	10.0	4.1
Fujian	49.1	13.9	10.0	4.1
Total	2041.8	11.1	211.9	100.0

Sources: State Statistical Bureau, *China Statistical Yearbook 1993* (Beijing: SSB, 1994); IMF, (1993).

1993 the share of exports in China's GNP almost doubled, increasing at a rate of 16 per cent a year in US dollar terms, while imports increased only marginally slower (World Bank, 1994e). The most dramatic growth was in manufactured exports. Total exports reached US$92 billion in 1994 (GATT, 1995); manufactured exports were 80 per cent of the total (Bell *et al.*, 1993). As in other Asian economies, exports have provided a dynamic source of economic growth.

Economic performance and liberalisation in major provinces

China's rapid economic growth and export expansion since 1978 can be linked strongly with the liberalisation programme (table 13.1). The contrast between the economic performance of Guangdong and Fujian where special economic zones were established early in the reform period, and Shanghai where liberalisation was delayed, is quite marked. In the decade 1981–90, Guangdong's real GDP grew the fastest of all of China's provinces (16.9 per cent a year) while Shanghai had the slowest rate of growth (only 6 per cent a year). Fujian province and other coastal provinces (except Shanghai) achieved real growth rates of around 13 per cent per annum, while the national average was 11 per cent per annum. Before the reforms began, Shanghai, in China's traditional industrial heartland, was the most important exporting province, but it fell behind Guangdong in 1986. Shanghai's exports slipped from 30 per cent of China's total in 1978 to only 10 per cent by 1990. In 1984, Guangdong, with 63 million people, exported only 10 per cent of China's exports but by 1990 its exports were 20 per cent of the total: the differences in the provinces' policy environment had caused marked divergence in performance.

Guangdong's growth has been driven by exports, which increased at an average annual rate of 29 per cent, more than twice the rate of output growth. The share of exports in Guangdong's GDP jumped from 13 per cent in 1978 to 34 per cent in 1990. Guangdong's export performance explains 80 per cent of the difference between economic growth in Guangdong and the average for China (Bell *et al.*, 1993). Most of these exports have come from special economic zones in the south of the province. Unofficial estimates indicate that in many counties in the Pearl River Delta, near Hong Kong, real growth has been around 20 per cent a year for the past ten years. In the three special economic zones in the Delta, growth is estimated to be 30 per cent a year for this period (Bell *et al.*, 1993; Lui Pak-Wui *et al.*, 1992)

Guangdong has also benefited from being close to Hong Kong and Macao. It received two-thirds of foreign direct investment (FDI) from these city states going to China in 1991, and one-third of China's total FDI (Bell *et al.*, 1993) Hong Kong markets Guangdong's manufactures. The province has also enjoyed relatively low fiscal transfers to the central government, compared with provinces like Shanghai and Zhejiang (Lui Pak-Wui *et al.*, 1992).

Guangdong's success has depended, however, on reform and liberalisation in a range of policy areas. When four special economic zones were established in 1984, three were located in Guangdong. One year later, the Pearl River Delta economic development zone was established and in 1988 the whole of Guangdong was made a reform experiment zone. Radical reforms were introduced in the financial sector, with the establishment of stock exchanges, joint stock companies and foreign exchange swap centres. Trade reforms introduced flexible import licensing and export marketing regimes to facilitate international trade. Price reforms were introduced and mandatory planning was removed. The provincial government was given freedom to invest in infrastructure, which was passed on to county and municipal authorities (Bell *et al.*, 1993).

In contrast, Shanghai is a very centrally planned province. Reforms on the entry of non-state firms, access for FDI, trade deregulation, price decontrol, labour and capital market liberalisation and enterprise management autonomy were delayed. Only a small proportion of China's total FDI went to Shanghai in the 1980s and only one-third the value received by Guangdong between 1979 and 1990 (Yun-Wing Sung, 1992; Ministry of Foreign Trade and Economic Cooperation, 1994). Shanghai's growth performance lagged. Not until 1990 was the first free-trade and investment zone opened at Pudong (adjacent to downtown Shanghai). At the same time, the Shanghai authorities attempted to improve the efficiency of the state-owned enterprise sector by merging small loss-making enterprises with more successful enterprises, selling loss-making enterprises to collective groups and forming joint ventures. A large injection of infra-structural investment and increased FDI inflows raised Shanghai's growth rate towards that of the southern coastal provinces (Shanghai Statistical Bureau, 1993).

Measuring the effects of policy reforms on economic performance

The divergent treatment given to different provinces under China's reform programme provides an opportunity to measure the benefits of liberalisation under controlled conditions. A survey of enterprises in four southern provinces (Guangdong, Fujian, Shenzhen and Shanghai) was undertaken in 1993 (Perkins, 1995a, 1995b; Zhang, 1994). This data is used to undertake two specific studies:

- *Using measures of total factor productivity.*[2] Comparisons are made between exporting and non-exporting enterprises with different ownership characteristics (state-owned, foreign-owned, joint ventures, collectives and private enterprises) in provinces with different policy regimes. Total factor productivity growth is the sum of output elasticities of labour, capital and materials (Perkins, 1995a, 1995b; Zhang, 1994).
- *Domestic resource cost ratios of enterprises estimated as a measure of financial benefits from exporting.*[3] An enterprise's annual net profit (domestic sales in local currency) *less* input costs (in local currency) is compared with the annual net foreign exchange earnings (exports *less* imports) (Bruno, 1967). If this domestic resource cost ratio is less than the effective rate of exchange (local currency/foreign currency), exporting from this enterprise is viable. These domestic resource cost ratios are compared for different ownership characteristics, in different industries and in different policy environments to assess the relative cost-effectiveness of their exports.

The survey data was collected from 300 state-owned, collective, joint venture and foreign-owned enterprises in four cities, Guangzhou, Shenzhen in Guangdong, Xiamen in Fujian and Shanghai. The questionnaire covered the period 1980–92 and included questions on enterprise decision making, freedom to trade, the impact of planning controls and subsidies, employment levels, capital sources, etc. The enterprises were representative of major manufacturing industries in the three provinces. All qualitative questions to managers were asked in mid-1993 and related to the situation in the firm at that time. Time series data (for 1980–92) was collected for all quantitative questions. This was provided by firms' accountants from their firm's accounts for previous years.

Enterprise export performance

In a market economy firms export if it is profitable. A country's export performance is enhanced by policy changes that increase profits from exporting. In a transitional economy like China, policy changes can also increase the incentive to export and to make profits. China and other countries have been urged to adopt policy reforms to expand exports (World Bank, 1993; Chow and Kellman, 1993).

Panel data on enterprises' export-orientation and policy environment in China were used to test these policy prescriptions (Perkins, 1995a). A specification based on an expanded export supply function was developed which anticipated that the proportion of total output exported would be determined by comparing domestic production costs with the local currency value of foreign exchange earnings from exports, the growth rate of domestic income and policy environment in which the enterprise operated. This included their exposure to reforms of ownership, factor markets and the trade regime that would influence enterprises' export performance.

The export-orientation of enterprises varied with different ownership structures in the period 1980–92 (table 13.2). State-owned enterprises were much less export-orientated than collective, township and village enterprises (TVE), joint ventures (JV) and foreign-owned enterprises (WFO). The collective enterprises steadily increased their export-orientation throughout the period covered. Foreign-owned enterprises produced principally for export. The export-orientation of enterprises in the survey according to industry classifications is shown in table 13.3.

Export-orientation of enterprises is related to total factor productivity (TFP) growth (table 13.4). Exporting state-owned and other enterprises in all industries experienced higher TFP growth rates than non-exporting enterprises. Exporting enterprises achieved 22–34 per cent higher TFP growth in the industries surveyed. This additional growth in TFP was experienced by export-orientated state-owned enterprises as well as export-orientated non-state firms.

Table 13.2. *Export performance of enterprises,
percentage share of exports in total sales,
1980–92*

Year	State	Collective	TVE	JV	WFO
1980	30	28	87	n.a.	n.a.
1982	26	29	n.a.	n.a.	n.a.
1984	19	33	n.a.	n.a.	n.a.
1985	22	52	98	34	n.a.
1986	12	45	n.a.	49	n.a.
1987	22	85	n.a.	50	n.a.
1988	23	55	n.a.	53	100
1989	33	82	n.a.	60	100
1990	29	76	58	62	98
1991	27	66	n.a.	59	81
1992	26	71	61	61	81
Obs.	91	10	13	45	13

Note:
n.a.=Not available.
Source: Survey data.

Table 13.3. *Export-orientation by industry, export/output share, 1980–92*

Year	Textiles	Garments	Electrical appliances	Machine tools	Iron and steel	Metal products	Other	Non-cotton textiles	Other appliances	High-tech
1980	34	78	n.a.	23	3	n.a.	25	27	29	1
1982	n.a.	29	57	26	n.a.	n.a.	n.a.	n.a.	n.a.	n.a.
1984	57	33	11	19	n.a.	n.a.	37	n.a.	n.a.	n.a.
1985	28	66	19	18	2	n.a.	21	31	18	1
1986	80	45	38	23	n.a.	n.a.	17	n.a.	n.a.	n.a.
1987	45	75	23	28	46	n.a.	21	n.a.	n.a.	n.a.
1988	75	58	26	31	77	n.a.	32	n.a.	n.a.	n.a.
1989	91	81	33	36	56	63	25	n.a.	n.a.	n.a.
1990	46	70	40	45	26	48	39	31	22	5
1991	52	75	36	32	27	39	33	32	19	6
1992	51	71	38	21	23	31	31	39	25	5

Note:
n.a.=Not available.
Source: Survey data.

Table 13.4. *TFP growth of export-orientated and non-exporting enterprises, by ownership and industry, 1982–92 (1980=100)*

	1982	1984	1986	1988	1990	1992	Obs.
State-owned							
• Non-export							
Textile	114.4	117.7	139.8	149.8	114.5	111.7	311
Garment	68.8	58.5	63.2	79.7	102.3	104.9	426
Elec. appliance	n.a.	n.a.	n.a.	n.a.	n.a.	n.a.	300
Machine tools	n.a.	n.a.	n.a.	n.a.	n.a.	n.a.	70
Iron and steel	98.8	105.5	94.9	89.6	106.4	114.1	165
Metal products	101.0	99.0	98.8	97.8	121.0	159.8	60
Total	102.3	105.0	110.2	114.0	102.4	122.7	1332
• Export							
Textile	108.4	123.3	145.1	159.6	140.6	144.1	311
Garment	114.3	124.4	115.9	118.3	109.5	129.9	426
Elec. appliance	96.9	101.0	90.8	117.8	64.4	122.2	300
Machine tools	101.6	106.0	123.5	148.2	162.6	180.7	70
Iron and steel	102.7	108.6	132.6	134.1	149.0	153.1	165
Metal products	n.a.	n.a.	n.a.	n.a.	n.a.	n.a.	60
Total	104.1	112.6	122.0	138.4	117.0	143.5	1332
Non-State							
• Non-export							
Textile	113.7	125.9	132.0	146.9	153.5	160.6	311
Garment	n.a.	n.a.	n.a.	n.a.	n.a.	n.a.	426
Elec. appliance	95.4	58.7	60.3	132.1	152.5	163.4	300
Machine tools	n.a.	n.a.	n.a.	n.a.	n.a.	n.a.	70
Iron and steel	n.a.	n.a.	n.a.	n.a.	n.a.	n.a.	165
Metal products	106.0	115.7	106.0	123.0	120.8	166.8	60
Total	105.0	108.3	109.7	126.4	123.8	147.2	1332
• Export							
Textile	n.a.	n.a.	n.a.	n.a.	n.a.	n.a.	311
Garment	115.8	121.4	131.2	139.1	160.1	171.3	426
Elec. appliance	112.0	163.3	135.4	177.7	148.8	198.9	300
Machine tools	n.a.	n.a.	n.a.	n.a.	n.a.	n.a.	70
Iron and steel	108.5	147.4	165.0	184.5	190.9	202.3	165
Metal products	n.a.	n.a.	n.a.	n.a.	n.a.	n.a.	60
Total	119.5	139.0	158.5	177.9	197.4	216.9	1332

Notes:
Obs.=no. of observations.
n.a.=Not available.
Source: Survey data.

Table 13.5. *Average domestic resource cost ratios, by type of ownership, 1980–92*

Ownership	1980	1984	1988	1990	1992	Obs.
State	0.65	0.62	0.65	0.95	0.82	85
Collective	0.89	0.79	0.92	0.97	0.94	14
TVE	0.96	n.a.	n.a.	0.90	0.85	11
JV	n.a.	n.a.	0.66	1.00	0.95	55
WFO	n.a.	n.a.	n.a.	0.91	0.93	13

Notes:
Obs.=number of observations.
n.a.=Not available.
Source: Survey data.

Comparisons of TFP growth of exporting and non-exporting enterprises in the cities surveyed show that export-orientated enterprises experienced consistently higher productivity growth than non-export-oriented enterprises. This was particularly marked in Shenzhen and Xiamen, but was also true for Guangzhou. On average, exporting enterprises achieved 32 per cent more productivity growth than non-exporting firms. These conclusions are consistent with productivity growth and efficiency increasing as exposure to international competition increases. This dissection of causality – from export-orientation to TFP growth – was supported by statistical testing (Granger, 1969; Perkins, 1995a).

Further evidence of the benefits from exporting was obtained by comparing the domestic resource cost ratio of different enterprises with effective exchange rates. Domestic resource cost ratios were calculated from recorded costs of enterprises; sales revenue *less* profits and input costs. At the beginning of the period covered, state-owned enterprises were using capital that had been installed under the Plan. No capital charges were paid. Furthermore, most raw materials and energy was supplied at Plan prices which were substantially below free market prices. Consequently, the reported costs of state-owned enterprises were significantly less than true economic costs of production. This is evident in the low estimated domestic resource cost ratios of state-owned enterprises at the beginning of the survey period (table 13.5). By 1990 state-owned enterprises were having to rely on loans to finance investment and were paying market prices for most production inputs. Export subsidies were abandoned in 1991. The domestic cost of state-owned enterprise's exports increased significantly (table 13.5).

The domestic resource cost ratios of collective enterprises in the survey

Table 13.6. *Average domestic resource cost ratios, by industry, 1980–92*

Industry	1980	1984	1986	1988	1990	1992
Cotton textiles	0.61	0.62	0.96	0.84	0.96	0.95
Non-cotton textiles	0.54	n.a.	n.a.	n.a.	0.76	0.96
Garments	0.93	0.79	0.91	0.86	0.94	0.95
Electrical appliances	1.05	0.64	0.81	0.88	1.06	0.90
Machine tools	n.a.	n.a.	0.45	0.53	0.91	0.89
Iron and steel	n.a.	n.a.	1.00	1.02	0.77	0.97
Heavy metal products	n.a.	n.a.	n.a.	n.a.	1.17	0.80
Non-electrical appliances	0.75	n.a.	n.a.	n.a.	0.90	0.87
Electronics, meters	n.a.	n.a.	n.a.	n.a.	0.79	0.77
Other	1.01	n.a.	n.a.	0.81	1.03	0.84

Note:
n.a.=Not available.
Source: Survey data.

Table 13.7. *Average domestic resource cost ratios, by region, 1980–92*

	1980	1982	1984	1985	1986	1987	1988	1989	1990	1991	1992
Guangzhou	0.76	0.75	0.79	0.59	0.66	0.71	0.76	0.76	0.89	0.69	0.68
Shenzhen	n.a.	n.a.	0.64	0.71	0.89	0.95	0.81	0.83	0.87	0.89	0.94
Xiamen	n.a.	0.65	0.62	n.a.	n.a.	0.73	0.87	1.12	1.15	1.04	0.90
Shanghai	0.80	n.a.	n.a.	0.80	n.a.	n.a.	n.a.	n.a.	1.10	1.17	1.10

Note:
n.a.=Not available.
Source: Survey data.

were stable, although they rose slightly. The costs of township and village enterprises were the lowest, despite having to secure all their capital, raw materials and energy at market prices, like the joint ventures and wholly foreign-owned firms.

In most industries, domestic resource cost ratios rose over the period 1980–92 as enterprises were exposed increasingly to market forces (table 13.6). The major exception was the iron and steel industry, whose domestic resource cost ratios fell in the 1990s, as artificially low fixed prices were raised towards international prices. By 1992, the domestic resource cost ratio of most industries were in a narrow band. This indicates that exporting enterprises in different industries were subject to a more uniform policy regime.

The average domestic resource cost ratios of enterprises in the four coastal cities surveyed are compared to see if differences in the policy environment influenced the financial profitability of exports (table 13.7).

The domestic resource cost ratios of surveyed enterprises in Guangzhou were significantly lower than those in Shanghai. This is consistent with the argument that a more liberal policy regime reduces enterprises' production costs. In addition, the close marketing ties with Hong Kong and the greater flexibility for firms to trade on their own account also increased export revenue of enterprises in Guangzhou. Domestic resource cost ratios of enterprises in Shenzhen are higher than in Guangzhou, and have been rising. This is consistent with the falling TFP growth and rising labour and land costs in Shenzhen in the late 1980s and early 1990s (Perkins, 1995b). Domestic resource cost ratios of enterprises in Xiamen were higher than in Guangzhou but lower than surveyed Shanghai enterprises. After peaking in 1990, the domestic resource cost ratios of Xiamen enterprises fell.

Determinants of export performance at the enterprise level

The enterprise survey data were employed to assess the major determinants of enterprises' export performance (details available from the author). For firms overall, decision making autonomy within the firm was the most important factor in explaining export performance. Firms which suffered less interference in their decision making by bureaucratic supervisors had good export records. The ratio of planned to total output was also significant in explaining export performance and, as could be expected, was negatively correlated with the export achievement of enterprises. As enterprises were given more freedom to sell their output in the market, they increased their capacity to export. This improvement in export performance may arise from the skills and attributes acquired in competing in the domestic market, including improved marketing, product quality and presentation.

The relationship of the domestic resource cost ratio to the effective exchange rate was significant in explaining export performance but had a positive sign: firms with a high domestic resource cost ratio exported more. In a market economy, an inverse relationship would be expected. The financial domestic resource cost ratio of all enterprises, and particularly state-owned enterprises, rose during the reform period, probably because of exposure to market forces. At the same time, and probably for similar reasons the export performance of Chinese enterprises improved. The regression shows a positive relationship between export performance and financial domestic resource cost ratios.[4]

Collective, township and village, and foreign-owned enterprises were significantly more successful exporters than state-owned enterprises. This supports the earlier conclusion that most export growth was generated in the non-state sector.

Enterprises located in the two special economic zones (SEZ), Shenzhen and Xiamen were significantly more successful exporters than enterprises outside the special economic zones (Shanghai and Guangzhou). The capacity of firms to export on their own account showed a positive impact on export performance. GNP growth rates had a small negative impact on export performance. In years of rapid growth in domestic demand, the availability of goods for export declined.

The average rate of protection was found to be significant in explaining export-orientation but had a positive sign. This may indicate that there is 'water' (an unnecessary component) in tariffs imposed by China on export-orientated sectors, such as garments and electronic appliances. There is product variation within these broad tariff categories (for example, fashion wear and basic clothing within garments and low- and high-quality electronic appliances). High tariffs on 'luxury goods' prevent 'waste' of foreign exchange, while for cheap products China is now a competitive exporter. Quantitative barriers and import licensing remain significant in China. The average rate of protection is an imperfect proxy for sectors' aggregate nominal protection. Moreover, no allowance is made for protection on inputs, so it is not a measure of effective protection.

The proportion of profits retained by enterprises and the proportion of loans in total investment were not found to be significant determinants of export performance. However, both had a positive effect on export performance.

Conclusion

The conclusions from this enterprise survey have several implications for China's entry to the WTO. First, from the point of view of China and the benefits expected from increased access to world markets, one of the most interesting findings was that export-orientated firms, regardless of ownership structure, industry or city surveyed, had higher growth of total factor productivity in the survey period than firms that did not export. Any trade liberalisation that increases access to overseas markets for China's exports, therefore, will tend to increase output from the most efficient enterprises.

Second, China's reform programme has reduced the significance of export subsidies. Domestic resource cost ratios of enterprises have declined. The rapid rise of the domestic resource cost ratios of state and collective enterprises was caused by their increasing exposure to market forces. Most inputs and outputs are now sold at market prices, and subsidies to the traded goods sector have declined.

Differences in the provincial policy regimes were evident from domestic resource cost ratios. Enterprises in Guangzhou, and to a lesser extent Shenzhen and Xiamen, had lower costs than those in Shanghai. Exporters from the former cities were more cost-efficient and profitable than those from Shanghai. Among the different ownership forms, the more market-orientated township and village enterprises had the lowest domestic resource cost ratios.

Finally, with respect to the domestic policy initiatives likely to improve export performance, the major determinants of export success by enterprises were autonomy in decision making and exposure to freer domestic markets. For non-state owned enterprises, the right to export on their own account contributed to export success. Collective, township and village and foreign-funded enterprises were all more successful exporters than state-owned enterprises. Enterprises located in the two special economic zones, Shenzhen and Xiamen, showed most success.

The results of this survey are all consistent with the benefits expected from free operation of markets and removal of government interference, especially directives and planning. Export performance is enhanced by withdrawing supervisory authorities from decision making roles by enterprises, revoking any obligations for firms to produce under the Plan and granting firms the right to trade on their own account. Extending duty drawbacks and foreign exchange and other privileges enjoyed by firms in the special economic zones to all enterprises, or preferably, dismantling China's heavy protection regime and establishing a truly market-based foreign exchange system, are other policies changes that are likely to increase export success. Finally, the continuing growth of the non-state sector is one of the most important factors improving China's export performance. Consequently, policies to encourage this sector, including capital market reform, should be given high priority.

For a country the size of China, it is not wise to talk in generalities about efficiency and competitiveness. In this study a survey of three of the most prosperous coastal provinces has been undertaken which shows that the effects of China's economic and trade reforms since 1978 have had the expected effects on productive efficiency and exports. This is a positive sign. The relaxation of regulations and planning in these provinces has improved the competitiveness of manufacturing industries. The signs are that China is moving towards a competitive market system. In these circumstances the doubts that remain about China's re-admission to the GATT should be eroded. The benefits of liberalisation have been demonstrated over the past decade. China's export growth is matched by similar growth in imports, for which GATT contracting parties will be free to compete once the protocol of accession is agreed.

NOTES

1. Foreign investment was attracted by permitting entry of joint Sino–foreign ventures and later wholly foreign-owned enterprises to an increasing number of sectors. Other inducements included a concessionary 15 per cent company income tax when the standard rate was 55 per cent (it is now set at 39 per cent for all enterprises). Foreign-funded enterprises (and others) in SEZ and other designated areas may obtain duty drawbacks on imported inputs used to produce exports and could 'retain' 100 per cent of foreign exchange earnings. Less regulated labour hiring and firing was supposed to be permitted, but it is doubtful whether this occurred. Foreign-funded enterprises can freely expatriate profits and are also allowed access to the local state-owned banking system, which in recent years has frequently offered negative real lending rates.

2. The Tornqvist index was used to define total factor productivity:

$$TFP=(\ln Q_t-\ln Q_{t-1})-\ell_L(\ln L_t-\ln L_{t-1})$$
$$-\ell_K(\ln K_t-\ln K_{t-1})-\ell_M(\ln M_t-\ln M_{t-1}) \tag{1}$$

where TFP is total factor productivity growth, ℓ_L, ℓ_K and ℓ_M are the output elasticities of labour, capital and materials respectively, estimated from (1) above and the terms in brackets are the first differences of the logs of labour, capital and materials.

3. The formula for a non-discounted domestic resource cost ratio is:

$$DRCR=\frac{(C_t^L-B_t^L)(\$L)}{(B_t^F-C_t^F)(\$US)} \tag{2}$$

where
C_t^L are the domestic input costs of the enterprise, measured in local currency
B_t^L are local sales made by the enterprise, measured in local currency, $L
B_t^F are the export earnings of the enterprise, measured in foreign exchange, $US
C_t^F are the import costs of the enterprise, measured in foreign exchange, $US.

4. It is possible that in future years, since the financial domestic resource cost ratio more closely reflects the true opportunity cost of domestic resources, this coefficient would have the expected negative sign.

14

Globalisation, East Asian trade and the Uruguay Round

DAVID ROBERTSON

International trade has played a major role in the economic development of the East Asian region. In the 1970s, export-led growth by the NIEs, based on labour-intensive manufactures, re-established the neo-classical model of economic development. More recently, research into the contributions that government strategies and imports have made to sustained economic growth in the region have enhanced further the role that trade has played. Opportunities also encouraged governments to embrace unilateral trade liberalisation and financial deregulation in the past decade which enhanced industrial growth and trade expansion in East Asia when other regions were experiencing economic recession.

'Globalisation of production' has added an extra dimension to the East Asian economies as well as integrating them into world markets. The efficiency and cost advantages of producing in this region promoted specialisation by process and attracted multinational enterprises to invest and to relocate production activities. This movement of technology, capital and 'firm-specific' assets (brand names, marketing, technical skills, management, etc.) across national frontiers increased intra-industry and intra-firm trade of East Asian countries through complex corporate systems of affiliation, association and subcontracting.

This integration into global markets, by commercial, financial and corporate links, encouraged the East Asian countries to participate more fully in the Uruguay Round of trade negotiations than they had in earlier negotiations. Over the seven years of negotiations many significant changes occurred in these economies and in their commercial relations with each other and with third countries, which intensified interest in the outcome. The Uruguay Round Final Act contains many agreements and decisions that will bear directly on their future economic performance – most positively, some negatively. The post-Uruguay Round trade regime will profoundly influence the trade and industrialisation of the East Asian economies.

Changing patterns of East Asian development

'Export-led development' was first identified in connection with the rapid development in East Asia's four NIEs (Little *et al.*, 1970). The same pattern is discernible in the ASEAN4 – Malaysia, Thailand, Indonesia, Philippines – where exports of labour-intensive manufactures (e.g. clothing, footwear, furniture, toys, electronic components, etc.) provided the stimulus for accelerating economic growth. Rapidly developing regions of China (Guangdong and Fuchen) are also following this path. Those similarities generated the term 'flying-geese' pattern of development. This portrays the development of East Asian economies as successive waves of industrialisation based on trade between countries at different stages of development. More advanced economies respond to 'catching-up' by their neighbours by moving up the technology ladder to exports requiring more human capital or higher technology, and withdrawing from labour-intensive, standardised products. At each stage, the evolution of the 'flying-geese pattern' depends on access to foreign markets, making the open, multilateral trading system, supported by GATT rules crucial.

The early stages of economic development in East Asia relied on exporting to OECD markets, and the United States in particular. Under-valued exchange rates early in the 1980s, especially against the US dollar, promoted expansion of East Asian exports, even though the world was in a slow recovery from recession. The share of exports from the four NIEs (and Japan) going to the US market increased strongly in the period 1980–6 (see table 14.3). After the currency realignments of 1986, the share of these exports to the United States and EC-12 declined, although export growth continued. Trade among the eight East Asian economies grew strongly (table 14.3). The ASEAN4 recorded strong growth in exports to all major destinations in the period 1986–92 and export shares to developed countries expanded as strongly as exports to East Asian neighbours. Similarly, China's exports to East Asia grew rapidly in the period 1986–92: in 1992, East Asia took over half China's exports. The rapid growth of trade in East Asia in the past decade was associated with rapid economic growth (table 14.1). As one of the world's leading growth poles, other major regions increased their trade with East Asia faster than their own regional trade (see table 14.4).

The rapid economic growth achieved by East Asian economies (except the Philippines) since 1986 derived from the strong growth in manufactured exports (table 14.2). The share of total exports and manufactured exports in GDP increased, which is consistent with 'the flying-geese theory'. Japan and its more advanced neighbours specialised in human

Table 14.1. *Economic indicators, average annual growth, percentages, 1980–93*

	GDP growth		Total exports growth		Exports as a percentage of GDP		GNP *per capita* (US$ current)	
	1980–6	1986–93	1980–6	1986–93	1980	1993	1980	1993
NIEs								
Hong Kong	6.5	5.7	10.7	15.8	88.0	143.8	5454	19150
Korea	9.1	8.2	11.6	9.6	34.0	28.9	1587	7513
Singapore	5.4	6.8	5.8	13.4	207.2	173.5	4680	19528
Taiwan	6.6	7.1	11.8	7.3	52.9	44.3	2290	10852
ASEAN4								
Indonesia	5.1	6.5	−2.0	8.0	33.0	29.3	504	714
Malaysia	4.5	8.1	8.6	13.8	57.5	78.0	1715	3163
Philippines	−0.5	1.6	−0.6	7.0	23.6	28.9	670	823
Thailand	5.5	8.2	8.5	17.1	24.3	36.0	683	2086

Source: World Bank (1995); Taiwanese data from Taiwanese government publications.

Table 14.2. *Gross domestic investment (GDI), 1980–93 and exports of manufactures, 1971–93*

	GDI share in GDP (%)		Manufactured exports annual average growth			Manufactures share of total exports (%)	
	1980–6	1986–93	1971–80	1980–6	1986–93	1980	1993
NIEs							
Hong Kong	30.7	28.1	13.1	1.3	18.3	96.5	95.3
Korea	28 1	35.8	28.0	7.2	12.2	69.5	92.3
Singapore	45.2	38.9	26.5	0.8	18.1	53.9	78.0
Taiwan	22.4	23.4	21.1	7.4	10.7	80.8	91.9
ASEAN4							
Indonesia	33.0	34.1	32.5	26.1	22.0	2.4	47.5
Malaysia	32.2	32.6	27.3	7.7	26.9	16.6	64.9
Philippines	22.9	20.7	33.7	−0.8	15.5	26.5	73.0
Thailand	26.0	38.0	29.3	8.5	32.4	20.9	67.9

Source: World Bank (1995); Taiwanese data from Taiwanese government publications.

Table 14.3. *East Asian exports to major markets, 1980–93*

	% share of exports 1980, 1986, 1993											
	United States			Japan			EC-12			8 EANICs		
	1980	1986	1993	1980	1986	1993	1980	1986	1993	1980	1986	1993
NIEs												
Hong Kong	26.7	32.0	23.4	4.7	4.8	5.2	23.4	14.9	15.1	13.4	9.7	8.9
Korea	26.4	39.7	21.6	17.4	15.5	13.8	15.5	12.3	11.2	12.4	9.5	21.7
Singapore	11.9	22.3	20.1	7.7	8.2	7.4	12.2	10.7	13.9	34.7	32.5	38.5
Taiwan	34.3	48.1	27.7	11.0	11.4	10.6	14.6	10.8	13.2	17.1	13.5	33.9
ASEAN4												
Indonesia	19.6	19.6	14.1	49.1	44.8	30.2	6.5	9.3	14.3	16.2	17.1	25.6
Malaysia	16.3	16.4	20.2	22.8	23.3	12.9	17.6	14.5	14.4	28.0	31.5	39.1
Philippines	27.4	35.5	38.5	26.5	17.7	16.0	17.4	18.2	17.3	15.0	16.6	16.7
Thailand	12.6	18.1	21.4	15.1	14.2	16.8	26.0	21.4	16.8	23.4	22.4	24.9
China	5.0	8.4	18.6	20.7	16.2	17.3	12.2	12.8	12.8	28.5	37.1	33.5
EC-12	5.6	9.3	7.5	1.0	1.4	2.0	55.7	56.7	56.0	1.9	2.2	4.5
Japan	24.5	38.9	29.1	. . .	. . .	. . .	14.0	14.8	15.7	21.8	17.9	31.7
United States	. . .	. . .	. . .	9.4	12.4	10.3	26.7	24.5	21.0	9.4	10.5	15.0

	Growth of exports 1980–93									
	United States		Japan		EC-12		8 EANICs		World	
	1980–6	1986–93	1980–6	1986–93	1980–6	1986–93	1980–6	1986–93	1980–6	1986–93
NIEs										
Hong Kong	13.6	15.3	10.5	20.8	2.2	20.9	4.4	18.1	10.3	20.1
Korea	20.2	1.6	10.1	8.6	8.0	9.9	7.4	27.1	12.3	11.4
Singapore	13.8	14.5	3.6	15.2	0.2	21.9	1.3	19.8	2.4	17.3
Taiwan	18.7	1.7	12.9	7.6	6.7	14.0	7.9	26.4	12.2	10.4
ASEAN4										
Indonesia	−6.4	7.2	−7.8	8.1	−0.6	22.5	−5.5	20.7	−6.3	14.3
Malaysia	1.4	21.2	1.6	9.9	−1.9	18.8	3.2	22.2	1.3	18.5
Philippines	1.2	13.2	−9.4	11.1	−2.4	11.7	−1.4	10.5	−3.1	11.7
Thailand	11.8	26.0	4.3	26.1	2.0	19.6	4.5	24.0	5.3	22.7
China	17.9	27.3	3.9	15.1	9.2	15.5	13.2	18.1	8.3	16.4
EC-12	11.5	3.5	9.2	12.3	2.7	8.4	5.1	17.7	2.4	8.0
Japan	17.0	3.0	. . .	. . .	9.3	9.4	4.9	16.2	8.3	7.8
United States	. . .	. . .	4.4	9.3	−1.7	10.0	1.6	16.6	−0.3	11.5

Note:
. . .=Negligible.
Source: IMF (1995).

Table 14.4. *Intra-regional and inter-regional trade for major regions, average growth rate of exports, 1981–93, percentage, per annum*

	NAFTA	Western Europe	East Asia	World
1981–93				
Exporter				
NAFTA[a]	8.0	4.0	8.4	5.9
Western Europe[b]	7.1	6.5	13.1	6.1
East Asia[c]	10.3	10.8	12.0	9.8
1986–93				
Exporter				
NAFTA	11.6	8.5	12.5	10.5
Western Europe	4.6	6.8	15.5	7.2
East Asia	7.8	12.9	18.0	12.7
1993 (share of world exports)				
Exporter				
NAFTA	7.7	3.2	3.7	17.2
Western Europe	3.5	26.3	3.1	39.9
East Asia	6.8	4.1	11.0	25.5

Notes:
[a]NAFTA=United States, Canada, Mexico.
[b]Western Europe=EC-12 plus EFTA-7.
[c]East Asia=Japan, ASEAN4, NIEs, China.
Source: International Economic Data Bank, The Australian National University; IMF Direction of Trade tapes (June 1994).

capital- and technology-intensive products, leaving labour-intensive products for the ASEAN4, which formed the basis for their rapidly growing exports to OECD markets since 1986.

Much of the trade among these East Asian economies (table 14.3) is promoted by foreign direct investment (FDI) and globalisation of production. After the 1986 currency realignments and continuing appreciation of the yen, Japan's economic growth came to depend on domestic demand as external competitiveness declined. This provided new trade opportunities for manufacturing in lower-cost neighbouring countries. Firms faced with rising production costs in Japan began to use imported components and to relocate production in Korea, Taiwan and Thailand, especially where the processes were labour-intensive. FDI from Japan into East Asia rose strongly after 1986 (table 12.3). The threat of exclusion from the European Single Market and NAFTA caused some diversion of investments to Europe and North America in the period 1990–2. Latest indicators suggest that Japanese investment in East Asia is rising again.

The four NIEs' dependence on export markets in the United States diminished after 1986, although it remains significant (table 14.3). For the

ASEAN4, however, the US market increased in significance as their low-cost manufactures became more competitive with realignments of exchange rates by Japan, Korea and Taiwan. Important economic links continued in spite of bilateral trade tensions. Much US FDI in East Asia related to the globalisation of production by US companies. 'Globalisation of production' refers to assembly and production in different countries based on imported parts and components from affiliated (intra-firm trade) or independent companies. Intra-industry trade between East Asia and the United States increased strongly in this period (Fukusaku, 1992).

After 1986, economic growth in the eight East Asian economies (except the Philippines) proceeded faster than growth in Japan (table 14.1). This trend has intensified since 1990. This results from the effects of the 'product-cycle' as labour-intensive production shifts to low-wage countries in the region (Vernon, 1966). In recent years foreign investment in East Asia has come increasingly from within the region (table 12.4); the data show that while Japanese investment has remained strong, the significance of US investment has declined even though annual investment flows into these economies have continued to increase. Hong Kong and Singapore have the largest stocks of US investment, while US investment in Indonesia has grown most rapidly. Since 1986, however, Japanese annual FDI flows have been two or three times US flows, and Japan's stock is rapidly catching up with US levels. The four NIEs now provide the biggest flows of investment to the ASEAN4, and China, where they provide more than half the inflows of FDI (table 12.4).

To demonstrate that rising investment flows are actually generating new types of trade is not easy; information on foreign investment flows in East Asia and from outside is difficult to obtain. Actual investment expenditures over time are not easily related to investment approvals. Because precise measurements are not possible, the impact of investment on production and trade flows is difficult to assess.

Intra-industry trade

The 'flying-geese' pattern of economic development is based on traditional theories of trade: comparative advantage based on factor endowments in East Asia established complementarity in production and promoted inter-industry trade flows. But as incomes rise (and wage costs) and as industries seek economies of scale, specialisation becomes narrower. Johnson (1968) synthesised several strands that had evolved to supplement neo-classical trade theory, to compose a dynamic theory of comparative costs. Vernon's 'product-cycle theory' (1966), which combined international investment and trade theories, was linked to the Hufbauer (1965)–Posner (1961) theory of 'technology-gap' trade to expand the theory of comparative costs; while Travis (1964) and Linder (1961) introduced the effects of demand (income levels and trade policies) on comparative advantage. This synthesis explains how differences in comparative advantage change over time, even in countries with similar factor endowments. Later the effects of imperfect competition on comparative advantage and the role of economies of scale were added (Krugman, 1987). This explains also why countries can trade in the same product, creating intra-industry trade (IIT). As specialisation by process increased and capital deregulation facilitated foreign investment flows, similarities in demand patterns and income levels provided scope for IIT to exploit cost differences.

Scepticism has surrounded measures of IIT since they were first introduced (Grubel and Lloyd 1975). IIT is measured according to a particular level of statistical aggregation (table 14.5): the fewer the categories, the higher an IIT coefficient is likely to be. Products with quite different uses may be incorporated in the same category. Measurement is commonly calculated at the 3-digit level of SITC. Since the aim is usually to show increases in IIT over time, any distortions caused by the aggregations should be present in all coefficients. The tendency for IIT in East Asia to rise is evident (table 14.5).

Research on IIT measures for manufactures in East Asian economies shows strong growth (Grant *et al.*, 1993; Noland, 1990). These coefficients vary positively with economic development. The sharp increase for the East Asian economies indicates their growing specialisation in manufacturing using high-tech methods and economies of scale. Interestingly, measures of IIT for Japan are lower than for the East Asian economies, with only a slow rise between 1970 and 1988. An OECD study of IIT (Fukusaku, 1992) shows the same trends, with all the East Asian economies, except the Philippines and Indonesia, recording higher IIT shares than Japan: all eight economies had faster increases in IIT than Japan. Japan's low IIT coefficient reflects its factor endowments making it an importer of raw materials and energy, and an exporter of finished manufactures.

Bilateral IIT coefficients among East Asian economies show strong links (table 14.5). Taiwan and Korea recorded the highest bilateral IIT coefficients with Japan, Singapore and Hong Kong. The ASEAN4 have strongest links with Singapore and each other, although intra-ASEAN4 trade is low. Malaysia, Singapore and Japan show high shares of IIT with OECD countries, especially the United States. Trade among the four NIEs shows increased intra-industry specialisation in technology-intensive production (Fukusaku, 1992). While globalisation is helping to bind together the East

Table 14.5. *Intra-industry trade (IIT) index of manufactures by main partner, 1980, 1986, 1993*

	NIEs			ASEAN4			China			EC-12		
	1980	1986	1993	1980	1986	1993	1980	1986	1993[a]	1980	1986	1993
NIEs												
Hong Kong	29.8	20.1	18.6	43.9	34.7	31.4	17.6	35.6	24.2	25.1	28.6	28.1
Korea	26.0	44.2	44.2	9.0	26.6	24.5	...	...	33.6	26.6	26.2	35.0
Singapore	44.5	50.4	72.6	48.1	64.6	63.7	8.9	20.2	46.5	35.9	39.9	34.2
Taiwan	27.1	31.5	54.3	16.1	17.7	28.2	...	...	...	20.8	28.3	33.9
ASEAN4												
Indonesia	13.3	17.2	35.1	19.8	20.8	33.3	...	1.4	11.1	3.3	5.3	12.8
Malaysia	49.6	68.4	65.7	54.9	51.1	57.6	1.9	9.6	15.9	21.4	36.6	41.4
Philippines	27.0	22.3	30.6	12.3	40.6	37.3	7.4	2.8	19.3	7.6	18.3	25.0
Thailand	30.7	41.3	65.1	25.7	29.0	60.4	6.9	22.8	22.8	7.1	19.8	29.0
China	37.2	56.8	46.5	6.8	13.8	20.5	...	...	...	14.6	12.2	17.9
EC-12	31.0	34.8	42.1	18.4	32.5	35.5	14.1	12.0	17.9	98.0	98.0	95.5
Japan	25.5	24.7	30.2	7.1	13.4	25.8	10.0	9.8	21.5	37.5	33.3	40.0
United States	30.4	25.8	43.9	39.5	48.6	34.2	9.2	9.7	13.2	59.4	53.3	67.7

	Japan			United States			World		
	1980	1986	1993	1980	1986	1993[a]	1980	1986	1993
NIEs									
Hong Kong	9.6	10.2	6.6	25.5	19.7	30.1	45.0	51.9	35.4
Korea	35.4	31.4	38.7	27.0	26.9	42.8	39.6	41.7	52.1
Singapore	8.4	17.9	31.5	43.7	47.8	45.4	65.1	73.2	74.1
Taiwan	20.1	27.6	33.2	20.8	19.0	34.6	34.9	39.3	52.1
ASEAN4									
Indonesia	1.1	2.0	9.6	1.4	2.7	12.6	7.7	10.3	25.0
Malaysia	7.9	25.4	32.6	56.8	61.7	41.4	37.5	60.6	59.8
Philippines	10.9	17.4	20.4	8.5	33.8	34.0	16.0	32.6	35.6
Thailand	4.4	10.4	25.7	14.8	35.9	38.6	23.3	37.4	48.8
China	10.0	9.8	21.5	9.3	9.7	13.5	28.2	30.0	35.8
EC-12	33.3	30.3	38.3	55.9	55.8	69.3	84.5	86.8	86.7
Japan	...	...	...	30.6	21.2	36.5	26.9	24.9	33.6
United States	26.4	18.4	30.0	...	...	...	61.6	57.8	69.8

Notes:
... = Negligible.
[a] Where 1993 data was unavailable 1992 data have been used. Hong Kong data exclude re-exports. Singapore data include re-exports.

Asian economies, these economies are also tending to become more integrated with US industries (table 14.5). Globalisation of production across the Pacific has continued the high rates of economic growth of East Asian economies in the past decade; their integration into the global economy offers further opportunities for IIT and specialisation to increase.

The focus on export-led growth in East Asia, and OECD governments' concerns about import penetration of their markets for manufactured goods on an ever-widening front, distracted attention from the opportunities offered by East Asian markets. (In the period 1985–90, exports to the four NIEs were a higher proportion of OECD exports than imports from these sources (OECD, *Economic Outlook*, December 1993).) Much of East Asia's rapid export growth was based on imports of capital equipment and services (Bradford, 1993). Imports by the East Asian economies have risen sharply, and import penetration has risen faster than in OECD countries (Hill and Phillips, 1993). The share of these imports originating in OECD countries (including Japan) has declined over the past two decades, but remains very high (60–80 per cent for the eight countries). Almost all the substitution has come from increased imports from East Asian neighbours.

These data on trade and foreign investment flows show that the strong trade performance of the East Asian economies has depended on the open, multilateral trading system provided by the GATT. Unilateral liberalisation in East Asia since 1986 has contributed to the growth of intra-regional trade. So far, there has been little interest in discriminatory regional trade agreements among East Asian economies; even the ASEAN free-trade agreement remains controversial. In consequence, expanding opportunities for intra-regional trade, as well as for world trade, depend largely on the implementation of the World Trade Organisation (WTO) and the Uruguay agreements. This is evident from the share of trade in GDP for the East Asian economies (even if the entrepôt trade of Hong Kong and Singapore is excluded). Discrimination by other regional groupings and experience with discriminatory impediments raised against East Asia's exports remain the major threats. OECD countries' use of GATT escape clauses in the past influence East Asian perceptions of the WTO and the new Uruguay Round agreements.

Discriminatory protection against East Asian exports

Obtaining information on 'administered protection' is extremely difficult. There is no reliable series of annual data. The GATT Secretariat provides data in the Director-General's *Annual Report*, but this depends heavily on notifications and cannot be comprehensive. The most recent report (July 1993) compiled figures using the Trade Policy Review Mechanism (TPRM). This should ensure more consistency once all contracting parties' trade policies have been reviewed according to the TPRM.

The Multifibre Arrangement (MFA) represented the first concerted effort by OECD countries to restrain access to their markets for East Asian exports of labour-intensive manufactures. In October 1994, importers under the MFA applied 145 bilateral restraint agreements affecting exports of textiles and clothing. Six importers (United States, EC, Canada, Austria, Norway, Finland) applied restraints on thirty exporters; in addition, twenty-eight import restraints applied to non-MFA countries were notified. In addition, several MFA exporters apply quotas against textiles and clothing imports. All eight East Asian economies are listed as exporters in the MFA. In July 1992, 127 trade restraints were applied to textiles and clothing outside MFA IV.

At the end of 1993, six safeguard actions according to GATT Article XIX remained in effect, down from fifteen in April 1993; ten actions were terminated and one new action taken. During the course of 1991–2, twenty actions had been in effect. One-third of these cases applied to agricultural products; only four remained in effect at the end of 1993. Many Article XIX actions have minor effects on world trade, being restricted in coverage to neighbouring countries; this discriminatory application of Article XIX safeguards contravenes Article I. The most serious restraint on trade still in effect is the German restriction on coal imports (introduced in 1958). Dissatisfaction with Article XIX among contracting parties leads to the use of so-called 'grey-area' measures applying various restraints bilaterally.

'Grey-area' measures affecting imports of industrial products (excluding textiles and clothing) are a notoriously difficult area to assess. These arrangements include unilateral export restraints (VERs), discriminatory import systems (quota allocations), orderly marketing arrangements (OMAs), and export forecasts. The most recent GATT figures (GATT, 1993b) has limited these measures to those applied by governments, whereas previous inventories included industry-to-industry arrangements. In consequence, the latest inventory contains only seventy-five measures affecting industrial products at the end of 1992. This compared with 284 arrangements in force at the end of 1990. It is possible, however, to reconcile these figures:

- In August 1990, EC member states had more than 120 products covered by national restrictions (allowed by Treaty of Rome, Article 115; EC Council Regulation, No. 288/82). This excluded measures covered by the MFA and imports from state-trading countries.

- Since the completion of the Single European Market at the beginning of 1993, the number of these national arrangements has been reduced. National restrictions on trade are not sustainable in a 'fully-integrated' market. France had seventy-one special arrangements, reduced to thirty in October 1992, and in Italy forty-eight was reduced to nineteen. Several of the remaining national restraints applied to fruit and vegetables (not included in the 1993 data), and consumer electronics from Japan and East Asia (GATT, 1993b).

- The end-1990 figure contained restrictions affecting fifty-nine agricultural products and thirty-nine steel products covered by the ECSC, which were excluded from the 1993 data. No measures affecting state-trading countries were included in the 1993 data.

Countervailing duties against 'unfair' subsidies have increased since 1989, with a marked increase in cases initiated in 1992–3 by the United States on steel products, following the expiry of steel VERs in July 1992. Outstanding actions (countervailing duties or price undertakings) remained fairly constant in the period 1989–93, until mid-1993 when a sharp increase was caused by US authorities announcing new duties. EC exports were by far the most frequent subjects of subsidy investigations (GATT, 1993b, table 7). Several EANIEs also featured in the period 1985–92: Thailand, Malaysia, Taiwan, Singapore, Korea (and China); together they accounted for 20 per cent of countervailing investigations in the period.

The GATT Anti-dumping Code came into force at the beginning of 1980. The data on initiations of anti-dumping actions up to 30 July 1994 show a marked increase since June 1990. The OECD noted that in the year to end-June 1993, more anti-dumping actions were initiated than in the previous five years (OECD, 1994a); the figure was only slightly smaller in the year to June 1994. This is in keeping with earlier experience during recessions when claims of 'unfair' competition tend to increase. The United States, EC, Australia and Canada are the main users of this form of protection, by a long way. Over the period 1990–4, these four accounted for 73 per cent of the 922 recorded initiations. There has been a tendency for middle-income developing countries to adopt anti-dumping measures recently; in the period mid-1990 to mid-1994, 20 per cent of new cases were initiated by Mexico, Poland, Korea, India and Brazil. (Mexico alone initiated 86 investigations.) Many countries have now introduced anti-dumping legislation which is likely to increase the use of anti-dumping measures in

Table 14.6. *Anti-dumping and countervailing actions, 1985–94*

Type of protection / Targets	OECD initiations (excl. Japan) (%)	East Asian 8	Japan	China	Total East Asia (%)
VRER in effect Dec. 1992 industrial products (excluding textiles and clothing)	65 (87)	50	19	1	70 (93)
CVD cases initiated 1985–92	154 (86)	32	. . .	5	37 (21)
Anti-dumping actions initiated 1985–94	1401 (85)	345	125	127	597 (36)

Source: GATT (1993b, 1994e, appendix tables).

future, especially after the unsatisfactory agreement on Article VI in the Uruguay Round.

Over the period mid-1985 to mid-1992, the East Asian economies were major targets for anti-dumping actions (GATT, 1993b). Of the total 1148 anti-dumping actions initiated and notified, 231 were targeted on the eight East Asian economies and sixty-nine against China. If Japan is included, one-third of anti-dumping actions were targeted at East Asia (Japan, China and the eight countries studied), and they were initiated mainly by EC, United States, Canada and Australia.

In the period mid-1992 to mid-1994, the targeting of East Asia was even more marked. Out of 498 anti-dumping cases initiated, 114 were against the eight East Asian economies, with in addition fifty-eight cases against China and twenty against Japan. Almost 40 per cent of anti-dumping cases initiated and notified to the GATT were brought against East Asia.

For all trade restraints considered as 'administered protection' (discriminatory and imposed unilaterally or under pressure by an importer), the East Asian economies (together with Japan and China) are major targets (see table 14.6).

The incomplete and patchy data available on administered protection is sufficient to demonstrate the reasons for East Asian interest in new agreements on trade rules in the Uruguay Round. They have been drawn progressively into GATT trade negotiations in an attempt to ameliorate discrimination against their exports and to contain OECD resort to GATT escape clauses. As the ASEAN economies became increasingly dependent on trade and more open to external forces through trade reforms, they adopted an active role in the Uruguay Round, too. The main fear of all these eight countries is that the GATT rules on which they depend will be weakened by discrimination resulting from bilateral trade disputes. US pressures on Japan and Korea resulted in better access for US plywood and rice than for competing ASEAN output.

These countries have participated actively in regional meetings of trade officials and three ASEAN countries are members of the Cairns Group. The ASEAN4 have not negotiated as a group, however, because of their disparate interests in agriculture and services. Over the seven years of negotiations, several issues regarded as controversial for ASEAN at Punta del Este have declined in importance (e.g. TRIMs, GATS).

Manufactured exports are significant for all these economies and here, without collaborating on offers, access to OECD markets was eased by tariff reductions and bindings. In keeping with their concerns about maintaining an open multilateral trading system, the major progress on codes of behaviour relating to contingent protection was most important:

- The Agreement on safeguards (and VERs);
- The Agreement on subsidies and countervailing measures;
- The Agreement on implementation of Article VI (1994);
- The Agreement on textiles and clothing (MFA);
- The Agreement on rules of origin;
- The Agreement on technical barriers to trade;
- The Understanding on rules and procedures governing the settlement of disputes.

These new agreements provide better security of market access for East Asian exporters. The Safeguards Agreement should see most VERs phased out over four years, following the establishment of the WTO. The new definitions of 'actionable' and 'illegal' subsidies should enable exporters to avoid countervailing actions for 'unfair' trade. Phasing-out the MFA over ten years means that benefits from relaxation of trade restraints will not appear until the end of the period. At the same time, in conjunction with the other changes, the opportunities for industrial countries to substitute new trade remedies should be limited.

East Asia and Uruguay Round outcomes

The seven East Asian representatives at the Marrakesh ministerial meeting that approved the Uruguay Round Final Act were all optimistic about the new trade regime that would come into effect with the WTO. (Taiwan is not a contracting party.) The most striking feature of these Ministers' statements was the support for the multilateral trading system over regional

256 *David Robertson*

economic groupings and managed trade, and the universal opposition to drawing links between trade and environmental and social policies (i.e. labour rights). Some disappointment was expressed about inadequacies in the agricultural agreement (Thailand, Indonesia), and imprecision in aspects of the GATS (Malaysia, Philippines, Indonesia). In addition, some concerns were expressed about the destabilising effect of unilateral trade measures taken to resolve bilateral trade disputes and the danger that trade remedies against 'unfair' trade may be substituted for 'quantitative restraints' (QRs) on trade to be removed according to Uruguay Round agreements (safeguards, and the phasing-out of the MFA).

Several East Asian ministers referred to the disincentive effect that trade remedies against 'unfair trade' can have on foreign investment in their countries. The phasing-out of VERs ('grey-area' measures) according to the Safeguards Agreement and the MFA should encourage investment in developing countries. But the definition of anti-circumvention in the Agreement on Article VI (anti-dumping) has the potential to damp investment flows to developing countries.

It is hoped that the strengthened consultation and dispute settlement mechanism will provide an effective defence for the trading interests of developing countries. This is perhaps the most significant, yet uncertain, aspect of the Uruguay Round Final Act. As trade frictions increased during the Uruguay Round negotiations, governments and industries have come to expect much of the dispute settlement procedure. Yet recent dispute panels, and some GATT Council decisions, have shown that many can be disappointed by the results. Only time and experience with the amended procedures will show how well they work. There is a danger of over-ambitious expectations that in themselves may undermine the new mechanisms. One of the major attractions of the WTO to environmental groups and social lobbies (labour rights) seems to be a belief that the dispute settlement mechanism will provide means for enforcing their goals. Such capture of the procedure would ensure its failure, as East Asian ministers demonstrated with their collective rejection of the WTO as an institution to handle environmental and social policies. Overburdening the new mechanism is a real danger; only by a steady accumulation of case law on disputes will an effective mechanism be established (Petersmann, 1993).

Quantitative assessments of the Uruguay Round Final Act (chapters 6–8 in this volume) estimate that most of the trade and welfare benefits expected to occur when all the agreements are fully implemented will come from tariff liberalisation, phasing-out the MFA and the Agricultural Agreement. Many other components in the Final Act are not easily quantified, but their effects on international transactions may be significant. The GATS is a framework agreement with many details to be decided; moreover, bene-fits from greater efficiency in service industries are more likely to appear in GNP measures than in international trade. Similarly, TRIPs and TRIMs will improve the competitive climate. Most of the other agreements and undertakings in the Final Act affect GATT rules, and their effectiveness still has to be tested. The major benefits for East Asia will arise from liberalisation of industrial trade and the tightening of GATT rules to prevent abuse of contingency protection under the escape provisions.

The strong growth in East Asia's manufactured exports in the past twenty-five years has been based on access to markets in developed OECD markets. More recently, trade growth in the East Asian region has augmented this export-led development. This dependence on OECD markets makes improvements in market access the most important aspect of the Uruguay Round Final Act. Industrial tariffs had been substantially reduced before the Uruguay Round negotiations began; an objective of the negotiations was to increase the number of tariff bindings and to remove residual low tariffs affecting developing countries' exports. According to the GATT Secretariat, the proportion of industrial countries' imports from developing countries entering at zero tariffs increased from 22 per cent to 45 per cent. At latest reckoning, 63 per cent of industrial countries' trade was subject to tariff reductions in the Round; 18 per cent was not subject to 'offers' (half being transport equipment). The main 'tariff peaks' (above 15 per cent) remaining in industrial countries affect textiles and clothing, leather, rubber and travel goods and transport equipment; these categories recorded below-average reductions in the round (GATT, 1993b).

Tariffs in industrial counties are thus not the main impediments to trade in manufactures. Concerns about market access relate to various forms of contingency protection (described above), and the uncertainties created by the threats of such action. Agreement to phase-out the MFA represents a major step, not only because of the importance of textiles and clothing exports to many developing countries, but also because it reduces the threat of similar multilateral protection arrangements. The build-up of bilateral trade restraints in motor vehicles, steel and electronic equipment give cause for concern, especially since the completion of the Single European Market. The Agreement on Safeguards requires the elimination of existing Article XIX actions and the phasing-out of 'non-conforming' measures (VERs) within four years. Clarification of the subsidies code will also remove some uncertainties.

The anti-dumping yardstick

The main area for continuing concern about discriminatory protection is anti-dumping actions. Some reassurance exists in the Rules of Origin Agreement. This sets out a work programme to harmonise rules of origin for non-preferential trade relations. It also contains provisions on administration of rules of origin to prevent their use to restrict or distort trade. This new Agreement applies to all contingency protection, including anti-dumping actions. In preferential trade regimes (GATT Article XXIV), the definition of 'origin' has yet to be defined. The Uruguay Round decision on anti-circumvention in the anti-dumping code still favours importers. Foreign suppliers are still at the mercy of domestic legislation in importing countries (United States, EC, Australia, Canada) for decisions on what constitutes 'unfair' trading, and for calculations of dumping margins (Hindley, 1988). Justifiably, exporters of manufactured consumer goods to OECD markets are concerned that anti-dumping remains a strong discriminatory instrument to use against competitive foreign suppliers. After the substantial amendments in the area of administered protection ('contingent' trade remedies) in the Uruguay Round Agreement, anti-dumping remains as the weak link in the 'safeguards complex' (Messerlin, 1990; Hindley, 1994).

Article VI of the GATT on anti-dumping was intended to limit this discriminatory form of protection to 'unfair' trade practices. In practice, the anti-dumping code sets out specific rules to regulate the use of anti-dumping measures, which have been adapted to the needs of domestic industries (Stegemann, 1991). Conformity of anti-dumping measures with the GATT code does not contribute to trade liberalisation; indeed, 'approved regulation of dumping has become a preferred tool of regulatory protectionism' (Stegemann, 1991, p. 376). The incidence of this protectionism is spreading because access to it is so easy. Research has shown how easy it is to obstruct (fabricate) dumping margins and how anti-dumping rules can be amended to suit the domestic needs of the major OECD countries that employ this form of protection (Hindley, 1988; Messerlin, 1990). Another concern is the spreading of anti-dumping legislation to developing countries, where it forms an acceptable form of insurance to accompany unilateral trade liberalisation and financial deregulation.

Anti-dumping measures are used to protect domestic producers against import competition. With 'grey-area' measures to be phased-out over five years and safeguards actions subject to new disciplines, anti-dumping provides the main loophole in GATT disciplines for would-be selective protection (Hoekman and Leidy, 1989). The failure to make anti-dumping actions more accountable in the Uruguay Round must be a major concern for East Asia's exporters. Manufactured exports to OECD countries have been targets for VERs and other market limitation agreements for many years, and anti-dumping measures are an emergency measure when all other forms of protection are denied.

Some hope of limiting anti-dumping actions, and possibly introducing new disciplines, comes from the globalisation of production that is integrating production and trade through corporate or contracting arrangements. Anti-dumping actions and procedures have tended to ignore domestic interests of consumers or users in favour of import-competing interests (Stegemann, 1991). But specialisation by process and intricate assembly/component associations will weaken the 'like-products' approach in anti-dumping. So far, governments have treated claims of 'unfair' trade in terms of import-competing industries seeking protection. As internationally integrated enterprises expand their sourcing and their markets this should create a countervailing force in determining protection, and their presence should be evident in the procedures to establish and measure dumping. This should become a valid component in the new agenda item on competition policy that will be considered by the WTO.

The agreement establishing the WTO requires all members to adopt a 'single undertaking'. For the first time, all members must accept GATT 1994 and all its agreements, except the plurilateral agreements which apply only to their signatory countries. This means that all the behaviour codes, interpreting and limiting GATT Articles, must be followed by all members of the WTO. (Formerly these codes applied only to signatories.) This gives non-OECD countries an interest in disputes arising under these codes, and particularly those relating to contingency protection. The new WTO dispute settlement procedures are central to this new comprehensive approach to trade relations.

15

An APEC postscript

DAVID ROBERTSON

During the three years of extended Uruguay Round negotiations in Geneva, economic events in the rest of the world were not in a similar state of suspension. Probably the largest change on the world trade landscape was the rapid evolution of regional trade arrangements. Some commentators saw the creation of the Single European Market (EU), the establishment of NAFTA and the intensification of Asia Pacific economic cooperation (APEC), as consequences of uncertainties surrounding the GATT system. In fact, history seldom provides such simple relationships of cause and effect. Each of these major regional developments – as well as some of the lesser regional trade arrangements among developing countries (AFTA, Mercosur, LAIA, etc.) – was probably a response to more complex needs and policy initiatives. After all, each of the major regional arrangements had been initiated before the irreconcilable differences that prolonged the Uruguay Round negotiations became apparent in 1990. Each of these arrangements had its own rationale.

- The Single European Market was intended to complete the process of eliminating EC internal borders.
- NAFTA was intended to reduce trade barriers faster then under multilateral negotiations, including instruments normally omitted from such negotiations (e.g. investment policies and trade safeguards). Canada expected that more favourable treatment would be granted under US trade laws, especially 'contingent' protection (anti-dumping and countervailing duties). NAFTA was also designed to lock-in Mexican trade liberalisation to the North American market.
- APEC was an attempt to increase economic cooperation in the world's fastest-growing region, and to bring Japan and the United States into a new forum to discuss their differences.

In all these processes, political as well as economic considerations played a part.

The major countries in the GATT negotiations evidently had designs on the opportunities offered by Article XXIV when the Uruguay Round began. Proposals for a review of Article I (non-discrimination) in the functioning of the GATT negotiating committee were rejected at an early stage. The amendments in the Uruguay Round Understanding on interpretation of Article XXIV were kept to a minimum, although the problems of interpretation and implementation were well known. The EC had had frequent recourse to Article XXIV for association agreements since the 1960s. The US Administration adopted bilateral free-trade areas as an active instrument of trade policy in the 1980s (Omnibus Trade and Competitiveness Act 1988). The declared US intention was to achieve further liberalisation of trade and investment through the negotiation of bilateral free trade arrangements, which would complement multilateral efforts.

Why regionalism is a threat

In the four years to the end of 1994, more than forty new regional trade agreements were notified to the GATT. Most of these involved the EU, but there were several important preferential agreements among developing countries (GATT, 1994e). Around half of merchandise trade already takes place within regional agreements, and the scope of new agreements has spread to trade in services. Special features in the new regionalism are the scope of the agreements and their spread into trade relations between industrial and developing countries.

The principal economic objection to trade preferences of any kind is that although they may promote trade among the participants, they do so at the expense of trade with other countries. These two effects are referred to as trade creation and trade diversion (Viner, 1950). While later analysts have modified these concepts, they remain useful. From the point of view of non-members of a preferential trade arrangement, however, they are discriminated against; demands for non-members' exports decline because of diversion of demand towards suppliers from preferred sources. Prices of output from member countries tend to rise, while falling demand for third countries' exports tends to reduce prices. The terms of trade facing non-members worsen. This could be offset by a reduction in protection against non-members. In a dynamic world, the terms of trade losses might also be compensated if higher incomes within the preference area spilled over into increased demand for imports (the income effect). Of course, price and income elasticities for imports from non-members vary according to product, so there will still be gainers and losers.

Regional trade agreements have positive and negative aspects. On the positive side, they are established to advance economic integration beyond conventional trade liberalisation. They can act against non-border barriers to trade in goods and services, and investment. On the other hand, regional trade arrangements often contain a defensive component, seeking to pre-empt future increases in protection or threats from 'contingent' protection. Countries outside regional arrangements are concerned about their effects on the multilateral system. There is a crucial difference between preferential trade arrangements that lead to zero tariffs and are open to new members, and agreements that have limited product coverage, differential treatment among members and are not open to new members. The former may complement a liberal multilateral system; the latter, by multiplying discrimination, weaken the system. Hence, the US' pursuit of bilateral free trade arrangements and the EU's association agreements and other preferential arrangements (e.g. Lomé IV) create a threat to the multilateral trading system. This has been referred to as 'hub-and-spoke' arrangements (Snape *et al.*, 1993). The United States and the EU form the 'hubs' with separate agreements representing spokes to another country, which may or may not have agreements with other 'spokes'. This process enhances the bargaining power of the 'hub' countries, which may set the terms for each bilateral agreement, or may refuse any agreement. A single free-trade treaty, open to new members who can meet specified requirements, is much less likely to distort trade. (Accession to the Treaty of Rome (EU) and NAFTA is circumscribed.)

A similar 'hub-and-spoke' structure is becoming established for foreign investment flows. The US Administration has signed seventeen bilateral investment agreements in the past three years, mostly with western hemisphere countries, and a similar number are being negotiated. Where countries exercise restrictions on foreign investment inflows, these agreements can amount to preferential arrangements. Increasingly commentators refer to complementarity between trade and investments. Proposals for a new multilateral investment agreement will have to confront such preferences (OECD Ministerial Council, May 1995).

Regionalism will be a permanent feature of the trading system. The contributions to multilateral liberalisation by EC and EFTA tariff dismantling may not be repeated by the new trading blocs with market power. The potential for non-cooperative behaviour will depend on the importance of their trade with non-members; that is the extent of continuing international economic interdependence. Nevertheless, the mechanics of new regional agreements could impede the process of 'internationalisation'; for example, the use of 'hub-and-spoke' agreements. The successful conclusion of the Uruguay Round, however, should diminish the incentives for non-cooperative behaviour between the major regional blocks.

The APEC surprise

In its present form, APEC does not come under Article XXIV because it does not comprise a free-trade agreement in the terms of that Article. APEC governments have studiously avoided any formal agreements that could be interpreted as discriminating against non-members, despite attempts by the United States to formalise trade and investment relations. Most Asian members of APEC emphasise the consultative character of the grouping, referred to as 'open economic association' or 'open regionalism' (Yamazawa, 1992). This requires the pursuit of trade liberalisation and deregulation through unilateral actions, without discrimination against non-members. A formal free trade agreement, as proposed by the APEC Eminent Persons Group, was rejected at the APEC Heads of State meeting in Seattle (November 1993). The revised proposal for 'free trade in the area', presented to leaders at Bogor in November 1994 was, however, adopted as a target by APEC, on the understanding that liberalisation would be introduced in accordance with GATT Article I, most-favoured-nation (Mfn) treatment. This 'free-trade objective' is to be achieved by 2010 by developed member countries, and by 2020 by developing countries. This commitment reached at Bogor was formalised into the Osaka Action Agenda at the APEC Leaders' meeting in November 1995.

Since the first APEC meeting in 1989, jointly sponsored by Australia and Korea, the outcomes from annual ministerial consultations have always exceeded expectations. While the Asian members continue to be cautious about new initiatives, the progress at the annual meetings is always carried along enthusiastically. This style of cooperation follows the ASEAN model. Decisions are taken by consensus and expressed joint statements of intent, without formally negotiated agreements. It is up to officials to implement the consensus.

The Seoul Declaration in November 1991 defined the scope of APEC activities:

- exchange of information and consultation on policies relevant to sustain growth, promote adjustment and reduce economic disparities;
- development of strategies to reduce impediments to trade and investment;

- promotion of regional trade, investment, human resource development, technology transfer and cooperation in specific sectors such
  as energy, environment, fisheries, tourism, transportation and telecommunications.

These objectives were to be pursued through technical cooperation at official level aimed at facilitating trade and investment flows in the region.
APEC commitments are phrased in the most general way. The acceptance
of the 'voluntary, non-binding investment principles' at Bogor (November
1994), illustrates this point. APEC exists on faith and trust, without the
support of formal legal agreements or schedules.

The reluctance to make commitments is founded on diversities in levels
and rates of development among the APEC countries, and the sensitivity
of existing national policies to change (i.e. sovereignty). Differences in
political regimes among the APEC countries, and widespread suspicions
about the motives of the larger member economies make detailed agreements difficult to achieve. The lowest common denominator in these circumstances is multilateral liberalisation and deregulation according to
Mfn treatment. Hence, APEC ministers always give priority in their statements to adherence to the GATT/WTO, regionalism in the sense of trade
preferences is rejected. And yet within APEC there are already several
regional trade arrangements (NAFTA, ANZCERTA and AFTA). The
ASEAN free-trade area (AFTA) has only gained real momentum since
APEC became an effective institution; a framework for AFTA was signed
in Singapore in 1992.

The major test for APEC will be to prepare schedules for the implementation of the Bogor Declaration to achieve free and open trade and
investment no later than 2020. In view of widespread opposition to the
free-trade area proposal before the Bogor meeting, because it involved
schedules for liberalisation, this declaration was another surprise. The
principal difficulty with the free-trade proposal (apart from diversified
membership mentioned above) seemed to be the interpretation that a free-
trade area meant integration along the lines of the EU. The correct model,
of course, would have been the EFTA, where the sacrifice of sovereignty
was minimal. A free-trade area requires a schedule of mutual reductions in
trade barriers by the members, but each member remains independent in
its trade policy with respect to non-members. Hence, adopting a zero tariff
against other member countries does not prevent the same rate being
applied on a Mfn basis against third-country suppliers. A free-trade area
(GATT Article XXIV) does not prescribe any kind of common tariff for
members. Hence, each APEC country would be free to adopt unilateral

free trade, but there would be a commitment to establish free trade with other member countries according to an agreed schedule of barrier dismantling (not necessarily the same schedule). This commitment by treaty would satisfy governments (like the United States) concerned with reciprocity in trade relations.

To achieve the Bogor Declaration to free and open trade and investment, the APEC governments will have to adopt schedules for dismantling barriers by 2010 or 2020, at the latest, depending on levels of economic development. This will be no mean task. It is common to hear that after the Uruguay Round tariffs and other trade barriers will have little impact on trade. The analysis in chapter 9 (p. 166) shows that bound tariffs remain generally high in many East Asian countries, and non-tariff and tariff barriers in some sectors are still important in industrial countries. Much will depend on the implementation of Uruguay Round agreements on textiles and clothing, safeguards and subsidies over the next ten years. Other trade and investment barriers, such as product standards, transport and communications bottlenecks, national treatment and rights of establishment, must also be dealt with during the next ten–twenty-five years.

APEC and the Uruguay Round

Slow progress in the Uruguay Round negotiations was one reason behind the Korea–Australia initiative to call the first APEC meeting. European foot-dragging, especially in agriculture, was delaying multilateral trade liberalisation and the strengthening of GATT rules that were anticipated by the export-hungry East Asian economies. Some also saw dangers in talk of a tripolar world, based on the dollar, the mark and the yen. Bringing the United States and Japan together in a Pacific group was viewed as one way to reduce the polarisation. The initiative was attractive in the United States, too, where multilateralism was giving way to more bilateralism in trade, and free-trade areas had become regarded as a route to liberal trade. The emphasis had shifted back to reciprocity at the expense of multilateralism.

In fact, it is unlikely that the establishment of APEC contributed much to the successful outcome of the Uruguay Round. Most Europeans regarded APEC as such a diverse group of economies that integration seemed a remote prospect. (The Europeans had experienced forty difficult years progressing towards a common market, based on inter-governmental agreements!) The cooperation achieved in APEC since 1989 has surprised the Europeans, but it seems unlikely that APEC had much influence on the GATT negotiations. An agreement as far-reaching as the Uruguay Round Final Act necessitated adjustments in officials' thinking, as well as a major re-education effort on domestic populations before it became acceptable. Only when all the stages had been completed could governments sign the treaties. This is illustrated by the 'softly-softly' approach adopted towards reform of the CAP in the EU. By the time the Agreement was signed, most of the policy changes had already been made, and adjustments in the industry were well under way.

Now the Uruguay Round Final Act has been ratified and the WTO is in place, APEC may have an important new role. In the period since 1986, the East Asian members of APEC have recorded rapid economic growth based on expansion of trade and investment. Trade among the East Asian economies (ASEAN, Taiwan, Korea, Hong Kong, Japan and China) has grown rapidly since 1986, and faster than trade with the rest of the world. But if allowance is made for faster growth of GDP in East Asia, trade with the rest of the world as a share of GDP has been unchanged. Trade with the rest of the world is still a higher proportion of GDP than trade within East Asia (see chapter 2). The US market remains the single most important market for most East Asian economies. The level of intra-industry trade (IIT) between several East Asian economies and the United States is also important (chapter 14, p. 250). Although foreign investment flows between East Asian economies have surged in recent years, especially to China, US foreign investment flows remain important, too. There is no evidence that Japan's investment is biased towards its East Asian neighbours (Frankel, 1992b).

All the APEC countries, regardless of their level of economic development, have vital interests in the full implementation of all the Uruguay Round agreements, in effective reviews of the agreements beginning in 1999, and in the smooth operating of the WTO and its disciplines. Moreover, because the APEC region represents almost half world output and 40 per cent of world trade in goods and services, any future round of trade negotiations will depend on initiatives and proposals from this region. The agenda for a new round will include domestic policies affecting trade and competition, investment policies, etc. But it will not neglect continuing protection provided by conventional trade instruments, including the tightening of conditions for using GATT escape clauses.

It is too early to forecast the agenda for a new round of trade negotiations. But the APEC approach to 'open regionalism' depends on an effective multilateral trading system, dominated by non-discrimination and transparency. If other countries resile from these principles, reciprocity could re-enter APEC's consideration of trade policy alternatives.

Bibliography

Anderson, K., 1991. 'Europe 1992 and the Western Pacific economies', *Economic Journal*, 101(409), November: 1538–52

    1993. 'Economic growth, environmental issues, and trade', chapter 11 in M. Noland (ed.), *Pacific Dynamism and the International Economic System*, Washington, DC: Institute for International Economics

    1994a. 'Agricultural policies and the new world trading system', in G. Raby (ed.), *The New World Trading System*, Paris: OECD

    1994b. 'Multilateral trade negotiations, European integration, and farm policy reform', *Economic Policy*, April: 14–52

Anderson, K. and Blackhurst, R. (eds.), 1992. *The Greening of World Trade Issues*, London: Harvester Wheatsheaf, and Ann Arbor: University of Michigan Press

    1993. *Regional Integration and the Global Trading System*, London: Harvester Wheatsheaf, and New York: St. Martin's Press

Anderson, K. and Norheim, H., 1993. 'Is world trade becoming more regionalized?', *Review of International Economics*, 1(2) June: 91–109

Anderson, K. and Snape, R., 1994 'European and American regionalism: effects on and options for Asia', *Journal of the Japanese and International Economies*, 8(4), December

Anderson, K. and Strutt, A., 1994. 'On measuring the environmental impacts of agricultural trade liberalization', paper presented to the IATRC Conference on *Trade and the Environment: Measuring the Critical Linkages*, Toronto, 17–18 June

Andrews, N., Roberts, I. and Hester, S., 1994. 'The Uruguay Round outcome: implications for agricultural and resource commodities', paper presented at the ABARE *Outlook 94* Conference, February

Armington, P.S., 1969a. 'A theory of demand for products distinguished by place of production', *IMF Staff Papers*, 14:159–78

    1969b. 'The geographic pattern of trade and the effects of price changes', *IMF Staff Papers*, 16:176–99

Asian Development Bank, 1993. *Asian Development Outlook 1993*, Manila

Bacha, E., 1984. 'Growth with limited supplies of foreign exchange: a reappraisal of the two-gap model', in Syrquin, M., Taylor, L. and Westphal, L.E. (eds.), *Economic Structure and Performance: Essays in Honor of Hollis B. Chenery*, New York: Academic Press

Backus, D., Kehoe, P. and Kehoe, T., 1992. 'In search of scale effects in trade and growth', *Journal of Economic Theory*, 58(2):377–409

Bahmani-Oskooee, M. and Alse, J., 1993. 'Export growth and economic growth: an application of cointegration and error-correction modelling', *Journal of Developing Areas*, 27(4):535–42

Bahmani-Oskooee, M., Mohtadi, H. and Shabsigh, G., 1991. 'Exports, growth, and causality in LDCs: a re-examination', *Journal of Development Economics*, 36:405–15

Baldwin, R., 1989. 'The growth effects of 1992', *Economic Policy*, 9:248–81

1992. 'Measurable dynamic gains from trade', *Journal of Political Economy*, 100(1):162–74

1995. 'Does sustainability require growth?', in Goldin, I. and Winters, L.A. (eds.), *The Economics of Sustainable Development*, Cambridge: Cambridge University Press

Bank for International Settlements, 1993. *Central Bank Survey of Foreign Exchange Market Activity in April 1992*, March, Basle: BIS

Bannister, G., 1992. 'Rent sharing in the MFA: the case of Mexico', mimeo

Belassa, B., 1978. 'Exports and economic growth: further evidence', *Journal of Development Economics*, 5:181–9

1985. 'Exports, policy choices, and economic growth in developing countries after the 1973 oil shock', *Journal of Development Economics*, 18:23–35

Belassa, B. and Associates, 1982. *Development Strategies in Semi-Industrial Economies*, Baltimore: Johns Hopkins University Press

Bell, M.E., and Kochhar, K. with Ma, J., N'guiamba, S. and Lall, R. 1993. *China at the Threshold of a Market Economy*, IMF, *Occasional Paper*, 107

Beltz, C., 1994. 'Don't stifle foreign investment', *Upside*, July: 14–15

Bergsten, F. and Williamson, J., 1983. 'Exchange rates and trade policy', in Cline, W. (ed.), *Trade Policy in the 1980s*, Washington, DC: Institute for International Economics

Bhagwati, J. and Patrick, H.T. (eds.), 1991. *Aggressive Unilateralism: America's 301 Trade Policy and the World Trading System*, Ann Arbor: University of Michigan Press

BIE (Bureau of Industry Economics), 1992. *Recent Development in the Theory of Economic Growth: Policy Implications*, Bureau of Industry Economics, Canberra: Australian Government Publishing Services

Bigman, D., 1987. 'The theory of variable levies', *Oxford Economic Papers*, 39: 357–77

Bilson, J., 1981. 'The speculative efficiency hypothesis', *Journal of Business*, 54(3):435–51

Boulton, L. *et al.*, 1990. 'Volatility of the Australian Dollar Exchange Rate', *Research Discussion Paper*, 9010, Research Department, Reserve Bank of Australia

Bradford, C.I., 1993. *From Trade-driven Growth to Growth-driven Trade: Reappraising the East Asian Development Experience*, Development Centre, Paris: OECD

Brandão, A. and Martin, W., 1993. 'Implications of agricultural trade liberalization for the developing countries', *Agricultural Economics*, 8:313–43

Branson, W. and Lowe, J., 1987. *US Manufacturing and the Real Exchange Rate*, paper presented to NBER Conference on 'Misalignment of Exchange Rates', Cambridge, MA: NBER, May

Brown, D., 1994. 'Properties of applied general equilibrium trade models with monopolistic competition and foreign direct investment', in Francois, J. and Shiells, C. (eds.), *Modelling Trade Policy: AGE models of North American free trade*, Cambridge: Cambridge University Press

Bruno, M., 1967. 'The optimal selection of export-promoting and import-substituting projects', in *Planning the External Sector: Techniques, Problems and Policies*, New York: UN

Burniaux, J.M., van der Mensbrugghe, D. and Waelbroeck, J., 1990. 'The food gap of the developing world: a general equilibrium modelling approach', in Goldin, I. and Knudsen, O. (eds.), *Agricultural Trade Liberalization*, Paris: OECD and World Bank

Burniaux, J.M., Martin, J.P., Delorme, F., Leinert, I. and van der Mensbrugghe, D., 1990. 'Economy-wide effects of agricultural policies in OECD countries: a GE approach using the Walras model', in Goldin, I. and Knudsen, O. (eds.), *Agricultural Trade Liberalization*, Paris: OECD and World Bank

Camps, M. and Diebold, M., Jr., 1983. *The New Multilateralism: Can the World Trading System be Saved?*, New York: Council on Foreign Relations, Inc

Cao, Y., 1992. 'The Chinese iron and steel industry in transition: towards market mechanism and economic efficiency', PhD dissertation, National Centre for Development Studies, Canberra: Australian National University

Chai, J.C.H. and Haishun, S., 1993.' Liberalising foreign trade: experience of China', Department of Economics, *Discussion Papers*, 135, University of Queensland, November

Charnovitz, S., 1987. 'The influence of international labour standards on the world trading regime: An overview', *International Labour Review* 126(5), September–October

Chia, S.Y. and Lee, T.Y., 1993. 'Subregional economic zones: a new motive force in Asian-Pacific development', chapter 7 in Noland, M. (ed.), *Pacific Dynamism and the International Economic System*, Washington, DC, Institute for International Economics

Chinn, M. and Frankel, J., 1992. 'Financial links around the Pacific rim: 1982–1992', in Glick, R. (ed.), *Exchange Rate Policies in Pacific Basin Countries*, Conference at Reserve Bank of San Francisco, 16–18 September

Choi, Y.P., Chung, H.S. and Marian, N., 1985. *The Multi Fibre Arrangement in Theory and Practice*, London: Frances Pinter

Chow, C.Y., 1987. 'Causality between export growth and industrial development', *Journal of Development Economics*, 26:55–63

Chow, P.C.Y. and Kellman, M.H., 1993. *Trade, the Engine of Growth in East Asia*, New York: Oxford University Press

Corden, W., 1993. 'Exchange rate policies for developing countries', *Economic Journal*, 103(416):198–207

Crockett, A., 1984. 'Exchange Rate Volatility and World Trade', *IMF, Occasional Paper* 28

Currie, D., 1993. 'International cooperation in monetary policy: has it a future?', *Economic Journal*, 103(416):178–87

270 *Bibliography*

Dagenais, M.G. and Muet, P.-A. (eds.), 1992. *International Trade Modelling*, London: Chapman & Hall, in the series *International Studies in Economic Modelling*

Darrat, A., 1986. 'Trade and development: the Asian experience', *Goto Journal*, 6:695–99

de Melo, J. and Robinson, S., 1990. 'Productivity and Externalities: models of export-led growth', *Working Papers*, Country Economics Department, Washington, DC: World Bank

Dean, J., Desai, S. and Riedel, J., 1994. 'Trade policy reform in developing countries since 1985: a review of the evidence', *Discussion Paper*, 267, Washington, DC: World Bank

Deardorff, A., 1984. 'Testing trade theories and predicting trade flows', in Jones, R.W. and Kenen, P.B. (eds.), *Handbook of International Economics*, vol. 1, Amsterdam: North-Holland: 467–517

  1994. 'Market access', in *The New World Trading System: Readings*, Paris: OECD

Department of Foreign Affairs and Trade (DFAT), 1993. *Uruguay Round: Outcomes for Australia*, 15 December (contains report of SALTER Modelling in conjunction with the Industry Commission), Canberra: Australian Government Publishing Service

  1994. *Outcomes of the Uruguay Round* (3 vol. set)., Canberra: Australian Government Publishing Service

  1995. *Trade in Services; Australia 1993–94*, Canberra: Australian Government Publishing Service

Dixit, A. and Norman, V., 1980. *Theory of International Trade*, Cambridge: Cambridge University Press

Dobson, W., 1993. *Japan in East Asia: Trading and Investment Strategies*, ISEAS Series on Japan and the Asia-Pacific, Singapore: Institute of Southeast Asian Studies

Dodora, S., 1993. 'Exports and growth: a reconsideration of causality', *Journal of Developing Areas*, 27(2):227–44

Dollar, D., 1992. 'Out-oriented developing countries really do grow more rapidly: evidence from 95 LDCs, 1976–1985', *Economic Development and Cultural Change*, 40(3):523–44

Dominguez, K. and Frankel, J., 1990. 'Does foreign exchange market intervention matter? Disentangling the portfolio and expectations effects for the mark', *Working Paper*, 3299, Cambridge, MA: NBER

Drysdale, P. and Garnaut, R., 1982. 'Trade intensities and the analysis of bilateral trade flows in a many-country world: a survey', *Hitostubashi Journal of Economics*, 22:62–84

  1989. 'A Pacific free trade area?', in Schott J. (ed.), *Free Trade Areas and US Trade Policy*, Washington, DC: Institute for International Economics

Eaton, J. and Ho, C. 1993. 'Trade and investment in the North America-Pacific region: does NAFTA matter?', in *Asian Economic Dynamism and New Asia-Pacific Economic Order: Post-Cold War US–Japan Economic Relations and New*

Regionalism, proceedings of Kyushu University International Symposium, Kitakyushu: Kyushu University, 279–307

Eaton, J. and Tamura, A., 1994. 'Bilateralism and regionalism in Japanese and US trade and direct foreign investment patterns', *Research Working Paper*, 4758, Cambridge, MA: NBER

Edwards, S., 1993a. 'Trade orientation, distortions and growth in developing countries', *Journal of Development Economics*, 39:31–57

1993b. 'Openness, trade liberalisation, and growth in developing countries', *Journal of Economic Literature*, 31(3):1358–93

Edwards, S. (ed.), 1987. *Hong Kong: A Guide to the Structure, Development and Regulation of Financial Services*, London: The Economist Intelligence Unit

EFTA, 1990. *EFTA Trade*, Geneva: EFTA economic affairs department

EPG (Eminent Persons Group), 1994. *Achieving the APEC Vision: Free and Open Trade in the Asia Pacific*, Singapore: APEC Secretariat, August

Esfahani, H., 1991. 'Exports, imports, and economic growth in semi-industrialised countries', *Journal of Development Economics*, 35:93–116

Eswaran, M. and Kotwal, A., 1993. 'Export-led development: primary vs. industrial exports', *Journal of Development Economics*, 41(1):163–72

Ethier, W., 1982. 'National and international returns to scale in the modern theory of international trade', *American Economic Review*, 72:950–59, June

Faini, R., de Melo, J. and Takacs, W., 1992. 'A primer on the MFA maze', Brussels: European Centre for Advanced Research in Economics, mimeo

Faruquee, H., 1991. 'Dynamic capital mobility in Pacific Basin developing countries: estimation and policy implications', IMF, *Working Paper*, 115

Feder, G., 1982. 'On exports and economic growth', *Journal of Development Economics*, 12:59–73

Feenstra, R. (ed.), 1988. *Empirical Methods for International Trade*, Cambridge, MA: MIT Press

Feketekuty, G., 1992. *The New Trade Agenda*, Washington DC: Group of Thirty

Feldstein, M., 1988. 'Thinking about international economic coordination', *Journal of Economic Perspectives*, 2(2):3–13

Finger, J.M., 1994. 'Can dispute settlement contribute to an international agreement (institutional order) on locational competition?', presentation at a conference on *Locational Competition in the World Economy*, Kiel, 22–23 June

Fischer, B. and Reisen, H., 1993. *Liberalising Capital Flows in Developing Countries: Pitfalls, Prerequisites and Perspectives*, Development Studies Centre, Paris: OECD

Flam, H. and Nordström, H., 1994. 'The single market(s) for cars in Europe', Geneva: GATT Secretariat, mimeo

Flickenschild, H. *et al.*, 1992. *Developments in International Exchange and Payments Systems*, World Economic and Financial Surveys, Washington, DC: IMF

Francois, J.F., 1992. 'Optimal commercial policy with international returns to scale', *Canadian Journal of Economics*, 25:184–95

1994a. 'Global production and trade: factor migration and commercial policy with international scale economies', *International Economic Review*, 35(3):565–81

1994b. 'Labour force growth, trade, and employment', Geneva: GATT Secretariat, mimeo

Francois, J.F., McDonald, B. and Nordström, H., 1993a. 'Economywide effects of the Uruguay Round', Uruguay Round background paper, Geneva: GATT

1993b. 'The growth effects of the Uruguay Round', Uruguay Round background paper, Geneva: GATT

1995. 'Assessing the Uruguay Round', paper presented at the World Bank Conference on *The Uruguay Round and Developing Countries*, Washington, DC, 26–27 January

Francois, J.F. and Shiells, C., 1993. 'The dynamic effects of trade liberalization', US International Trade Commission Publication 2608, February

Franke, G., 1991. 'Exchange rate volatility and international trading strategy', *Journal of International Money and Finance*, 10:292–307

Frankel, J.A., 1992. 'Is a yen bloc forming in Pacific Asia?', in O'Brien, R. (ed.), *Finance and the International Economy:5*, New York: Oxford University Press

1993. 'Is Japan creating a yen bloc in East Asia and the Pacific?', in Frankel, J. and Kahler, M. (eds.), *Regionalism and Rivalry: Japan and the United States in Pacific Asia*, Chicago and London: University of Chicago Press, 53–85

Frankel, J.A. and Wei, S.-J., 1993. 'Trade blocs and currency blocs', *Research Working Paper*, 4335, Cambridge, MA: NBER

Frenkel, J. and Goldstein, M., 1989. 'Exchange rate volatility and misalignment: evaluating some proposals for reform', *Working Paper*, 2894, Cambridge, MA: NBER

Froot, K. and Frankel, J., 1989. 'Forward discount bias: is it an exchange risk premium?', *Quarterly Journal of Economics*, 104(1):139–61

Froot, K. and Stein, J., 1991. 'Exchange rates and foreign direct investment: an imperfect capital markets approach', *Quarterly Journal of Economics*, 106(2):1191–1217

Fukusaku, K., 1992. *Economic Regionalization and Intra-industry Trade: Pacific-Asian Perspectives*, Development Centre, Paris: OECD

Gao, X., 1993. 'China's foreign exchange regime and its impact on exports and growth', PhD dissertation, National Centre for Development Studies, Canberra: Australian National University

Garnaut, R., 1994. 'The floating dollar and the Australian structural transition: some Asia Pacific context', paper presented at the Department of Economics, Research School of Pacific and Asian Studies, Canberra: Australian National University, 10 May

GATT, 1974. *Arrangement Regarding International Trade in Textiles*, Geneva: GATT Secretariat

1984. *Textile and Clothing in the World Economy*, Geneva: GATT Secretariat

1987. *International Trade 1986–87*, Geneva: GATT Secretariat

1989. *International Trade 1988–89*, Geneva: GATT Secretariat

1991. *Draft Final Act*, Geneva: GATT Secretariat

1992a. *Annual Report*, Geneva: GATT Secretariat

1992b. *International Trade 90–91*, vol. II, Geneva: GATT Secretariat

1992c. *Trade Policy Review, Japan 1992*, vol. I, Geneva: GATT Secretariat

1992d. *Trade Policy Review, Korea 1992*, vol. I, Geneva: GATT Secretariat

1993a. *An Analysis of the Proposed Uruguay Round Agreement, with Particular Emphasis on Aspects of Interest to Developing Economies*, Geneva: GATT Secretariat

1993b. *International trade and the trading system:* report by the Director-General 1992–93, Geneva: GATT Secretariat

1993c. *International Trade 1993: Statistics*, Geneva: GATT Secretariat

1993d. *The Uruguay Round, A Giant Step for Trade and Development*, Geneva: GATT Secretariat

1994a. *Analytical index: guide to GATT law and practice*, 6th edn, Geneva: GATT Secretariat

1994b. *Final act embodying the results of the Uruguay Round of multilateral trade negotiations*, Geneva: GATT Secretariat

1994c. *International Trade Statistics 1993*, Geneva: GATT Secretariat

1994d. *News of the Uruguay Round of Multilateral Trade Negotiations*, Geneva: GATT Secretariat, April

1994e. 'Director-General's Annual Report to the Council', Geneva: GATT Secretariat, December

1994f. *International Trade Statistics 1994*, Geneva: GATT Secretariat

Glen, J., 1993. 'How firms in developing countries manage risk', *Discussion Paper*, 17, Washington, DC: International Finance Corporation, World Bank

Goldin, I., Knudsen, O. and van der Mensbrugghe, D., 1993. *Trade Liberalisation: Global Economic Implications*, Paris: OECD and World Bank

Goldsborough, D. and Teja, R., 1991. 'Globalization of financial markets and implications for Pacific basin developing countries', *Working Paper*, 34, IMF

Goto, J., 1989. 'The Multifibre Arrangement and its effects on developing countries', *World Bank Research Observer*, 4:203–27

Graham, E. and Richardson J.D. (eds.), forthcoming. *Global Competition Policies*, Washington, DC: Institute for International Economics

Granger, C.W.J., 1969. 'Investigating causal relations by econometric models and cross-spectoral methods', *Econometrica*, 37:424–38

Grant, R.J., Papadakis, M. and Richardson, J.D., 1993. 'Global trading flows: old structures, new issues and empirical evidence', chapter 2 in Bergston, C.F. and Noland, M. (eds.), *Pacific Dynamism and the International Economic System*, Washington, DC: Institute for International Economics

Grossman, G., 1995. 'Pollution and growth: what do we know?', in Goldin I. and Winters, L.A. (eds.), *The Economics of Sustainable Development*, Cambridge: Cambridge University Press

Grossman, G. and Helpman, E., 1991. *Innovation and Growth in the Global Economy*, Cambridge, MA: MIT Press

Grubel, H.G. and Lloyd, P.J., 1975. *Intra-industry Trade: The Theory and Measurement of International Trade in Differentiated Products*, London: Macmillan

Gylfason, T., 1992. 'Output gains from economic liberalization: a simple formula', *Seminar Paper* 514, Stockholm: IIES

Haaland, J.I. and Norman, V.D., 1992. 'Global production effects of European integration', chapter 3 in Winters,. L.A. (ed.), *Trade Flows and Trade Policy After '1992'*, Cambridge: Cambridge University Press

Haaland, J.I. and Tollefsen, T., 1994. 'The Uruguay Round and trade in manufactures and services. general equilibrium simulations of production, trade and welfare effects of liberalization', CEPR, *Discussion Paper*, 1008

Hamada, K., 1972. 'Japanese investment abroad', in Drysdale, P. (ed.), *Direct Foreign Investment in Asia and the Pacific*, Canberra: Australian National University Press: 173–96

Hambley, J., 1995. 'Early stage processing of international trade and input–output data for SALTER', SALTER, *Working Paper*, Canberra: Industry Commission

Hamilton, C., 1984. 'ASEAN systems for allocation of export licenses under VERs', in Findlay, C. and Garnaut, R. (eds.), *The Political Economy of Manufacturing Protection: Experiences of ASEAN and Australia*. Sydney: Allen & Unwin (1986)

    1986. 'An assessment of voluntary restraints on Hong Kong exports to Europe and the USA', *Economica*, 53: 339–50

    1992. *Textile Trade and the Developing Countries: Eliminating the MFA in the 1990s*, Washington, DC: World Bank

Hamilton, C. (ed.), 1990. *Textiles Trade and the Developing Countries*, Washington DC: World Bank

Hanslow, K., 1993. 'Later stage processing of international trade data for SALTER', SALTER, *Working Paper*, 16, Canberra: Industry Commission

Haque, N. and Montiel, P., 1990. *Capital Mobility in Developing Countries – Some Empirical Tests*', IMF, *Working Paper*, 117

Harris, R.G., 1984. 'Applied general equilibrium analysis of small open economies with scale economies and imperfect competition', *American Economic Review*, 74: 1016–32

Hathaway, D.E., 1987. *Agriculture and the GATT, Rewriting the Rules*, Washington DC: Institute for International Economics

Hathaway, D.E. and Ingco, M.D., 1996. 'Agricultural liberalization and the Uruguay Round', in Martin, W. and Winters, A. (eds.), *The Uruguay Round and the Developing Countries*, New York: Cambridge University Press

Healey, D., 1991. *Japanese Capital Exports and Asian Economic Development*, Paris: OECD

Helpman, E., 1981. 'International trade in the presence of product differentiation, economies of scale, and monopolistic competition: a Chamberlin–Heckscher–Ohlin approach', *Journal of International Economics* 11, August, 305–40

Helpman, E. and Krugman, P., 1985. *Market Structure and Foreign Trade: Increasing Returns, Imperfect Competition and the International Economy*, Cambridge, MA: MIT Press

Hertel, T. and Tsigas, M., forthcoming. 'GTAP model documentation', in Hertel, T. (ed.), *Global Trade Analysis Using the GTAP Model*, New York: Cambridge University Press

Hertel, T., Horridge, J. and Pearson, K., 1992. 'Mending the family tree: a reconciliation of the linearized and levels schools of AGE modelling', *Economic Modelling*, 9, 385–407

Hill. H. and Phillips, P., 1993. 'Trade is a two-way exchange: rising import penetration in East Asia's export economies', *The World Economy*, 16(6):687–97

Hindley, B., 1988. 'Dumping and the Far East trade of the EC', *The World Economy*, 11(1)

1994. 'Safeguards, VERs and anti-dumping action', chapter 8 in *The New World Trading System*, Paris: OECD Secretariat

Hoekman, B., 1994. 'General Agreement on Trade in Services', chapter 20 in *The New World Trading System*, Paris: OECD Secretariat

1995. 'Tentative first steps: an assessment of the Uruguay Round Agreement on Services', World Bank, mimeo

Hoekman, B.M. and Leidy, M.P., 1989. 'Dumping, anti-dumping and emergency protection', *Journal of World Trade*, 23

Hoekman, B.M. and Mavroidis, P.C., 1994. 'Competition, competition policy, and the GATT', *The World Economy* 17(2): 121–50

Hsiao, M.W., 1987. 'Tests of causality and exogeneity between export growth and economic growth', *Journal of Development Economics*, 12 December: 143–59

Hufbauer, G.C., 1965. *Synthetic Materials and the Theory of International Trade*, London: Duckworth

Industry Commission, 1994. *Annual Report 1993–94* (Appendix H), Canberra: AGPS

Ingco, M., 1994. 'How much agricultural liberalization was achieved in the Uruguay Round?', Washington, DC: World Bank, mimeo

International Agricultural Trade Research Consortium, 1994. 'The Uruguay Round Agreement on Agriculture: an evaluation', *Commissioned Paper*, 9, Department of Agricultural Economics, University of California at Davis, July

International Monetary Fund (IMF), 1970–93. *International Financial Statistics*, Washington, DC: IMF

1976–8. *Exchange Restrictions – Annual Report*, Washington, DC: IMF

1979–93. *Exchange Arrangements and Exchange Restrictions – Annual Report*, Washington, DC: IMF

1993. *Annual Report*, Washington, DC: IMF

Jackson, J.H., 1989. *The World Trading System: Law and Policy of International Economic Relations*, Cambridge, MA and London: MIT Press

1990. *Restructuring the GATT System*. New York: Council on Foreign Relations Press for the Royal Institute of International Affairs

Joelson, M., 1993. 'Antitrust aspects of NAFTA', *Federal Bar News & Journal*, 40(9), October: 573–8

Johnson, H.G., 1968. *Comparative Cost and Commercial Policy Theory for a Developing World*, Stockholm: Wicksell Lectures

Jomini, P., Zeitsch, J.F., McDougall, R., Welsh, A., Brown, S., Hambley, J. and Kelly, J., 1991. 'SALTER: a general equilibrium model of the world economy, vol 1, model structure, database and parameters', Canberra: Industry Commission

Jones, R., King, R. and Klein, M., 1993. 'Economic integration between Hong Kong, Taiwan and the coastal provinces of China', *OECD Economic Studies*, 20, Winter: 114–44

Julius, D., 1990. *Global Companies and Public Policy*, London: RIIA, Chatham House

Jung, W.S. and Marshall, P.J., 1985. 'Exports, growth and causality in developing countries', *Journal of Development Economics*, 18:1–12

Jupp I., 1993. 'Survey of foreign exchange market activity', *Reserve Bank Bulletin*, 56(1), New Zealand Reserve Bank

Kalirajan, K.P. and Shand, R.T., 1991, 'Causality between technical and allocative efficiencies: an empirical testing', *Journal of Economic Studies* 19:2:317

Kawai, M., 1994. 'Accumulation of net external assets in Japan', in Sato, R., Levich, R. and Ramachandran, R. (eds.), *Japan, Europe, and International Financial Markets: Analytical and Empirical Perspectives*, Cambridge: Cambridge University Press: 73–123

Keesing, D.B. and Wolf, M., 1980. 'Textile Quotas against Developing Countries', *Thames Essay*, 23, London: Trade Policy Research Centre

Kehoe, T., 1992. 'Modelling the dynamic impact of North American free trade', in *Economy-Wide Modelling of the Economic Implications of a FTA with Mexico and a NAFTA with Canada and Mexico, USITC Publication*, 2508, Washington, DC: United States International Trade Commission

Khanna, S.R., 1991. *International Trade in Textiles: MFA Quotas and a Developing Exporting Country*, New Delhi: Sage

Kohli, I. and Singh, N., 1989. 'Exports and growth: critical minimum effort and diminishing returns', *Journal of Development Economics*, 30(2):391–400

Kojima, K., 1968. 'Japan's interest in the Pacific trade expansion', in Kojima, K. (ed.), *Pacific Trade and Development*, papers and proceedings of a Conference held by the Japan Economic Research Center, Osaka: Japan Economic Research Center: 153–93, January

    1985. *Nihon no Kaigai Chokusetsu Toshi (Japan's Direct Investment Abroad)*, Tokyo: Bunshindo

Komiya, R., 1990. 'Japan's foreign direct investment', in Komiya, R., *The Japanese Economy: Trade, Industry, and Government*, Tokyo: University of Tokyo Press: 111–56

Komiya, R. and Wakasugi, R., 1991. 'Japan's foreign direct investment', *Annals of the American Academy of Political Social Sciences*, 513:48–51

Krishna, K., and Tan, L.H., 1993a. 'Implementation in the MFA: the effects of rules on outcomes', mimeo

    1993b. 'Rent sharing in the Multifibre Arrangement: evidence for US apparel imports from Korea', mimeo

Krishna, K., Erzan, R. and Tan, L.H., 1994. 'Rent sharing in the Multifibre Arrangement: theory and evidence from US apparel imports from Hong Kong', *Review of International Economics* 2: 62–73

Krueger, A.O., 1978. *Liberalization Attempts and Consequences*, Cambridge, MA: Ballinger

    1980. 'Trade policy as an input to development', *American Economic Review*, 70(2):288–92

    1985. 'Importance of general policies to promote economic growth', *The World Economy*, 7(2):93–108

    1992. 'Free trade agreements as protectionist devices: rules of origin', Duke University, September, mimeo

Krugman, P.R., 1980. 'Scale economies, product differentiation, and the pattern of trade', *American Economic Review*, 70, December: 950–9

1987. 'Is free trade passe?', *Economic Perspectives*, Fall:131–44

Landesman, M. A. and Petit, P., 1992. 'Trade in producer services: international specialisation and European integration', *Working Paper*, 9217, Department of Applied Economics, University of Cambridge

Lardy, N., 1992. *Foreign Trade and Economic Reform in China, 1978–1990*, Cambridge: Cambridge University Press

Lau, L. (ed.), 1990. *Models of Development*, San Francisco. International Center for Economic Growth

Lawrence, R.Z., 1992. 'How open is Japan?', chapter 1 in Krugman, P. (ed.), *Trade With Japan: Has the Door Opened Wider?*, Chicago: University of Chicago Press

1993. 'Regionalism, multilateralism and deeper integration', draft monograph for the Brookings Institution project on 'Integrating The World Economy', Washington, DC, December, mimeo

1994. 'Trade, multinationals, and labour', in Lowe, P. (ed.), *International Integration of the Australian Economy*, Sydney: Reserve Bank of Australia

Leamer, E., 1984. *Sources of International Comparative Advantage; Theory and Evidence*, Cambridge, MA: MIT Press

1987a. 'Paths of development in the three-factor, n-good general equilibrium model', *Journal of Political Economy* 95(5): 961–99, October

1987b. 'Cross-section estimation of the effects of trade barriers', chapter 3, in Feenstra, R. (ed.), *Empirical Methods for International Trade*, Cambridge, MA: MIT Press (1988): 51–82

1988. 'Measures of openness', in Baldwin, R.E. (ed.), *Trade Policy Issues and Empirical Analysis*, Chicago: University of Chicago Press

Leung, S., 1991. 'Financial liberalization in Australia and New Zealand', in Ostry, S. (ed.), *Authority and Academic Scribblers: The Role of Research in East Asian Policy Reform*, San Francisco: International Center for Economic Growth

1992. 'An empirical investigation into Australia's asset markets and exchange rates', *Working Paper in Economics and Econometrics* 244, Canberra: Australian National University

1993. 'Exchange rate regimes and outward looking growth', Economics Division, *Working Paper* 93/4, Canberra: Australian National University, forthcoming in Garnaut, R. (ed.), *Sustaining Export Oriented Development in East Asia*, Cambridge: Cambridge University Press (1995)

Lin, Shujuan, 1991. 'Application of cost-benefit analysis in China: a case study of the Xiamen special economic zone', PhD thesis, National Centre for Development Studies, Canberra: Australian National University

Linder, S.B., 1961. *An Essay on Trade and Transformation*, New York: Wiley

Little, I., Cooper, R. and Rajapatiran, S., 1993. *Boom, Crisis and Adjustment: The Macroeconomic Experience of Developing Countries*, New York: Oxford University Press

Little, I., Scitovsky, T. and Scott, M., 1970. *Industry and Trade in Some Developing Countries: A Comparative Study*, Oxford: Oxford University Press for OECD

Lucas, R., 1988. 'On the mechanics of economic development', *Journal of Monetary Economics*, 22:3–42
    1993. 'Making a miracle', *Econometrica*, 61(2):251–72
Lui Pak-Wui, Yun-Wing Sung, Wong, R. Yue-Chim and Lau, Pui-King, 1992. *China's Economic Reform and Development of the Pearl River Delta*, Study for Nanyang Commercial Bank Ltd, Hong Kong
Lynde, M.R., 1992. 'Testing an imperfect competition trade model', chapter 2 in Dagenais, M.G. and Muet, P.-A. (eds.), *International Trade Modelling*, London: Chapman & Hall
MacDonald, R. and Taylor, M., 1991. 'Exchange rate economics: a survey', IMF, *Working Paper*, 91/62
Magee, S., 1972. 'The welfare effects of restriction on US trade', *Brooking Papers on Economic Activity*, 3
Markusen, J.R., 1990. 'Micro-foundations of external economies', *Canadian Journal of Economics*, 23, 495–508
Martin, W., 1990. 'Two tier pricing in China's foreign exchange market', *China Working Paper Series*, National Centre for Development Studies, Canberra: Australian National University
Martin, W. and Francois, J., 1994. 'Bindings as trade liberalization', paper presented to the *Festschrift* for Bob Stern, University of Michigan
Mathieson, D. and Rojas-Suarez, L., 1992. 'Liberalization of the Capital Account: experiences and issues'. IMF, *Working Paper*, 46.
Matsushita, M., 1994. 'Harmonization of competition laws through bilateral trade negotiations – Japanese experience', Gaston, Sigur Centre, George Washington University, Washington, DC: mimeo
McCleary, R.K., 1992. 'An inter-temporal, linked, macroeconomic CGE model of the United States and Mexico, focusing on demographic change and factor flows', in *Economy-Wide Modelling of the Economic Implications of a FTA with Mexico and a NAFTA with Canada and Mexico, USTIC Publication*, 2508, Washington, DC: US International Trade Commission
McKibbin, W. and Sundberg, M., 1993. 'Macroeconomic linkages between the OECD and the Asia-Pacific region', in Currie, D. and Vines, D. (eds.), *North–South Linkages and International Macroeconomic Policy*, New York: Cambridge University Press
McKinnon, R., 1988. 'Monetary and exchange rate policies for international financial stability: a proposal', *Journal of Economic Perspectives*, 2(1):83–103
    1993. *Dollar and Yen: The Problem of Financial Adjustment Between the United States and Japan*, Asia Pacific Research Center, California: Stanford University
McKinnon, R. and Fung, K., 1993. 'Floating exchange rates and the new interbloc protectionism: tariffs versus quotas', in Salvatore, D. (ed.), *Protectionism and World Welfare*, Cambridge: Cambridge University Press
Messerlin, P., 1990. 'Anti-dumping', chapter 6 in Schott, J.J. (ed.), *Completing the Uruguay Round*, Washington DC: Institute for International Economics
Michaely, M., 1977. 'Exports and growth: an empirical investigation', *Journal of Development Economics*, 4:49–53
Ministry of Foreign Trade and Economic Cooperation (MOFTEC), 1994. *Almanac of MOFTEC*, Beijing

Morgan Guaranty Trust Company, 1984–93. *World Financial Markets*, New York
  1984. 'Import quotas on textiles: the welfare effects of United States restrictions
  on Hong Kong.' *Bureau of Economics Staff Report to the Federal Trade Commission*,
  Washington, DC: US Government Printing Office
Morkre, M.E., 1979. 'Rent seeking and Hong Kong's textile quota system', *The
  Developing Economies*, 18: 110–18
Musgrove, P., 1985. 'Why everything takes 2.71828. . . times as long as expected',
  American Economic Review, 75(1): 250–2
New Zealand Reserve Bank, 1993. *Bulletin*, 56(3)
Nguyen, T., Perroni, C. and Wigle, R., 1993. 'An evaluation of the draft final Act of
  the Uruguay Round', *Economic Journal*, 103:1560–9
Nishimizu, M. and Robinson, S., 1984. 'Trade policies and productivity change
  in semi-industrialized countries', *Journal of Development Economics*, 16:
  177–206
Noland, M., 1990. *Pacific Basin Developing Countries Prospects for the Future*,
  Washington, DC: Institute for International Economics
Nordic Statistical Secretariat, 1993. *Yearbook of Nordic Statistics 1993*, Copenhagen:
  Nordic Council of Ministers
Ocampo, J., 1986. 'New development in trade theory and LDCs', *Journal of
  Development Economics*, 22(1):129–70
OECD, 1990. PSE/CSE Calculations, Paris: OECD, mimeo
  1991. *Agricultural Policies, Markets and Trade: Monitoring and Outlook 1990*, Paris:
  OECD
  1992. *National Accounts 1978–1990: Detailed Tables*, vol. 2, Paris: OECD
  1993. 'Assessing the effects of the Uruguay Round', *Trade Policy Issues*, 2, Paris:
  OECD
  1994a. *Main Developments in Trade 1993: Annual Report*, Paris: OECD Secretariat
  1994b. *Monitoring and Outlook Report on Agricultural Policies, Markets and Trade*,
  Paris, OECD
  1994c. *The New World Trading System; Readings*. Paris: OECD Secretariat
Ohlin, B., Hesselborn, P.-O. and Wijkman, P. M. (eds.), 1977. *The International
  Allocation of Activity*, London: Macmillan
Osband, K. and Villanueva, D. 1993. 'Independent currency authorities', *IMF Staff
  Papers*, 40(1): 202–16
Pacific Basin Working Paper, Center for Pacific Basin Monetary and Economic
  Studies, 1993, PB93–01, Federal Reserve Bank of San Francisco
Panagariya, A., 1981. 'Variable returns to scale in production and patterns of spe-
  cialization', *American Economic Review*, 71: 221–30
Park, K. and Schoenfeld, S., 1992. *The Pacific Rim Futures and Options Markets*,
  Chicago: Probus
Perkins, F.C., 1994. *Practical Cost Benefit Analysis*, Melbourne: Macmillan
  1995a. 'Export performance and enterprise reform in China's coastal provinces',
  Economics Division Working Paper Series – East Asia, 95/2, Research School of
  Pacific Studies, Canberra: Australian National University
  1995b. 'Productivity performance and priorities for the reform of China's state
  owned enterprises', *Economics Division Working Paper Series – East Asia*, 95/1,
  Research School of Pacific Studies, Canberra: Australian National University

Petersmann, E.V., 1993. 'International trade law and international environmental law', *Journal of World Trade,* 27(1), February

Petri, P., 1994. 'Trade and investment interdependence in the Pacific', paper presented at the 21st Pacific Trade and Development Conference, *Corporate Links and Direct Foreign Investment in Asia and the Pacific,* Hong Kong, 1–3 June

Polasek, M. and Lewis, M., 1985. 'Australia's transition from crawling peg to floating exchange rate', *Banca Nazionale del Lavoro Quarterly Review,* June

Posner, M.V., 1961. 'International trade and technical change', *Oxford Economic Papers,* 31

Powell, A.A., 1993. 'Integrating econometric and environmetric modelling', *General Paper,* G-102, Melbourne, Centre of Policy Studies and the Impact Project, November

Pratten, C., 1988. *A Survey of the Economies of Scale,* Luxembourg: Commission of the European Communities

Qian, Y. and Varangis, P., 1992. 'Does exchange rate volatility hinder export growth?', *Working Paper,* WS 911, Washington, DC: World Bank

Quirk, P. *et al.,* 1988. 'Policies for developing forward foreign exchange markets', IMF *Occasional Paper,* 60

Radetski, M., 1992. 'Economic growth and environment', in Low, P. (ed.), *International Trade and the Environment, Discussion Paper* 159, Washington, DC: World Bank

Ramstetter, E. (ed.), 1991. *Direct Foreign Investment in Asia's Developing Economies and Structural Change in the Asia-Pacific Region,* Boulder: Westview Press

Rhee, Y.W., Ross-Larson, B. and Pursell, G., 1984. *Korea's Competitive Edge: Managing the Entry into World Markets,* World Bank/Johns Hopkins University Press

Richardson, J.D., 1993. 'Global trade flows: old structures, new issues, empirical evidence', in Bergsten, C.F. and Noland, M. (eds.) *Pacific Dynamism and the International Economic System,* Washington DC: Institute for International Economics

Robertson, D., 1992. 'GATT rules for emergency protection', *Thames Essay,* 57, London: Harvester-Wheatsheaf for Trade Policy Research Centre

    1994. 'New burdens for trade policy', in R. O'Brien (ed.), *Finance and the International Economy 8,* The Amex Bank Review Prize Essays, London: Oxford University Press: 108–18

Romer, P., 1987. 'Crazy explanations for the productivity slowdown', in *NBER Macroeconomic Annual,* Cambridge, MA: MIT Press

    1990. 'Endogenous technological change', *Journal of Political Economy,* 98(5):S71–S102

Rutherford, T., 1994a. 'Applied general equilibrium modelling with MSPGE as a GAMS subsystem', University of Colorado, mimeo

    1994b. 'Extensions of GAMS for complementarity problems arising in applied economic analysis', University of Colorado, mimeo

Saad, I., 1993. 'The impact of trade reforms and the Multifibre Arrangement on Indonesian clothing and textile exports', PhD thesis, National Centre for Development Studies, Canberra: Australian National University

Sampson, G. 1989. 'Protection in agriculture and manufacturing: meeting the objections of the Uruguay-Round', chapter 10 in *The Balance between Industry and Agriculture in Economic Development*, Proceedings of the Eighth World Congress of the International Economics Association, London: IEA and Macmillan Press

Sarris, A. and Freebairn, J., 1983. 'Endogenous price policies and international wheat prices', *American Journal of Agricultural Economics*, 65:214–24

Schott, J.J., 1990. *The Global Trade Negotiations: What Can Be Achieved?*, Washington, DC: Institute for International Economics

Schott, J.J. (ed.), 1989. *Free Trade Areas and US Trade Policy*, Washington, DC: Institute for International Economics

Sengupta, J., 1993. 'Growth in NICs in Asia: some tests of new growth theory', *Journal of Development Studies*, 29 (2):342–57

Sercu, P., 1992. 'Exchange risk, exposure, and the option to trade', *Journal of International Money and Finance*, 11:579–93

Shanghai Statistical Bureau, various years. *Statistical Yearbook of Shanghai*, Shanghai

1993. *Shanghai Pudong New Area, Statistical Annual Report*, Shanghai

Sheard, P., 1993. '"Keiretsu" business organization, competition, and access to the Japanese market', in Graham and Richardson, forthcoming

Slayter, W. and Carew, E., 1993. *Trading Asia-Pacific Financial Futures Markets*, Sydney: Allen & Unwin

Smith, M.A.M., 1976. 'Trade, growth and consumption in alternative models of capital accumulation', *Journal of International Economics*, 6: 371–84

1977. 'Capital accumulation in the open two-sector economy', *Economic Journal* 87: 273–82

Snape, R.H., Adams, J. and Morgan, D., 1993. *Regional Trade Agreements: Implications and Options for Australia*, Canberra: Australian Government Publishing Service for the Department of Foreign Affairs and Trade

Solow, R., 1957. 'Technical change and the aggregate production function', *Review of Economics and Statistics*, 39(3):312–20

Song, L. and Chen, T., 1993. 'On exports and economic growth: further evidence – a cross-county analysis', Australian Japan Research Centre, Canberra: Australian National University, mimeo

Soon, C., 1994. *The Dynamics of Korean Economic Development*, Washington, DC: Institute for International Economics, March

Sprout, R., and Weaver, J.H., 1993. 'Exports and economic growth in a simultaneous equations model', *Journal of Developing Areas*, 27(3):289–306

Srinivasan, T.N., 1991. 'Is Japan an outlier among trading countries?' chapter 11 in de Melo, J. and Sapir A. (eds.), *Trade Theory and Economic Reform: Essays in Honour of Bela Balassa*, Oxford: Basil Blackwell

Stegemann, K., 1991. 'The international regulation of dumping: protection made too easy', *The World Economy*, 14(4)

Stewart, T., 1993. *The GATT Uruguay Round, A Negotiation History (1986–1992)*, Dordrecht: Kluwer Law and Taxation

Stoeckel, A., Pearce, D. and Banks, G., 1990. *Western Trading Blocs: Game, Set or*

Match for Asia Pacific and the World Economy, Canberra: Centre for International Economics

Sung Yun-Wing, 1992. 'A comparative study of foreign trade and investment in Shanghai and in Guangdong', unpublished paper, Chinese University of Hong Kong

Sutherland, P., 1994. *Aftermath of the Uruguay Round*, statement to the 27th General Meeting of the Pacific Basin Economic Council, Kuala Lumpur, 25 May

Tangermann, S., 1994. 'An assessment of the Uruguay Round Agreement on Agriculture and on Sanitary and Phytosanitary Measures', Institute of Agricultural Economics, University of Göttingen, mimeo

Tavlas, G. and Ozeki, Y., 1991. 'The internationalization of the yen', *Finance and Development*, Washington, DC: IMF and World Bank

Travis, W.P., 1964. *The Theory of Trade and Protection*, Cambridge, MA: Harvard University Press

Trela, I. and Whalley, J., 1990. 'Global effects of developed country trade restrictions on textiles and apparel', *Economic Journal*, 100, December: 1190–1205

    1991. 'Internal quota allocation schemes and the costs of the MFA', NBER, *Working Paper*, 3627. Cambridge, MA: NBER

Tumlir, J. and Till, L., 1971. 'Tariff averaging in international comparisons', in Grubel, H. and Johnson, H. (eds.), *Effective Tariff Protection*, Geneva: GATT and Graduate Institute of International Studies

Tyers, R. and Anderson, K., 1992. *Disarray in World Food Markets: A Quantitative Assessment* Cambridge: Cambridge University Press

Tyler, W.G., 1981. 'Growth and export expansion in developing countries', *Journal of Development Economics*, 9:121–30

US Department of Agriculture, 1990. 'Estimates of producer and consumer subsidy equivalents: government intervention in agriculture 1986–87', *Statistical Bulletin*, 803, Washington, DC: Agricultural Trade Analysis Division, Economic Research Service

    1994a. 'Effects of the Uruguay Round Agreement on US agricultural commodities', Office of Economics, Economic Research Service, March

    1994b. 'Uruguay Round: implications for US agriculture', Office of Economics, Economic Research Service, presented at the American Agricultural Economics Association meetings in San Diego, August

US International Trade Commission, 1991. *The Economic Effects of Significant US Import Restraints, Phase III: Services, with a CGE Analysis of Significant US Import Restraints*, September

    1993. *The Economic Effects of Significant US Import Restraints, An Update*, November

Urata, S., 1993a. 'Changing patterns of direct investment and the implications for trade and development', in Bergsten, F. and Noland, M. (eds.), *Pacific Dynamism and the International Economic System*, Washington, DC: Institute for International Economics: 273–97

    1993b. 'Japanese foreign direct investment and its effect on foreign trade in Asia', in Ito, T. and Krueger, A.O. (eds.), *Trade and Protectionism*, Chicago: University of Chicago Press: 273–99

1994. 'Trade liberalization and productivity growth in Asia: introduction and major findings', *Developing Economies*, 32(4):363–72

Vernon, R., 1966. 'International investment and international trade in the product cycle', *Quarterly Journal of Economics*, 80

Viner, J., 1950. *The Customs Union Issue*, New York: Carnegie Endowment

Vousden, N., 1990. *The Economics of Trade Protection*, New York: Cambridge University Press

Wall, D., 1990. 'Special economic zones and industrialisation in China', paper presented to a Conference on *Trade and Industrial Performance in Developing Countries*, University of Bradford, 21–22 June

Wang, G., 1994. 'China's return to the GATT: legal and economic implications', *Journal of World Trade*, 28(3)

Warner, M. and Rugman, A., 1994. 'Recent US protectionist R&D policies: are Canadian multinationals exempted?', *Canadian Business Law Quarterly*, 23(3), June

Whalley, J., 1992. 'The Multifibre Arrangement and China's growth prospects', in Anderson, K. (ed.), *New Silk Roads*, Cambridge: Cambridge University Press

Willett, T., 1986. 'Exchange-rate volatility, international trade, and resource allocation: a perspective on recent research', *Journal of International Money and Finance*, 5:S101–S112

Williamson, J., 1985. 'The exchange rate system', *Policy Analyses in International Economics*, 5, Washington, DC: Institute for International Economics

1992. 'FEERs and the ERM', *National Institute Economic Review*, 137:45–50

1993. 'Exchange rate policies for developing countries', *Economic Journal*, 103:88–97

Winters, A., 1994. 'Import surveillance as a strategic trade policy', in Krugman, P. and Smith, A. (eds.), *Empirical Studies of Strategic Trade Policy*, Chicago: The University of Chicago Press

Wolter, F., 1994. 'GATT: The practicalities of implementation', Geneva: GATT secretariat, mimeo

Woo Wing Thye and Hirayama, K., 1994. 'Monetary autonomy in the presence of capital flows: never the twain shall meet?', paper presented to National Bureau of Economic Research 5th Annual East Asian Seminar on Economics, Singapore, June 15–18

World Bank, 1987. *World Development Report*, New York: Oxford University Press, for World Bank

1991. *World Development Report*, New York: Oxford University Press, for World Bank

1992a. *Philippines Capital Market Study*, vol. 1: *Main Report*, Washington, DC: World Bank

1992b. *China: Reform of the Plan in the 1990s*, Washington, DC: World Bank

1993. *The East Asian Miracle: Economic Growth and Public Policy*, New York: Oxford University Press for World Bank

1994a. 'Developing countries, firms, and risks', *Development Brief*, 30, Washington, DC: World Bank, March

1994b. *East Asia's Trade and Investment*, Washington, DC: World Bank

1994c. *World Development Report 1994*, New York: Oxford University Press for World Bank

1994d. *World Tables*, Washington DC: World Bank

1994e. *China: Foreign Trade Reform*, World Bank Country Study, Washington, DC: World Bank, February

Wu, Rong-I. 1994. 'On possible areas of cooperation on competition policy', prepared for Sixth APEC EPG Meeting, Hong Kong, 30–31 May

Yamazawa, I., 1992. 'On Pacific economic integration', *Economic Journal*, 102

Yang, Y., 1992. 'The impact of MFA on world clothing and textile markets with special reference to China', PhD dissertation, Canberra: Australian National University

1994a. 'Trade liberalization with externalities: a general equilibrium assessment of the Uruguay Round', National Centre for Development Studies. Canberra: Australian National University, mimeo

1994b. 'The impact of the MFA phasing out on world clothing and textile markets', *Journal of Development Studies*, 30, July

1995. 'A global general equilibrium model incorporating trade externalities – an extension of GTAP', mimeo

Yang, Y., Martin, W. and Yanagishima, K., 1995. 'Evaluating the benefits of MFA liberalization in the Uruguay Round', in Hertel, T. (ed.), *Global Trade Analysis Using the GTAP Model*, New York: Columbia University Press

Yoffie, D.B., 1983. *Power and Protectionism: Strategies of the Newly Industrializing Countries*, New York: Columbia University Press

Young, S., 1993. 'East Asia as a regional force for globalism', chapter 6 in Anderson, K. and Blackhurst, R. (eds.), *Regional Integration and the Global Trading System*, London: Harvester Wheatsheaf and New York: St. Martin's Press

Zhang, X., 1994. 'How successful is China's trade reform: an empirical assessment', *Economics Division Working Paper Series – East Asia* 94/4, Research School of Pacific Studies, Canberra: Australian National University

Index